SUPERHEROES

ON

WORLD SCREENS

SUPERHEROES ON WORLD SCREENS

Edited by Rayna Denison and Rachel Mizsei-Ward

UNIVERSITY PRESS OF MISSISSIPPI
JACKSON

www.upress.state.ms.us

The University Press of Mississippi is a member of the Association of American University Presses.

Manufactured in the United States of America

First printing 2015
∞

Library of Congress Cataloging-in-Publication Data

Superheroes on world screens / edited by Rayna Denison and Rachel Mizsei-Ward.
pages cm
Includes bibliographical references and index.
ISBN 978-1-62846-234-0 (hardback) — ISBN 978-1-62674-674-9 (ebook)
1. Superhero films—History and criticism. 2. Motion pictures and globalization. 3. Heroes in motion pictures. I. Denison, Rayna, editor. II. Mizsei-Ward, Rachel editor.
PN1995.9.S76S87 2015
741.43'652—dc23
2014042288

British Library Cataloging-in-Publication Data available

CONTENTS

ACKNOWLEDGMENTS

Rayna and Rachel would like to thank the contributors for their expertise and insights, Peter Coogan for his kind feedback, and the editors at University of Mississippi Press for all their help. We would also like to thank Derek Johnston for his involvement with the *Superheroes on Screen* blog and early stages of this book project.

Rayna would like to thank her father, Raymond Denison, for inspiring her love of comic books. It is thanks to my Dad that I knew about telekinesis before I could read most other words. I also want to thank my mother, Sheila, for introducing me to classic TV science fiction and my partner, John Taylor, for indulging my love of world cinema. It is thanks to all of you that I love what I do.

Rachel thanks her husband Adam. I couldn't have done it without you. This book is dedicated to those who have inspired us, and to the memory of Muriel, who continues to inspire me.

SUPERHEROES ON WORLD SCREENS

INTRODUCTION

RAYNA DENISON, RACHEL MIZSEI-WARD, AND DEREK JOHNSTON

Superheroes are everywhere. Their iconic logos reach around the world, gracing everything from pizza boxes to blockbuster film posters. Their images have been co-opted for purposes commercial and political, and those creating superhero texts range from media conglomerates to grassroots fans. As a consequence of their long global exchanges, not all superheroes now trace their histories back to US comic books. Many national cultures have created (or re-imagined) superheroic figures, and the world of superheroes now contains many icons whose histories borrow from local folklore, myths, and legends. Consequently, the superhero needs to be reconsidered, to be seen as part of both local *and* global culture, and examined for the rich meanings that such divergent origins and re-workings can create. This collection is the first concentrated attempt to think through the meanings and significance of the superhero not just as a product of US culture, but as a series of local, transnational, and global exchanges in popular media.

These exchanges in superhero cultures have generated a broad spectrum of superhero types across many media formats. According to Peter Coogan, the difficulty with previous superhero studies has been the tendency to accept all heroic characters as superheroes; or, conversely, to stay very close to the US superhero canon. Coogan's response to this conundrum is to run potential superheroes through a series of content-based genre tests (2005). However, this may paint too neat a picture of contemporary superheroes and their shifting global genre histories. One central question that this collection deals with is: where is the superhero genre located? Superheroes have commonly crossed media formats since their earliest existence in comic books, radio, film, television, children's toys, and other epiphenomena. Moreover, superheroes have been created for distinct audiences. Compare, for example, the recent "dark" film revisions of Batman and Superman (Brooker 2012), with the superheroes of global children's cartoons.

Japan's *Anpanman* (created by Takashi Yanase in 1973) might usefully be considered as a significant national superhero franchise, as might the French *Asterix* (Rene Goscinny and Albert Uderzo 1959–), while the UK's *Bananaman* (created by John Geering in 1980) and *SuperTed* (Mike Young 1982–1986) respectively provide satirical and sweet local superheroes, all of which have been aimed at younger audiences. As these examples suggest, if superheroes form a genre, then it has long been a transnational genre, one with myriad sub-categories and disparate local originating myths, producing texts aimed at a wide range of audiences in a range of cultural milieus. However, studies of film genres have tended to focus on singular production contexts, seen for example, in a consistent body of scholarship around Hollywood genres (for examples, see: Schatz 1981; Altman 1984; Neale 2000).

Genre studies have, however, introduced the importance of understanding genre production in context, and have increasingly come to see "genrifiction" as a continual process (Altman 1999; Langford 2005). Our contributors follow similar paths towards an understanding of superheroes in world media, but by tracing the appearances of superhero texts as part of wider cultural negotiations between globalizing media exchanges and local histories and tastes. In this way, they suggest that the superhero's meanings are culturally and contextually dependent, and that the superhero genre is often subject to local reinterpretations and remodeling (Loock and Verevis 2012).

The superhero is also an emphatically transmedia phenomenon; or, at very least, needs to be conceptualized as a genre whose wide-ranging manifestations are hard to pin down to an original or even dominant source. Moreover, superheroes, as a type of character, do not always appear within superhero narratives or in "superhero genre" texts. Though arguably always reliant on their genre for meaning, superheroes are now routinely de- and re-contextualized within media culture. Take, for example, the satirical Bagram Batman, a series of military safety videos posted to YouTube; or, consider the various superheroes (among them Superman and Batman) featuring in the USA's "Got Milk" advertising campaigns, each of which takes a superhero out of its normal media surrounding, re-imagining it as a public health or military safety advisor. These ancillary uses of iconic superheroes suggest just one way in which superheroes have been dispersed throughout global media culture. By thinking across media formats and by considering the transnational reach of superheroes, this collection goes beyond a textual formulation of the superhero genre, instead reconsidering superheroes as parts of larger cultural matrices (Brooker 2012) or intertextual networks (Meehan 1991).

The fact that superhero texts have already been analyzed as parts of wider textual relays is significant. As Hiroki Azuma suggests, this means that fans of superheroes need not be fans of comic books, and that their fandom can begin from any point of the intertextual relay in which a character appears (2009). For this reason, the chapters in this collection are not organized around media platforms, but are presented through wider frames, so that superheroes from a range of media are granted attention. We focus on screen representations, from films and television to computer screens, because these have commonly provided the most highly exchanged iterations of superheroes, particularly in the case of superheroes whose local fame is greater than their international distribution. This works, too, for chapters highlighting transnational exchanges in US-derived superheroes. Rayna Denison's chapter, for example, offers an historical analysis of a 1970s Japanese television adaptation of Marvel's Spider-Man, a text that transnational fans were only recently given access to through Marvel's official website. The re-release and subtitling of *Supaidāman* online acted as a cross-promotional stunt preceding the release of a new live-action Hollywood film, *The Amazing Spider-Man* (2012). Initially made for a local Japanese television audience, *Supaidāman* is now shifting frames to become a fully transnational part of Spider-Man's larger intertextual network. Because of the fluidity of such exchanges, and their high profile, we have chosen to focus not on comic book adaptations for the screen, but on the superhero as a mutable local and global screen presence.

Because of the quickly shifting frames of reference for superheroes, our contributors take a range of approaches to the local and transnational production of superhero texts, viewing them alternately as part of a wider cultural moment, and as a product of collisions between local and transnational superhero formations. This allows our contributors to place superheroes within a wide range of spaces, times, and socio-cultural milieus, ranging from superheroes' connections to local myths to their engagements with contemporary politics. In these ways, the essays contained in this collection work to expand our understanding of the superhero in global culture in order to include a wide range of character types borrowed from multiple, often hybridized, genres and traditions. Our authors' approaches have been divided into three sets of frameworks, which will be detailed further in this introduction, working outwards from local superheroes, through to transnational superheroes and considerations of the ideological ramifications of superhero exchanges.

Not Just the American Way

Rethinking the "Americanness" of US Superheroes

The conceptualization of superheroes as national symbols is common, with Ryan Edwardson noting in his exploration of the Canadian superhero Captain Canuck:

> Distinctively national comic books . . . are vessels for transmitting national myths, symbols, ideology and value. They popularize key elements of the national identity and ingrain them into their readers – especially, given the primary readership, younger generations experiencing elements of that identity for the first time. (2003, 186)

While this comment relates to comic books as a whole and not simply superheroes, the superhero, whether Captain America, Captain Canuck, or Captain Britain, can be specifically related to the values of the nation that it represents, even if, as is the case with Captain Britain, these conceptions are actually generated by members of another nation.

Bart Beaty has claimed, "Not only do superheroes serve to protect the national interest within superheroic narratives, but they also serve to illuminate national interests in the real world as iconic signs" (2006, 428). The most famous example of this is probably Superman, representing truth, justice, and the American Way, even as individual comics' storylines question the closeness of the connection between Superman and the USA, and adaptations into other media have increasingly left "the American Way" unsaid. These shifts in the depiction of Superman not only indicate an awareness of the global audience that needs to be engaged by the character in order for its representations to be profitable, but also a re-engagement with the political aspects of the character. After all, Superman's early adventures depicted him as an active supporter of the ideals of the New Deal, combating the selfishness of criminals and slumlords. By associating him with "the American Way," the writers were thus adopting a political stance and saying that Roosevelt's ideals should be understood as the true American Way. As the character developed, and his adventures became more fantastical, this particular political association became less clear; however, the catchphrase stuck.

With the popularity of the character of Superman in various media, this image has thus come to associate the superhero as a whole with the idea of the United States of America. This also means that the idea of "America" that is seen as being represented by superheroes is one that has developed in a particular US context and around particular US concepts of national identity and individual action in the service of particular political and social ideals that may not be seen as desirable or useful in other parts of the world (for more, see Dittmer 2012). The New Deal ideals of individual action to serve the community can seem like a rash tendency to aggression, particularly if separated from the framework required by an action-adventure narrative told through visual media. As Ryan Edwardson's article also points out, there is a long tradition of characterizing nations as individuals: Uncle Sam, Britannia or John Bull, Johnny Canuck; and this use of the superhero figure in such roles could be seen as merely continuing the personification of the nation (2003, 186).

However, this is a simplification of the way superheroes function within cultures. Emphasis is placed on different characteristics depending on writer, national mood, and the commercial demands of producing a successful ongoing comic book, television series, or film. Even those that are most perceived as being representations of their nations are not personifications in the same way that Uncle Sam or Britannia are. Instead, they are an embodiment of certain conceptions and ideals about the nation, and their involvement in narratives, particularly with long-running characters, means that they can be used to question and explore those conceptions and ideals. This is why Captain America, introduced in comics in December 1940, could be depicted punching Hitler in an issue cover-dated March 1941, almost a year before the United States abandoned its isolationist policy to enter World War II on 8 December 1941. As Captain America co-creator Joe Simon has said, "Other superheroes were in the business of fighting crime, but the war in Europe was of far greater significance" (quoted in Fingeroth 2007, 57). Simon goes on to identify the creation of Captain America as perhaps a means "of lashing out against the Nazi menace" for co-creator Jack Kirby and himself, and against the isolationist and right-wing elements of American society at the time.

However, while a superhero character may enjoy "mainstream" success, its origins frequently lie within a particular social or ethnic group. This theme is central to Danny Fingeroth's exploration of the creation of

American comic book superheroes, *Disguised as Clark Kent: Jews, Comics, and the Creation of the Superhero* (2009), where he claims that the Jewishness of many of the early superhero comics creators in America influenced their creations, albeit in a fairly general, subconscious way. He connects the broader immigrant experience of the comics' creators, many of whom were the children of immigrants, with superhero concepts relating to the persecution of outsiders, the desire to retain cultural identity while also becoming part of the host culture, and the desire for justice and the ability to act for justice. However, these desires and conceptions can be seen as part of a wider immigrant desire, as opposed to a specifically Jewish one, and, while Fingeroth's book offers an interesting view of a particular aspect of American superhero comic book history, it does not speak to the creation or use of superheroes outside the USA. Arguably, the connection of the superhero with the outsider is part of the appeal of these characters and narratives, regardless of the specific national culture within which the stories are created and presented.

Furthermore, superheroes do not have to be representative of their nation to display national characteristics. As with any cultural product, they are informed and shaped by spoken and unspoken cultural mores and beliefs, whether reflected in their characterization, their origin story, their costuming, or their narratives. Indeed, as Will Brooker's work on Batman has shown (1999, 2001, 2012), a superhero's meanings shift across time. Brooker argues that "Batman belongs not to the fans, but to the world at a specific point in history" (1999, 197). The superhero's mythos, then, becomes part of a wider socio-cultural moment, speaking to one or more cultures in a dialogic relationship. Though this commonly happens at the level of intra-national discourse, this collection aims to demonstrate the reach of superheroes across transnational and even global boundaries. Central to the work of many of our contributors is the understanding that this broader level of debate continuously refigures the superhero during a dynamic exchange of (inter-)cultural texts.

While superhero characters can be taken as products of a general mythos working in concert with specific socio-cultural moments, they are more normally conceptualized as American phenomena. As such, their appearances in other cultures often emphasizes the differences between American culture and local experiences. George Orwell, writing in 1946, decried American comics as a debased form of previously exemplary American children's literature, a form that projected power fantasies unsuitable for English children.

> English children are still Americanized by way of the films, but it would no longer be generally claimed that American books are the best ones for children. Who, without misgivings, would bring up a child on the coloured 'comics' in which sinister professors manufacture atomic bombs in the underground laboratories while Superman whizzes through the clouds, the machine-gun bullets bouncing off his chest like peas, and platinum blondes are raped, or very nearly, by steel robots and fifty-foot dinosaurs? It is a far cry from Superman to the Bible and the woodpile. (2000, 400)

Even at this relatively early moment in superhero history, Orwell clearly perceived this representation of power and sensationalism as unsuitable for the English national character. This perception of difference between American individualist power and local national characteristics frequently leads to a fairly mocking look at the superhero figure, as Jochen Ecke and Patrick Gill contend in their chapter on the British television superhero in this volume. Focusing on the series *My Hero* (2000–2006), *No Heroics* (2008), and *Misfits* (2009–2013), Ecke and Gill demonstrate how characteristics typically associated with the British national character, such as understatement, ridicule, and a distrust of the gung-ho hero figure, are played out through these programs.

This suggests that national superheroes are frequently deployed as a form of cultural resistance to American soft power. However, the deployment of the superhero in East Asia seems to have been more deeply absorbed into expressions of national culture, developing its own forms that have, at times, influenced American superheroes in return. Daniel Martin's chapter in this collection examines the problematic adaptation of folklore figures into superhero narratives, focusing on South Korean animation's adaptation of Chunhyang, a mythic suffering beauty who becomes amalgamated over time into Japanese anime notions of the super-ninja. This super-ninja figure, a preternaturally skilled warrior (often a woman), has also found its way back into US superhero culture, perhaps most evidently in comic book figures like Elektra and Shi. Trans-Asian to begin with, the re-appropriation of this "local" Asian character type within a co-production between South Korea and Japan opens up new spaces in which to rethink the regional and transnational circulation of such martial-arts-derived superheroes and their roots in local folklore.

Such questioning of national stereotypes can be seen in superhero comics as well as screen representations, as J. Richard Stevens has discussed in relation to the discourses that took place in the letter pages of *Captain America*. From 1969 to 1976 *Captain America*'s letters pages debated the superhero's position as a voice of the establishment, versus his status as an independent-thinking patriot (2011). While Stevens' article examines a period of particular division in American society, it is clear that these questions are still important to superheroes. Even more so, they are relevant to the broader media representation of superheroes, as the burgeoning field of screen superheroes extends these conceptualizations of national characteristics into transnational arenas. Of course, American comics have been central to the spread of the concepts and images of these superheroes around the world, but the wider market for superheroes needs also to be understood through the lens of increasing globalization within screen cultures.

Superheroes on World Screens

From Local Productions to Transnational Blockbusters

Despite American comic book culture's creation of archetypes, genres, and mythoi, other national contexts have also had an impact on how we might understand the figure of the superhero. Take Lincoln Geraghty's assertion in this volume that Doctor Who might be considered "the quintessential British superhero," with his alien nature, quirky costumes, and cerebral approach to protecting the innocent. Geraghty examines the ways that *Doctor Who*'s global export from the UK to the USA might challenge US definitions of how superheroes operate within world culture. As a British response to American superheroes, *Doctor Who*'s presence at the heart of US comic book culture at Comic-Con suggests a transnational fandom for superheroes that shifts across genres and national contexts to embrace a world of super-possibilities.

Viewed industrially, the reach and importance of superhero origins often fades the further they travel, and the more often they are translated. For example, when *Captain America: The First Avenger* (2011) was released, the superhero's name, "Captain America," was dropped from the film's title in Russia, South Korea, and the Ukraine. Brooks Barnes, writing for the *New York Times*, notes that

> selling a quaintly patriotic war hero in a politically divided United States would be tricky enough. What about overseas, where movies can

> generate over 70% of their total box-office revenue and the word "America" can be a downright dirty one? (2011)

In this example, the political and commercial imperatives driving large blockbuster films towards ever-broader definitions of what it means to be an "American" superhero film are made explicit. Barnes speaks to the challenges facing US superheroes as they travel around the world; as they are translated, censored, cut, and reshaped by the local cultures in which they are shown, something our authors tackle in analyzing the transnational lives of superheroes from within and beyond the USA. In their chapters on very different periods of Marvel's transnational history, for instance, both Vincent Gaine and Rayna Denison argue for the decentering of "America" in discussions of core US superheroes like Thor and Spider-Man. In the former case, Gaine develops a complex picture of Thor's multiple threads of transnational influence, first within his comic book history, and then within the production of this god/superhero as a blockbuster film character played by an Australian and surrounded by British and European actors.

These competing industrial and technological endeavors, and the way they alter the nature and local perceptions of superheroes, offer alternative lenses through which world cinema might be framed by an examination of superhero films and television. From their translations and re-editing for local tastes through to their dispersal by the global branches of Hollywood's big producer-distributors (Toby Miller et al. 2005), superheroes are ever-changing figures in global culture. Moreover, in addition to licensed programs and filmmaking, there are whole worlds of audience engagement and industrial production enacting unlicensed versions of "American" superheroes, reimagining them in relation to a wide range of national and subaltern cultures. Iain Robert Smith's chapter on popular Hindi cinema's many legal and less-than-legal adaptations and variations of superheroes attests to the difficulties of parsing the local within the transnational and vice versa. Smith's analysis of the development of local cycles of Bollywood superhero production also suggests how sensitive even powerful transnational cinemas can be to shifts in US production styles and techniques.

As blockbusters palimpsest notions of the nation (intentionally or through fan re-workings), nationality becomes increasingly hard to discern (for example, when a location in one nation stands in for that of another; or, when blockbusters are localized through re-dubbing by local stars). When transnational cinema meets world cinema, both come to mean something new, forging new understandings of superheroes. These moments of collision go back some time, as Kevin Patrick's chapter in this volume shows. Patrick takes the example of *The Phantom* (1996), an American comic book film that was interpreted as a local film in Australia, thanks to the presence of key personnel, such as its Australian director Simon Wincer. Despite being a relative box office disappointment, *The Phantom* film offers a new lens through which to consider notions of the popular, national, and transnational in superhero filmmaking. Through such examples, it is possible to see how "American" films are co-opted by local communities, aware of high-profile American superhero texts being produced by and in their local communities. Consequently, chapters like Patrick's have the potential to challenge understandings of how the superhero operates (as genre, character, and cultural archetype), providing a means to reconceptualize these figures as less intrinsically American.

Furthermore, Chris Berry, following Arjun Appadurai, has usefully posited that we can think of blockbusters (and with them, many superhero films) as they are "made sense of and practiced according to local cultural and filmmaking contexts" (2003, 218). In making this case for locally produced blockbuster equivalents, Berry makes a space for conceptualizing national superheroes without an American origin point, for reading them instead on their own terms and turf. Ian Gordon, Mark Jancovich, and Matthew P. McAllister are also quick to point out that "too often comics are associated with American comics, and comics-based films with Hollywood blockbusters" (2007, xiv). Too often, superhero films are assumed to have comic book precursors; whereas world cinema and television is replete with superheroes who borrow from disparate sources, often without recourse to comic books or Hollywood filmmaking. Therefore, the chapters in this collection take care to map the relationships between their superheroic subject matter and the local and global histories from which they emerge.

The Politics, Morality, and Socio-Cultural Impact of Superheroes on World Screens

Ideology and politics are two of the most consistent threads running through the analyses of superheroes to date. Jason Dittmer, for example, has claimed that "superheroes serve as a crucial resource for legitimating, contesting, and reworking states' foreign policies, and as such have arguably grown in importance over the past several decades" (2012, 3). The global and local blockbuster cultures featuring superheroes are not, as his statement shows, only important for their commercial potential. Rather, as Marc DiPaolo notes, "Superheroes make morals their business" (2011, 5), a practice meaning that

> comic books have always been political, and have taken stands on controversial issues such as the death penalty, abortion, gay rights, and the environment. They have also reflected the mood of the public by being pro-war during wartime and pacifistic during peacetime almost as often as they have served as the voice of the minority opinion, crying out for peace during wartime and advocating going to war when the public is reluctant to do so. (11)

These practices are visible throughout the on-screen careers of superheroes as much as they are found in comic books. Consequently, the chapters in this volume all note various sorts of politics, power relations, and sociocultural concerns running through the superhero texts under scrutiny, regardless of where those texts originate from.

These political wranglings form the third frame of this collection, as our contributors explore the implicit and explicit politics and ideologies of superhero screen texts. However, while some claim that superheroes have always been political, others demur. Jamie A. Hughes, for example, argues that

> no superheroes claim to have an affiliation with a political party, none of them are particularly jaded by education, racism, sexism or bigotry, and many of them, while in the news regularly, are not influenced by the images they see. Also, no superheroes fight crime or the forces of evil because they believe God is on "their side." (2006, 547)

Hughes' claim is diametrically opposed to the Superman catchphrase of "Truth, Justice, and the American Way," and to the perceived need to drop the ideologically loaded "Captain America" from the title of Marvel's recent superhero film. As our authors show, and contrary to Hughes' claim, there seems to be a high degree of politicization to the figure of the superhero. Our contributors argue that to fight crime and protect the weak is an inescapably political, ideologically informed act.

Superhero characters have been politicized in many ways, and this process has happened at different stages in their creation, development over time, official expansion through intertextual networks, and in their unofficial exploitation by fans. Characters such as Captain America and Johnny Canuck were purposely created as propaganda figures, while the 99 were developed to provide role models for children in the Middle East, to influence positively how Islam was represented and perceived. The importance of such superheroes to global understandings of Islam has been raised recently in media coverage of Pakistan's first superhero film, *Nation Awakes* (2013), with one commentator writing, "Some Western viewers will doubtlessly be perplexed by an Islamic stronghold, all too often pigeonholed by the media as a poverty-ridden terrorist breeding ground, revealed to be embracing and adapting some hearty red, white and blue pop culture" (Waddell 2013, 108). While it is possible to read *Nation Awakes* as a capitulation to America's culturally imperialist agenda, the importance of this film is at once national(istic) and transnational(ist).

In her chapter in this collection, Rachel Mizsei-Ward explores the impact of the religious and political ideologies that shaped right-wing US responses to *The 99* (2007), which began life as a comic book but which has now been made into a cartoon series. In doing so, her work highlights the Judeo-Christian ideologies that often linger within the mythos of the superhero. At the same time, Mizsei-Ward also demonstrates the ingrained negative sexualization of female US superhero characters, which DiPaolo concurs are "dreadful portrayals of women" as "masturbatory fantasies for the predominantly male readership" (2011, 42). She does so by examining the uproar about "burqa"-based costumes among right-wing commentators, who struggled to reconcile their outrage against the backdrop of exploitative representations of US superheroines.

Tracing the ideology and politics of superheroes becomes problematic as superhero media spreads across formats and between nations. Moreover, the long-running transmedia nature of many superhero narratives means that the depiction of the superhero may not be coherent across time *or* media. Popular superhero characters rarely get long periods of inactivity, or at least not ones that the consumer sees, in which to consider their worldview. As a result, it is often the narrative drive and the writer's choice of enemy that provides us with the clearest view of the politics of the superhero—and consequently, those of their creators.

It is perhaps unsurprising, therefore, that superheroes with distinctive national or ethnic connections often exhibit more extreme (or at least overt) political awareness than those representing white, middle-class American ideological positions. For example, Zorro, the Spanish-American pulp superhero precursor of the 1920s, while being himself a scion of the nobility, is defined in opposition to the authorities and defends the

Mexican and Native American peasants, who are often portrayed as the underdogs. Zorro is therefore defined by a politics of "otherness," thrown into relief by a normatively perceived white, US superheroism. To similar ends, Jeffrey A. Brown has examined how "new [African American] heroes rework existing paradigms by including African American identities within the conventional narratives and iconography of the superhero formula" (2000, 8). Distinctive and disparate forms of "otherness" continually work on the superhero genre, as Jochen Ecke and Patrick Gill illustrate in their chapter in this collection in which they map otherness within the British superhero tradition. This collection aims to provide more new perspectives on how the superhero is being thought through and how one culture's mainstream superhero can function at another culture's margins. However, it is just as often in the less overt political and ideological spaces of the superhero that contentious transnational grabs for power can be read.

National, inter-generational political and ideological shifts can be read, for example, in Mary Jane Ainslie's chapter on Thai superhero Insee Daeng (The Red Eagle), whose 2010 re-imagining as an urban superhero provides a stark departure from the character's working class roots. Likewise, Iain Robert Smith's examination of the superhero subgenre of Indian popular cinema brings to the fore a set of contradictory, competing ideologies and political wrangles over identity. On the one hand, he sees cross-fertilization, the borrowing from other cultures, as a crucial aspect of these films. On the other hand, Smith reads the disavowal of the superhero film genre (in the repeated claims by filmmakers to be producing India's first superhero film), as a political marketing technique designed to localize the subgenre while at the same time making associational appeals to US superhero counterparts. What these chapters show, along with others in this collection, is that the superhero may be enmeshed in local politics while concomitantly providing stark examples of transnational postmodern palimpsest.

These competing politics and ideologies, wherein films can be read through multi-tiered hierarchies of local and transnational meaning, offer perhaps the most crucial reason driving the creation of this collection. By complicating the understanding of the superhero, by analyzing a range of local, transnational, and global superhero characters, our contributors reveal the complex meanings that such superheroes hold for their audiences. For example, the British super- and anti-hero Judge Dredd can be understood as one such contradictory character. Judge Dredd can be alternately read as a political character supporting an authoritarian government; as a satire about politics and law enforcement; or as a science fiction narrative about a dystopian future. All of these represent different political stances, and contradict each other (Barker and Brooks 1998). As a result, Judge Dredd's "Britishness" becomes inherently problematic, particularly as the narrative is set primarily in a future city in what was the United States, and as the character moves through a future world where the concept of the "national" has itself become obsolete. As the recent film version, *Dredd* (2012), exemplifies, this British superhero throws into relief questions of acceptable politics and ideology, especially after the production of the film was relocated to South Africa, and made to contend with the local political history of that nation.

Inherent in asserting that the superhero has wide-ranging meaning beyond the USA is an understanding of the superhero as a global phenomenon that is locally inflected, transnationally distributed and transculturally exchanged. What such super-characters mean to nations outside of the USA has not been widely discussed, and this collection is intended to create a space for future debates about the figure of the superhero. Rather than seeing these characters as inherently bound up in US politics and ideology, this collection offers a broad spectrum of readings which are intended to show the potential for the creation of new kinds of "super" beings, creations that have the potential to extend and expand our understanding of what it means to be a hero. To this end, this collection is organized in ways intended to shift the frameworks for analyzing the superhero, with chapters grouped together in three sections. The first deals with the ways superheroes have been localized within specific contexts. The second deals with the transnational flows in superhero texts and concepts; and the third with the shifting ideological and political landscapes within which such textual exchanges take place. Through these means, we believe that this collection will offer new ways to approach the superhero as sets of local and transnational textual matrices.

SECTION ONE

Not Just the American Way

Rethinking the "Americanness" of US Superheroes

THE TRANSPLANTED SUPERHERO

The Phantom Franchise and Australian Popular Culture

KEVIN PATRICK

In December 2008, comic book fan sites and online media outlets were abuzz with the news that an Australian company, Sherlock Symington Productions, had purchased film rights to the American comic strip character the Phantom. Aside from announcing that the script was penned by an Australian filmmaker, Tom Boyle, few details about the project—titled *The Phantom: Legacy*—were confirmed. But the company's spokesman, Bruce Sherlock, felt confident enough to predict that the film, budgeted at $130 million, would go into production by the end of 2009. "I think we did it okay before," he added, "but I really honestly feel we can do it better. A lot better" (quoted in Clayfield 2008).

The Phantom: Legacy would be Sherlock's second encounter with the superhero popularly known as "The Ghost Who Walks." Almost twenty years beforehand, Sherlock had made similar pronouncements as the head of an Australian consortium that bought the film rights to the comic strip, a deal which—nearly a decade later—culminated with the release of *The Phantom* (1996), starring Billy Zane. However, the character's marginal status as a comic strip "superhero," coupled with the film's lackluster box office performance, has meant that *The Phantom* has received scant attention. Yet the story behind the making of the first *Phantom* feature film (dotted by a string of coincidences) is a remarkable case study of how the internationalization of film production has meant that commercial and creative genesis for ostensibly "American" film projects can emanate just as easily from peripheral sites, like Australia, as they can from the traditional filmmaking epicenter of Hollywood.

However, the pronounced level of Australian involvement in the production of *The Phantom* only hints at the character's intriguing cultural status "Down Under." This chapter will explain how *The Phantom* has resonated with generations of Australian readers since the mid-1930s, by charting the series' successful transition from popular women's magazines to comic books. It will be argued that Australian publishers' deliberate efforts to mask the comic strip's American origins played a significant part in encouraging Australian audiences to appropriate the Phantom as an "indigenous" superhero. Both in print and on screen, *The Phantom* offers unexpected and telling insights about the global circulation of the superhero phenomenon far beyond its American homeland.

Who Is The Phantom?

The Phantom comic strip, created by author Lee Falk, debuted in the *New York Journal* on February 17, 1936. Midway through the first story, titled "The Singh Brotherhood," Falk created an epic legend around the Phantom, revealing that he was the twenty-first descendant of an English nobleman who, in 1525, on the skull of his father's murderer, swore an oath "against all piracy, greed and cruelty." He further pledged, "As long as my descendants walk the earth, the eldest male of the family shall carry out my work." And so began the unbroken dynasty of the Phantom, who many believed was immortal and thus came to be known as "The Ghost Who Walks—Man Who Cannot Die" (Falk and Moore 2010 [1936], 115).

Clad in a skin-tight costume, his face concealed by an eye-mask and cowl, and sporting a distinctive skull symbol on his gun belt, the Phantom was the first costumed crime fighter to appear in American newspaper comic strips and became the visual prototype for the costumed superhero, predating the debut of Superman in *Action Comics* (1938). Yet the Phantom also bore many of the hallmarks of the pulp-magazine heroes of the early 1930s, such as The Shadow (1931) and Doc Savage (1933). Like them, the Phantom lived in a secret locale, known as the Skull Cave, and had a loyal band of followers, the Bandar pygmy tribe, who alone knew the secret of the Phantom dynasty. He relied on his physical strength and, occasionally, his Colt .45s to defeat his adversaries, instead of using fantastic powers that defined the next generation of comic book superheroes. The Phantom also fought the standard retinue of pulp magazine-era villains, such as gangsters, pirates and feudal warlords, instead of the costumed super villains typically found in superhero comics. For these reasons, Peter Coogan has argued that, although he "laid important groundwork for the superhero genre," the Phantom did not represent a seismic break "from the conventions of the [pulp magazines'] mystery man" formula, and thus failed to generate the same level of popular imitation caused by the debut of Superman, who instigated the vogue for costumed superheroes in American comic books throughout World War II (2006, 184).

There were other aspects of the Phantom's fictional scenario that made him a problematic superhero. Whereas most superheroes' adventures took place in recognizably urban American settings, such as Batman's Gotham City, the Phantom's earliest exploits occurred in the sort of faraway locales found in pulp magazines, such as the Himalayas and the Netherlands East Indies, before Lee Falk eventually reassigned him to the quasi Afro-Asian region known as "Bengali" (later "Bangalla"). The Phantom's ancestry was even more porous than the geographical boundaries of his jungle realm, as his forefathers had wed Scandinavian maidens, English actresses, Indian princesses and Native American tribeswomen (Falk and Barry 1990 [1989–1990], 7–9; Falk and Barry 1991 [1979], 258). According to Lee Falk, the Phantom's colorful lineage was a key reason for his enduring popularity:

> My stuff translates very simply because it's not American in background, or necessarily in temperament. . . . They're international strips. The Phantom is not even American. . . . He's multi-cultured. (Quoted in Murray 2005, 49)

The factors that arguably militated against the Phantom's popular acceptance in his American homeland—such as his lack of superpowers, or recognizably American origin or setting—did much to enhance his international appeal. King Features Syndicate (which held copyright ownership) sold *The Phantom* to newspaper and magazine publishers in Italy (1937), France (1938), Turkey (1939), and Sweden (1940) soon after the series' American debut.[1] And nowhere would *The Phantom* enjoy a more ardent following than in Australia.

Making *The Phantom* "Australian"

The Phantom made its antipodean debut in *The Australian Woman's Mirror* on 1 September 1936, where it was promoted, not as a juvenile comic strip, but as an "exciting picture serial" intended for an adult audience (*Australian Woman's Mirror* 1936, 49). Such a publication may seem an unlikely venue for a masked adventurer, but the inclusion of *The Phantom* in the *Woman's Mirror* was driven by commercial urgency. Launched in 1924, the *Woman's Mirror* was pitched squarely at Australian housewives, who were awarded prizes for contributing recipes and household tips to the magazine. By 1925, this successful editorial formula helped the *Woman's Mirror* achieve the highest circulation of any weekly periodical in Australia (Rolfe 1979, 290). However, the magazine's once unassailable market dominance was challenged by the arrival of *The Australian Women's Weekly* in 1933. This sophisticated, upmarket rival posed a direct challenge to the "homely" and "dowdy" *Woman's Mirror* (300). The *Women's Weekly* had begun boosting its already impressive circulation with the addition of Lee Falk's first comic strip, *Mandrake the Magician*, in December 1934 (O'Brien 1982, 55). *The Woman's Mirror* was therefore understandably keen to purchase the local serial rights to Falk's newest comic strip from its Australian licensor, the Yaffa Syndicate.

The Phantom's lengthy tenure in the *Woman's Mirror*—where it remained until the magazine's closure in 1961—cemented the character's popular status within Australian print culture. Appearing in a respectable publication like the *Woman's Mirror* meant *The Phantom* was deemed acceptable "family entertainment" and could be read in households that would not otherwise admit disreputable, American-styled comic books. The character's exposure to a large, predominantly female readership may also explain why the present-day edition of *The Phantom* comic book retains a strong following among older Australian women.

More significant, however, were the magazine's deliberate attempts to promote *The Phantom* as an Australian, rather than American, comic strip. References to American dollars were changed to sterling currency, while American spelling and slang was replaced by their "correct" Australian equivalents. Diana Palmer, the Phantom's long-suffering fiancée, was referred to as a "young Sydney girl" (Falk and Moore 1938 [1936], 5), while the setting of the opening episode was changed from New York Harbor to somewhere "off Sydney Heads" (9). Although such devices were later abandoned, they helped foster the widespread belief among Australian readers that *The Phantom* was a home-grown comic strip.

The Phantom became an undeniably popular feature for the *Woman's Mirror* and appealed to all members of the family, particularly children. Keen to exploit this ancillary market, the magazine's publisher released *The Phantom* comic book in 1938, compiling previously published episodes from the *Woman's Mirror* in a single edition, but its success was cut short by the imposition of wartime newsprint rationing in 1940. Nonetheless,

Australia became the second country in the world—after Italy—to issue *The Phantom* in comic book format. By comparison, *The Phantom* had to wait until 1962 before receiving its own, self-titled comic book in the United States.[2]

The Comic Book "Cult" of *The Phantom*

The ongoing presence of *The Phantom* in the *Woman's Mirror* proved beneficial for Frew Publications, a small Sydney firm which acquired the rights to produce a brand new edition of *The Phantom* comic book, commencing in September 1948. The character's weekly exposure in the *Woman's Mirror* served as free advertising for the series, which gradually achieved a monthly circulation of ninety thousand copies by 1950 (Snowden 1973, 6). By the late 1950s, however, Australia's comic book industry was facing competition from the introduction of television broadcasting in 1956 and the re-admission of imported American comics in 1960 (Patrick 2012a, 166 and 170–71). Frew Publications was not immune to these disruptions and drastically cut back its publishing output to just a handful of comics by the early 1960s. Yet contemporary press reports noted that *The Phantom* continued to exert a "phenomenal grip on the juvenile market" (*The Observer* 1960, 6).

Nor did the demise of the *Woman's Mirror* deny any further publicity for Frew's flagship comic book hero. In 1960, Australian Consolidated Press (publisher of the *Women's Weekly*) acquired the *Woman's Mirror*, before merging it with *Everybody's*, a youth-oriented weekly dedicated to "show business and pop culture" (O'Brien 1982, 143). *The Phantom* duly reappeared in *Everybody's*, where it remained just prior to the magazine's closure in 1968. By this time, Yaffa Syndicate was selling *The Phantom* comic strip to growing numbers of regional and metropolitan newspapers throughout Australia, thus maintaining the character's public profile (Shedden 2006). For example, the wedding of the Phantom and Diana Palmer in 1977 received considerable (albeit tongue-in-cheek) press coverage in Australia (Cook 1978, 12; Gardiner 1982; Kennedy 1980, 35), culminating in a satirical sketch performed by the future star of *Crocodile Dundee*, Paul Hogan, on his top-rated television program, *The Paul Hogan Show*, in 1978. *The Phantom* enjoyed an unusually high media profile, with reports noting the character's popularity among politicians and sporting celebrities (Jones 1986, 130–31), the high prices paid by collectors for old *Phantom* comics (Stretton 1985, 16), and how his devoted readers came from all walks of life, from stockbrokers to fire fighters (Brown 1988, 25–26). That such levels of media coverage were rarely extended to any other comic book character attests to the Australian public's enduring fascination with the character.

However, by the mid-1980s, Australia's remaining comic book publishers, including Yaffa Publications and Federal Comics, gradually left the field, unable to compete with color television, videocassette films and computer games (Porter 1981, 30). Only Frew Publications remained, with *The Phantom* still reportedly selling forty thousand copies per issue, making it the last "Australian" comic book left standing (Henderson 1986, 14). Despite the local comic industry's straitened circumstances, *The Phantom* continued to command astonishing loyalty, even as its readership grew progressively older. Ian Jack, an expatriate Australian fan, recalled *The Phantom*'s popularity among his white-collar workmates:

> A lot of accountants I know followed [The Phantom]. Every second week, when the book came out, the accountants would disappear from the office and take up watch at the newsstand, waiting for the new issue to appear. (Quoted in Benjamin 1985, 73)

When set against this historical backdrop, it now becomes easier to understand why the impetus for developing *The Phantom* feature film came, not from American, but Australian producers, who were nevertheless Hollywood "outsiders."

The *Crocodile Dundee* Connection

Bruce Sherlock would have perhaps identified with Jack's former colleagues, as the founder of Lion Insurance Brokers freely admitted to being "a Phantom freak." So too were many of his clients, who Sherlock noticed wore Phantom "skull rings," observing that "the Phantom has this great facility for taking ... serious [business] people back to their childhood" (quoted in Jacques 1988, 25). Among Sherlock's clients was Peter Sjoquist, production manager on the Australian film *Crocodile Dundee* (1986), who put the idea of co-producing a new film to Sherlock. Casting around for ideas, Sherlock bought a copy of *The Phantom* and, wondering why no one had yet made a film about his favorite comic book hero, suggested to Sjoquist that they approach Lee Falk to see if the film rights were available (Ward 1989, 12).

Crocodile Dundee turned out to be the perfect calling card for the aspiring producers. The film was already on its way to becoming the highest grossing domestic film in Australian box office history and would eventually break US box office records for a foreign film (Goldsmith, Ward and O'Regan 2010, 53).[3] Falk invited them to meet him in New York, largely on the basis of Sjoquist's association with *Crocodile Dundee*, later declaring that "*Crocodile Dundee* was exactly the tone and class" that he wanted for *The Phantom* (quoted in Clark 1988, 3). Once negotiations were concluded with King Features Syndicate, Falk was retained as a story consultant and visited Australia in March 1988 to discuss his initial concepts with the production team's newest member, Ken Shadie, who co-wrote the screenplay for *Crocodile Dundee*. Sherlock was undoubtedly convinced about the potential audience interest in the film, claiming that *The Phantom* comic strip was followed by an estimated one hundred million readers worldwide (Jacques 1988, 25; Ward 1989, 12). While Shadie declared that his script would portray "a 1990s Phantom [who would be] a modern-day hero" (quoted in Watson 1989, 83), Sherlock maintained that the film would remain loyal to Falk's vision of the Phantom as a deeply moral hero. There would be "no blood and guts on the screen," insisted Sherlock, adding that it would be a "mixture of [James] Bond and *Raiders of the Lost Ark*" (quoted in *Sydney Morning Herald* 1988, 3). The comparison with Steven Spielberg's retro-styled adventure film would turn out to be both prescient and, ultimately, ill-advised.

Hollywood on the Gold Coast

Sherlock's acquisition of the film rights to *The Phantom* coincided with the American film industry's growing pursuit of "runaway" film production opportunities—a trend that would have a direct bearing on the eventual production of *The Phantom* feature film. Throughout the 1990s, American film studios sought to overcome escalating domestic production costs by mounting "runaway" film shoots in offshore locations. Hollywood studios' choice of foreign production sites was influenced by three key factors: favorable exchange rates between the US dollar relative to local currencies; financial incentives offered by foreign governments; and the availability of adequate studio facilities and skilled foreign film crews (Herd 2004, 23).

Queensland was the first Australian state to aggressively pursue "runaway" foreign investment for the development of local film-production facilities. In 1986, the Queensland government announced that it had struck a deal with the US-based De Laurentis Entertainment Group (DEG) to build a film studio and a theme park at Coomera, near the Gold Coast, a popular tourist destination. The Queensland government, which offered DEG a generous assistance package estimated to be AUD$12.5 million (Goldsmith, Ward, and O'Regan 2010, 58), hoped the studio would stimulate economic growth and job opportunities by expanding the Gold Coast's existing tourism infrastructure and service industries (Goldsmith and O'Regan 2003, 26). However, DEG'S ongoing financial woes, compounded by the global stock market crash in October 1987, saw the company's Australian subsidiary (De Laurentis Entertainment Limited) absorbed into the Village Roadshow Corporation (Goldsmith, Ward, and O'Regan 2010, 68–69). Despite its turbulent financial beginnings, the site, renamed the Village Roadshow Film Studio, was formally opened in July 1988. Shortly thereafter, Village Roadshow sold 50 percent of its stake in the Queensland studio site to Warner Bros. (US), with whom it would jointly develop a theme park on land adjacent to the film studio (Ketchell, 1998).[4] The Warner Bros. Movie World Theme Park was opened to the public in 1991 and was widely promoted as "Hollywood on the Gold Coast."

Village Roadshow's ongoing involvement with the Warner Roadshow Movie World Studios (as it became known) played a key role in the production of *The Phantom* feature film. The company was founded by Roc Kirby, who built Australia's first drive-in cinema in suburban Melbourne in 1954 as part of his fledgling Village Cinemas chain (Groves 1995, 58 and 64). The business gradually expanded its interests in cinematic exhibition and distribution and became a publicly listed company in 1989, with majority control retained by the Kirby family. By the mid-1990s, Village Roadshow was a vertically integrated media and entertainment company, with interests in "hardtop" cinemas, film and video distribution, theme parks and commercial radio throughout Australia and Southeast Asia (*Variety Deal Memo* 1995, 10–11). The formation of a US-based film production unit, Village Roadshow Pictures, in 1989 therefore seemed a logical extension of the Australian parent company's activities. The new venture was helmed by Greg Coote (President), who was the former joint-managing director of Village Roadshow, and was now tasked with the job of developing new film and television projects in Hollywood.

The Phantom became one of the first such projects on Coote's production slate, when Village Roadshow Pictures agreed to act as the Sherlock-led consortium's international representatives in searching for a distribution partner (Watson 1989, 83). Coote foreshadowed that *The Phantom* would be filmed outside the US, claiming it "could easily be made anywhere, certainly in Mexico [or in] Kenya," but said his ultimate goal was to ensure "the film [gets] finished in Australia" (quoted in Urban 1989, 14). Despite the character's American provenance, Coote maintained that the film would be an essentially Australian production—not because of the Phantom's ersatz status as an "Australian" comic book hero, but because the majority of the film's budget "will stay in [Australia]" (quoted in Urban 1989, 14).

Touting access to world class production crews and facilities, along with proximity to spectacular shooting locales, the combined efforts of both state and national government-backed film production offices had, by 1993, succeeded in attracting US$70 million (AUD$100 million) in foreign film and television production to Australia—a task made easier by the favorable currency exchange rates between the Australian and American dollar (*Variety* 1994, 45). The Pacific Film and Television Commission, established by the Queensland State Government in 1991, used a raft of financial incentives to lure overseas productions to the Warner Roadshow Movie World studios, declaring it to be "the largest purpose-built lot in the southern hemisphere" (Pacific Film and Television Commission, ca.1990s). By 1994, the Warner Roadshow facilities were hosting film projects valued at AUD$116.3 million (US$89 million), of which up to 80 percent was derived from offshore productions (Murdoch 1995, S-3). As Robin James, CEO of the Pacific Film and Television Commission, bluntly observed, "we can offer the same production values as the US at a lower cost – that's the bottom line" (*Variety* 1994, 45). *The Phantom* film project would ultimately benefit from these developments, whereby the economic imperatives of the US film industry happily coincided with Australian state governments' regional development policies, which in turn successfully promoted Queensland as an economically viable offshore film production site.

The Phantom and "Comic Book Movies"

Superheroes were, of course, no strangers to Hollywood, with many of the genre's earliest stars, such as Superman and Captain Marvel, making the transition from print to screen throughout the 1940s. The Phantom also made his cinematic debut during this period. Columbia Pictures produced a fifteen-episode serial-film version of *The Phantom* (1943), starring Tom Tyler, but the cheap production values caused only painful memories for Lee Falk (Steinbrunner 1997 [1970], 204). The pilot for a planned television version of *The Phantom* was filmed in 1960, but the series was not picked up by American television networks and the episode remained unseen for decades. Big screen adaptation of comic book superheroes were, for decades, thereafter consigned to cheaply made matinee serials, which were ostensibly produced as disposable children's entertainment—much like comic books themselves. Nor did superheroes fare well in the analog era of film production, when special effects techniques could not convincingly duplicate the spectacular feats that were the hallmark of comic book superheroes. However, the attitudes of both filmmakers and filmgoers towards cinematic superheroes changed following the success of *Superman: The Movie* (1978), which treated its central character with a winning blend of mythic reverence and tongue-in-cheek humor, ably abetted by the film's relatively unknown star, Christopher Reeve. Furthermore, filmmaking technology had begun to catch up with comic book visuals and could now fulfill the promise embedded in *Superman*'s promotional tagline: "You will believe a man can fly."

But it was not until the release of *Batman* in 1989 that Hollywood truly appreciated how a comic book superhero could be transformed into a global box office phenomenon. The film's estimated global box office takings (US$411 million) were augmented by an unprecedented merchandising campaign, orchestrated by Warner Communications Inc. across its varied publishing, audio-visual entertainment, theme park and retailing interests (Meehan 1991, 47–65). The astonishing success of *Batman* led to a scramble among American film studios to snap up film rights to comic book properties, creating the kind of feverish marketplace demand that, theoretically, should have worked in favor of *The Phantom* being acquired by a major studio. Some of the most commercially successful "comic book movies" of the 1990s were based on obscure titles, such as *Teenage Mutant Ninja Turtles* (1990) and *Men in Black* (1997). If these relatively unknown comic book characters could be profitably adapted for film, then *The Phantom*, with its worldwide readership numbering in the millions, would seem assured of equal, if not greater success.

Yet the glut of comic book movies that followed in the early-to-mid-1990s was marred by several US box office failures, including *Tank Girl* (1995) and *Judge Dredd* (1995). More ominous was the lukewarm performance of *The Rocketeer* (1991), which earned just US$46.7 million against its estimated US$35 million budget. This 1930s-period action film was based on a retro-superhero comic that enjoyed a cult following among comic book fans, but failed to excite mainstream audiences. Did its relatively poor performance indicate that moviegoers no longer cared for its evocation of "old-fashioned," Saturday matinee adventure—the very qualities which had underscored *The Phantom*'s popularity for decades?

Paramount Pictures
The "Reluctant" Partner

The Phantom was eventually picked up by Paramount Pictures, but the studio's level of financial commitment to the project was confined to covering the costs of developing film prints, advertising and distribution fees (Busch 1994, 1, 91). This was in keeping with Paramount's cautious film financing strategy, which was predicated on sharing development costs with co-production partners. Michael Douglas and Steve Retuer's company, Constellation Films, was originally named as a co-production partner on *The Phantom* (Sheehy 1994, 5), but Robert Evans and Alan Ladd Jr. were eventually named as producers.

Remarkably, many of the aspirations that Lee Falk and Bruce Sherlock had expressed for the project were realised during this period. Ken Shadie's original treatment calling for a modern day, 1990s hero was overturned by the film's new screenwriter, Jeffrey Boam, whose credits included *Indiana Jones and the Last Crusade* (1989). Drawn to the character's "old-fashioned" sense of integrity, valor, and courage, Boam opted to retain the series' original 1930s setting, saying that "it had to be in that period, because I don't think a lot of those ideas translate well into the present" (quoted in Scapperotti 1995, 8). Lee Falk initially declared that *The Phantom* wouldn't need a "big-name" actor, explaining that "if the picture's a hit, he'll [become] a star like Christopher Reeve, who was such a wonderful choice for *Superman* ... well, we need a Phantom like *that*" (quoted in Murray 1988, 68). Billy Zane was therefore a near perfect casting choice when it was announced in 1994 that he would play the Phantom; the up-and-coming actor was best-known to Australian audiences as the villain menacing Nicole Kidman in *Dead Calm* (1989), which was filmed off the Queensland coast. It was there that Zane first read *The Phantom* comic book, later recalling, "I thought this [character] was the greatest and soon I was having [the comics] flown to Hamilton Island so I could read more" (quoted in Stanley 1994, 9). Zane became a zealous fan of the character, declaring him "the end-all as far as role models and superheroes" were concerned, and undertook a rigorous training regimen to "bulk up" for the role (Paramount Pictures 1996).

The film's pre-production phase was not without disruption. The disappointing box-office performance of *The Shadow* (1994), which, like *The Phantom*, was based on a 1930s-era hero, apparently unnerved Paramount Pictures, which was already anxious about *The Phantom*'s estimated $53 million production budget.[5] Joe Dante had been chosen to direct *The Phantom* and was visiting Queensland to scout locations when Paramount temporarily shut down production until it could secure additional co-production financing. The delays meant that the sets already built on the Warner Roadshow Movie World Studios lot were dismantled and the local crew was dismissed in September 1994, with filming pushed back to the following year (Partridge 1994). When production resumed, Dante stayed on as an executive producer, but was replaced as director by the Australian filmmaker Simon Wincer, whose credits included *Free Willy* (1993), and the Emmy Award-winning TV mini-series, *Lonesome Dove* (1989).[6] Wincer, aside from being a lifelong *Phantom* reader, was no stranger to 1930s period drama, having directed several episodes of *The Young Indiana Jones Chronicles* for US television in 1992 and 1993.[7] Crucially, Wincer suggested changes that allowed shooting to recommence, arguing that the exterior jungle scenes could be cheaply filmed in Thailand, while the New York street scenes could be built on Hollywood backlots. By filming the remaining interior scenes on specially constructed sets in Queensland, as Wincer later claimed, "The budget was trimmed by nearly US$10 million—and we were off and running" (Paramount Pictures 1996). Filming began in Los Angeles in October 1995, before relocating to Thailand for a seven-week location shoot. The production was transferred to the Warner Roadshow Movie World Studios in mid-December 1995, where filming concluded on February 13, 1996—nearly sixty years to the day from when *The Phantom* comic strip made its debut (Paramount Pictures 1996).

Mobilizing the "Phans"

The quest to bring *The Phantom* to movie screens was, in many key aspects, a fan-driven endeavor; Bruce Sherlock's decision to purchase the film rights was, after all, influenced by his lifelong enthusiasm for the character. Yet just as Sherlock began negotiations with King Features Syndicate, *The Phantom* was undergoing a popular renaissance in Australia, thanks to the dedicated efforts of an organized fan movement and the arrival of a new publisher determined to revitalise the comic's commercial fortunes. As the film project gathered momentum, the Phantom's fans (or "phans," as they called themselves) and his official gatekeepers entered into a symbiotic, and occasionally adversarial, relationship. Yet both parties hoped that *The Phantom* movie would mark the successful culmination of their parallel campaigns to restore the character's prominence in Australian public culture.

The Phantom Club, launched in 1981, was a business venture created and operated by fans. King Features Syndicate licensed Hendo Industries (formed by the Club's President, John Henderson) to produce *Phantom* merchandise for sale throughout Australasia (Robson 1985, 83). The club was indefatigable in its promotion of *The Phantom* within the region, with Henderson doing media appearances dressed in his tailor-made Phantom costume (*Jungle Beat* 1987, 8). The Club lent its support to *The Phantom* film project, with Henderson offering to play the character himself and pledging to donate his fee towards the construction of a *Phantom* fun park in Queensland (*The Sun* 1988). Despite recruiting over 3,500 members by the mid-1980s, the Club's license was withdrawn by King Features Syndicate in 1988, due to alleged copyright infringements (Shedden 2007).

In 1987, Frew Publications' surviving founders, Ron Forsyth and Lawford "Jim" Richardson invited Sydney journalist Jim Shepherd to suggest ways of rejuvenating *The Phantom* comic book which, according to Shepherd, was "getting a bit dog-eared" (quoted in Patrick 2007). After canvassing readers' memories of their favorite adventures, Shepherd set about reprinting previously censored *Phantom* stories by recruiting prominent Australian "phans," such as Barry Stubbersfield (Hammond 2006), to conduct archival research and retrieve lost artwork (Shepherd 1988, 9). Shepherd introduced a letters column ("Phantom Forum") to gauge readers' reactions to the new publishing program and answer their questions about various aspects of Phantom lore. The "Phantom Forum" also gave Australian readers an opportunity to express their affinity for the character. Some liked the Phantom because "he does not fly ... and does not have x-ray vision" and was therefore not a "superhero" in the modern sense of the word, but simply "a law-enforcer" (Skender 1996, 34). Others admired the Phantom because he was a "strong, virtuous and true hero" (Davis 1996, 33), whose positive beliefs and actions made him, in the eyes of one reader, "a role model ... that I can hold up to my boys with confidence" (Furlong 1996, 34). Australians, it seemed, admired the Phantom because they saw him as the very antithesis of the American "super" hero.

King Features Syndicate, in conjunction with its Australian merchandising representative, Gaffney International Licensing, embarked on a publicity campaign in 1991, dubbed "The Year of the Phantom," to commemorate the strip's fifty-fifth anniversary. Key events included the widely publicised release of the one thousandth edition of *The Phantom* comic book and the opening of a *Phantom* art exhibition at Sydney's DC Art Gallery. Coinciding with this campaign was the re-launch of The Phantom

Official Fan Club Australia, now operated by the gift retailer Famous Faces (Melbourne). The club's newsletter became a sales catalogue for the growing array of *Phantom* merchandise now available in Australia, as well as a publicity outlet for Frew Publications, which provided news about forthcoming *Phantom* comics. Nonetheless, the newsletter remained dependent on readers' contributions for most of its editorial content (Shedden ca.2007).

Ongoing Australian press coverage of the film's casting and production delays kept *The Phantom* movie in the public spotlight throughout the 1990s. *The Phantom* comic book carried reports of Jim Shepherd's meeting with Lee Falk, together with the film's cast and crew, accompanied by "Frew historian" Barry Stubbersfield, thus acknowledging the vital role that "phans" have played in rejuvenating *The Phantom* franchise (Frew Publications 1996, 40–41). The cumulative effect of these publishing, merchandising and marketing campaigns was to foster an active "phan" community, who not only represented a burgeoning market for *Phantom* merchandise, but who could also be potentially called upon to help generate "buzz" about *The Phantom* prior to the film's local release. Australian "phans," therefore, provided the kind of dedicated audience that the film's American distributors simply could not call upon in the United States, largely because of the character's dormant public profile.

Twilight of the (Matinee) Heroes

The Phantom, however, seemed destined to join the growing list of failed "comic book movies," despite holding sixth-place in US box-office rankings upon its first week of release from 7 June 1996, when it took in over US$7 million (*Variety* 1996, 10). Movie industry sources swiftly declared *The Phantom* to be "among the early [US] summer losers," generating just US$16 million in ticket sales against an estimated budget of US$45m (Hindes 1996, 10), dropping to 93rd place in the top-100 domestic grosses for the US market in 1996 (*Box Office Mojo*). *The Phantom* enjoyed a comparatively better performance upon its Australian release (26 September), earning nearly AUD$1.6 million by the end of its first week and eventually taking AUD$4.9 million at the Australian box-office, ultimately scoring thirty-third place among the top fifty highest grossing films in Australia for that year (Screen Australia 2012c). To be fair, *The Phantom* faced formidable competition from such Hollywood blockbusters as *Independence*

Day, *Twister* and *Mission: Impossible*, which dominated American and Australian cinema circuits throughout 1996.

Critical reactions to the film, both in Australia and America, were essentially positive, but not without reservations. While some critics admired Billy Zane's "bright and breezy" portrayal of the Phantom (Creed 1996), and lauded the film's evocation of "old-fashioned adventure" (Stratton 1996), others felt that these very qualities handicapped the film, and found it compared poorly with the "blockbuster" adaptations of Superman or Batman (Cheshire 1996, 40; Van Gelder 1996). Even the reaction among diehard "phans" was lukewarm: Paul Sheehan, writing in the *Sydney Morning Herald*, said that, despite the film's undeniable charms, many fans "will not like the now formulaic Indiana Jones feel of the film, which reflects the Indiana Jones affiliations of the film-makers" (1996, 5). The built-in nostalgia of *Raiders of the Lost Ark*, which the producers tried so hard to emulate in *The Phantom*, ultimately alienated audiences. Not only did the film's lo-tech thrills and improbable plot device (involving a search for three magical skulls) fail to impress moviegoers, but the heroic persona of the Phantom himself seemed out of step with audience tastes.

Even Simon Wincer acknowledged this trend when he made the following crucial observation:

> Most American superheroes . . . need a psychiatrist. It's the darker side of the heroes that appeals to the American market. *The Phantom* has never really been successful in America because he doesn't have flaws. He is almost too straight. (Quoted in Beck 1996, 4)

The Phantom became an unintended victim of the phenomenal success of Tim Burton's *Batman*, which did more than just demonstrate the commercial potential of comic book movie franchises; it also proved that audiences were more than ready to embrace darker, morally ambivalent superheroes. For even as Bruce Sherlock and his consortium partners were negotiating film rights for the character in the late 1980s, *The Phantom* was already a film whose time had passed.

Conclusion

The production of *The Phantom* movie was made possible by a remarkable confluence of events that allowed the project to be instigated, and largely driven by, film industry outsiders who were themselves unabashed fans of the character. Their endeavors to bring *The Phantom* to the screen benefited from the internationalization of American film production, which actively fostered commercial collaboration with foreign industry and government-backed production partners. The logistical outsourcing of Hollywood movies ultimately led to *The Phantom* being partly filmed on Australian shores—a fitting turn of events, given the character's enduring popularity in that country.

Yet the commercial failure of *The Phantom* challenges popular notions about the ubiquitous appeal of comic book movies among mainstream audiences and the influence that comic book fans supposedly wield in steering filmmakers towards "preferred" interpretations of their cherished heroes, as well as fans' collective ability to determine positive box office outcomes. Despite the best efforts of the film's production team—several of whom were avowed fans of the Phantom—to ensure fealty to Lee Falk's creative vision, *The Phantom* simply failed to resonate with the majority of moviegoers who had little prior engagement with the character in its original comic strip form. In the end, there were simply not enough "phans" to make *The Phantom* a resounding financial success, even in foreign markets like Australia, where the character had been an integral part of popular print culture for generations.

The Phantom remains a problematic franchise for King Features Syndicate to this day. A determined effort to reboot the character as a modern-day urban adventurer in *The Phantom* (2009), a TV mini-series produced by RHI Entertainment for the SyFy Channel (US), was met with critical disdain (Powers 2010), and even greater audience indifference. Nonetheless, Bruce Sherlock remained upbeat about the prospects for *The Phantom: Legacy*, assuring "phans" that it will have "the makings of a blockbuster" and would contain "some surprises that will thrill Phantom fans worldwide" (*Comingsoon.net* 2008). Yet given his troubled on-screen career, it is far from certain if "The Ghost Who Walks" will rise again.

Acknowledgments

The author would like to thank John Clements (Australian comics historian), Bryan Shedden (*The Deep Woods*), the staff of the Australian Film Institute Research Collection, RMIT University (Melbourne) and the Motion Picture Distributors Association of Australia.

Notes

1. By the 1960s, the character's international popularity had reached such heights that several foreign comic book publishers began commissioning new episodes of *The Phantom*, produced and written by local writers and illustrators, to satisfy domestic demand. This was especially notable in Sweden, where *Fantomen* (as it was known) had become one of the country's top-selling comic books since its debut in 1950, second only to *Kalle Anke* (*Donald Duck*). From 1963 onwards, Swedish publisher Semic Press began producing new Fantomen stories for the Scandinavian market, which were subsequently reprinted under license in the Austrialian edition of The Phantom comic book (Pilcher and Brooks 2005, 246–48; Patrick 2012b, 133–58).

2. *The Phantom* made its first appearance in American comic books as one of several King Features Syndicate serials to be reprinted in *Ace Comics* No.11 (David McKay Publications, February 1938). *The Phantom* subsequently appeared as a solo feature in six editions of the *Feature Book* series, commencing with No.20 (David McKay Publications, December 1938), but it was not a self-titled series devoted entirely to the Phantom.

3. *Crocodile Dundee* earned AUD$47.7 million at the Australian box office, making it the highest grossing domestic film in Australian cinema history, and the sixth most profitable film overall ever screened in Australia (Screen Australia, 2012a, 2012b).

4. Village Roadshow had distributed Warner Bros. films in Australia since 1971 (Shoebridge 1996, 37).

5. *The Shadow* earned US$32 million against its estimated US$25 million production budget. Source: *Box Office Mojo* (http://boxofficemojo.com), accessed: 19/04/2012.

6. Lee Falk had apparently suggested Simon Wincer as a potential director for *The Phantom* after watching *Lonesome Dove* (Kahn 2011, 298).

7. In a further coincidence, Wincer had also directed one of *The Phantom*'s future co-stars, Catherine Zeta-Jones (who played Sala, leader of the Sky Band), in a 1993 episode of *The Young Indiana Jones Chronicles*.

THOR, GOD OF BORDERS

Transnationalism and Celestial Connections in the Superhero Film

VINCENT M. GAINE

The trailer for the Marvel-Paramount release *Thor* (2011) features the supertext: "TWO WORLDS," "ONE HERO," and "THE BATTLE COMES TO EARTH." These words are a fair description of the film's narrative, as Thor (Chris Hemsworth) is exiled from his home on Asgard to Earth, where he must battle both internal and external forces in the process of becoming a hero. In addition, the trailer draws attention to the film's concern with liminality and border crossing, perhaps a surprising concern in a film that is, ostensibly, an "American" product. *Thor*, like many superhero films and indeed Hollywood films in general, problematizes the notion of "Americanness," both as a cultural text and as a commercial product. This essay argues that the problematization is achieved through *Thor*'s transnational elements, and that these elements can be identified through analysis of the film's production, distribution, and marketing, through the cultural appropriation involved in making a *Thor* film, and in the diegetic elements of the film itself.

Some Assembly Required

The Superhero Genre and Transnational Hollywood

Aihwa Ong observes that "*Trans* denotes moving through space or across lines" (quoted in Hunt and Wing-Fai 2008, 3), and a common feature within the discourse of transnational cinema is that of *movement* of both commercial and cultural content across borders. Commercially, funds travel across borders to allow location shooting and post-production such as visual effects, and personnel are brought together for filmmaking from multiple nations. These form the new international division of cultural labor (Miller et al. 2005), which describes the manufacture of cultural products in a global context. These practices result in culturally transnational film texts. "Transnational" in this sense means that an element of one nation moves between its place of origin and another site where it joins with elements of other nations into an assembly of different cultural forms. The central site in this case is "Hollywood." Not Hollywood as a district of Los Angeles, but Hollywood as an industrial concept, a filmmaking practice and aesthetic that is understood as specific and recognizable within world cinema (Olson, 2000, quoted in Miller et al. 2005, 7). It is the assembly of transnational elements within filmmaking that have led authors to argue for a reading of "global Hollywood" filmmaking.

The superhero genre has frequently featured transnational talent, including high profile examples like Taiwanese Ang Lee acting as director of *Hulk* (2003), which starred Australian actor Eric Bana. Other Australian performers featuring prominently in "American" superhero filmmaking include Heath Ledger as the Joker and Hugh Jackman as Wolverine, Jackman sharing the *X-Men* franchise with British actors Patrick Stewart, Ian McKellen, Michael Fassbender, James McAvoy, and Nicholas Hoult. Furthermore, British actors Christian Bale, Andrew Garfield, and Henry Cavill have, respectively, recently played the most iconic of all US superheroes: Batman, Spider-Man, and Superman. Furthermore, Bale shares the Dark Knight Trilogy with fellow Brits Michael Caine, Gary Oldman, and Tom Hardy. This is hardly a new phenomenon, as Hollywood has featured international personnel almost since its inception, suggesting that, as an entertainment industry, Hollywood has long imported global talent into its production culture. Behind the camera too, many of Hollywood's most famous directors are not American, including such recent examples as Peter Jackson, Guillermo Del Toro, Gavin Hood, Alfonso Cuarón, and, of course, Kenneth Branagh, the director of *Thor*, whose first film, *Henry V* (1989), garnered considerable attention including Academy Award nominations for Branagh as both director and leading actor. Taken together, the variety in such multi-national production members in the superhero genre suggests a significant investment in transnational production strategies.

In the case of *Thor*, its transnational cast and crew demonstrate the difficulty in describing the film as simply or entirely "American."[1] Within its key cast and crew members, *Thor*'s appeal to a wide range of national identities is emblematic of the kinds of transnational filmmaking currently dominant in Hollywood. Branagh is Irish-born, but Royal Shakespeare

Company trained, speaking with an English accent and consequently possessed of a hybridized British identity. Costume designer Alexandre Byrne is also English, while the composer, Patrick Doyle, is Scottish. One of the producers, Victoria Alonso, hails from Argentina and the cinematographer, Haris Zambarloukos, from Cyprus. Performers include the British Anthony Hopkins as Odin, Idris Elba as Heimdall, and Tom Hiddleston as Loki, alongside the Australian Chris Hemsworth and the Americans Natalie Portman as Jane Foster, Kat Dennings as Darcy Lewis, Rene Russo as Frigga, and Clark Gregg as Agent Coulson. To add further international variety, Canadian Colm Feore appears as Laufey, the Swedish Stellan Skarsgård as Erik Selvig and the Japanese Asano Tadanobu as Hogun. With prominent figures from at least five continents, *Thor*'s production offers extensive evidence of Hollywood's complex transnationalism.

Industrial elements also join the transnational mix. The London Philharmonic Orchestra performed the soundtrack of *Thor*, while thirteen special effects companies worked on the film, including the French BUF and the Australian Fuel VFX. However, it would be nonsensical to suggest that the contributions of such companies mean that some of the effects are "French" or "Australian," and therefore distinct from those made by American FX houses Gentle Giant Studios and Evil Eye Pictures. Nor does the London Philharmonic Orchestra make a more "English" sound than, say, the Boston Philharmonic Orchestra, but the contribution of companies and personnel based outside the USA does indicate Hollywood's transnational ambitions and the scope of their global recruitment strategies. On one level, this demonstrates the flow of global capital—non-American companies hired and paid for by American Hollywood studios. On another, it also demonstrates the global dissemination of product—music played by the London Philharmonic Orchestra travels the world on the soundtrack of *Thor*, while the effects of BUF and Fuel VFX effects houses dazzle viewers the world over.

Furthermore, while the immediate domestic audience for Hollywood filmmaking may still be in the United States, the overseas market is often more lucrative. *Thor*, for example, made over $181 million from its domestic release and over $268 million from theaters outside the USA, while *The Dark Knight Rises* grossed $636.3 million overseas as opposed to $448.1 million in the States (Box Office Mojo). Similarly, the highest grossing superhero film to date, *The Avengers* (2012), in which Thor also appears, earned over $1.5 billion, and $895.2 million of that was taken outside the USA (Box Office Mojo). The new international division of cultural labor, combined with the importance of the overseas market, thereby reveals the transnational production of Hollywood cinema—as resources from multiple countries are assembled into products that are then consumed in myriad countries.

However, these transnational elements do not stop *Thor* from being an American commercial product. American companies Marvel and Paramount hired other companies to contribute to a film that the studios would ultimately own, and their legal ownership of the product confers upon it an American identity as a piece of intellectual property. Intellectual property has been the source of much legislation and litigation, ensuring that Hollywood can maximize profits from such diverse blockbuster properties as *Star Wars* and *Harry Potter* (Miller et al. 2005, 216–35), as well as Marvel's superhero films (which, like *Star Wars*, are now owned by Disney). This legal ownership allows studios to be the beneficiaries of the production, in the case of *Thor*, of a global box office take of $449 million from a budget of $150 million.

Marketing Complex "Americanness"

Thor and the Promotion of a Transnational Blockbuster Film

Thor may be an American industrial product like beer brewed by Minnesota or Aerospace Manufacturing in Washington State, but as a cultural text its identity is more complex. This product's appeal to as broad a market as possible is strongly influenced by the film industry's perception of "an emergent global hegemony of taste" (Miller et al. 2005, 262). This perception is responsible for a perceived standardization of cinematic product, avoiding risk by producing genres and styles of film with proven track records. It is claimed that this standardization means that Hollywood produces

> empty and costly cinematic spectacles that, in order to maintain their mainstream inoffensiveness, must be subjected to increasingly thorough forms of cultural and ideological cleansing before being released into the global cinemascape. (Ezra and Rowden 2006, 2)

This "cleansing" minimizes the risk of "cultural discount": the notion that texts with culturally specific content do not travel (or sell) well (Hoskins and Mirus 1988). In a global market, "media products with sufficient cultural transparency" (Davis and Nadler 2009, 2), namely Hollywood films, can be distributed and consumed across borders because they do not require any specific cultural upbringing or background in order to be understood.

This transparency leads to the criticism encapsulated by Ezra and Rowden that Hollywood films are "empty," lacking in complex plots or sophisticated ideas. More perniciously, Hollywood cinema can be viewed as a form of cultural imperialism, exporting American values to a global audience, with an emphasis on "transcendental modernity – fixing social and individual problems via love, sex and commodities" (Miller et al. 294), values which celebrate "the cult of the individual" (Gray and Kaklamanidou 2011, 4). Claims about the ubiquity of this ideology likely stem from the success of Hollywood cinema in penetrating local film markets (not to mention American television, music and other popular culture) that saturates perception and understanding. Since American commercial texts are imbued with American values, they also appear as American cultural texts, eagerly consumed by audiences the world over. But this consumption is not simply a matter of cultural discount, transparency or simplistic material. The ubiquity of Hollywood product might also suggest a "global hegemony of taste," but this ignores the ruthless control of theatrical exhibition by Hollywood distributors: Hollywood product is found everywhere because distributors put it everywhere (Miller et al. 2005, 91–110). Moreover, such perceptions rest on an understanding of Hollywood films as straightforwardly American, and not as carefully managed transnational film productions, made with the world in mind. Nor is this careful transnational positioning solely tied to film narrative, as transnational elements such as personnel, settings, and themes can create selling points for the film, which can then be emphasized in the films and their marketing. *Thor* demonstrates such emphasis.

The representations of Asgard that appeared in *Thor*'s marketing campaign, and later in the film itself, offer a useful case study of the film's transnational aspirations and roots. In a deviation from the comic books, crowd shots of Asgard indicate people of multiple races—the various characters by no means look Nordic or Scandinavian. This creates a sense of universalism in Asgard, preventing it from appearing as a Northern European version of the heavenly realm. This universalism is, however, becomes problematic in *Thor*'s marketing campaign. For example, Hogun, Thor's close comrade, is played by the Japanese actor Asano Tadanobu, and the Guardian of Asgard, Heimdall, is portrayed by Black English actor Idris Elba. Their inclusion in the cast was surprising enough to some that it led to cries from a white supremacist group for the film to be boycotted

(Smith 2010; Hauman 2010). Close-ups of Hogun and Heimdall appear in the trailer for *Thor*, receiving greater emphasis than some of the film's more major characters. Hogun and Heimdall are minor characters in *Thor*, so their presence in the publicity rather than other actors such as Ray Stevenson (Volstagg) and Josh Dallas (Fandral) suggests a deliberate emphasis being placed on non-Caucasian characters and their performers. This is demonstrated by the use of marketing images featuring Tadanobou and Elba. In Europe and the USA, posters featured the faces of Hemsworth, Hopkins, Portman, Hiddleston, and Elba , whereas in Japan, Elba was replaced with Tadanobu.

These different posters suggest multiple meanings. Firstly, that Paramount took its global film and localized it for different territories by emphasizing different performers. The presence of Tadanobou could "position" the film in the mind of the Japanese cinemagoer as a point of familiarity among the Caucasian star faces, while the presence of the black (and British) Elba might be used as a potential draw for domestic African American audiences as well as overseas audiences. More specifically, the shifting deployment of stars reveals the competing ideologies at work in "global" film promotion. While Hemsworth's most prominent Hollywood appearance prior to *Thor* was a brief role as George Kirk in *Star Trek* (JJ Abrams, 2009), he may have been a draw for Australian audiences who knew him from a three-year stint on television show *Home and Away* (1988–). Hemsworth's appearance as Thor in the film's promotional posters, in combination with the film's other major stars, does suggest that his was not expected to be a fulsome draw for audiences.

Consequently, a shifting rostrum of stars appeared above the titular character in *Thor*'s poster campaign. Prior to *Thor*, Tadanobou had appeared in over sixty films, including *Ichi The Killer* (2001) and *Mongol: The Rise to Power of Genghis Khan* (2007), the latter of which received an Academy Award nomination for Best Foreign Language Picture. His presence on the Japanese poster suggests that his star profile was used to market the film in his home nation, while his absence from the US poster implies that he had yet to achieve a "global" star status. In the case of Elba, his presence in television shows like *The Wire* (2002–2006) and *Luther* (2010–), as well as films like *American Gangster* (2007), and *28 Weeks Later . . .* (2007) (which also featured fellow *Thor* alumnus, Jeremy Renner) would have made him a significant transmedia star for certain groups of potential viewers. However, the inconsistent presence of Elba in the marketing also indicates the limits of his fame, seen in his omission from the poster for

Japan in favor of Tadanobou. Superhero films may have demonstrated that they do not need A-list stars in order to attract audiences, but the shifting use of stars from ensemble film casts like *Thor*'s indicates that known performers remain important when marketing superhero blockbusters.

Just as marketing is not completely standardized, nor is the incorporation of cultural elements into Americanness complete. The transnational elements of different nations and cultures converse and interact in the site of global Hollywood, which may prescribe "Americanness" to its cast and characters, but equally may emphasize difference. For example, in the X-Men film franchise, the character of Charles Xavier is clearly coded as English, whether played by Patrick Stewart or James McAvoy (although a homogenization of "Britishness" takes place here, as McAvoy is actually Scottish). Xavier speaks with an English accent (despite his privileged New England upbringing) and in *X-Men: First Class* (Matthew Vaughn, 2011) is educated at Oxford University. Combined with the Canadian Wolverine and the German Nightcrawler, the British Xavier forms part of the diversity of the X-Men (his disability also adds to this). A key theme of the franchise is acceptance versus prejudice towards those who are different. In the case of *Thor*, difference pervades the film text as well as its paratextual materials. The transnational cast and mixture of Earthly and alien characters is key to the film's meaning, to which I return later.

The Stories I Heard as a Child

Norse Mythology and Thor's Transmedia Remakes

As noted above, the film *Thor* is a product of Marvel Studios, but Marvel's version of Thor is itself a cultural appropriation from Norse mythology. Stan Lee explains,

> I thought it would be fun to invent someone as powerful as, or perhaps even more powerful than, the Incredible Hulk. But how do you make someone stronger than the strongest person?
>
> It finally came to me; don't make him human – make him a god.
>
> I decided readers were already pretty familiar with the Greek and Roman gods. It might be fun to delve into the old Norse legends. . . . Besides, I pictured Norse gods looking like Vikings of old, with the flowing beards, horned helmets, and battle clubs. . . . I picked Thor . . . to headline the book. (2002, 157–58)

Richard Reynolds discusses the appropriation of Thor into established comic book conventions, including why this mythological character was successful:

> Jack Kirby's original artwork for the title rendered Thor, the supporting cast, Asgard and its inhabitants, the rainbow bridge Bifrost and all the villains and monsters in an accessible, science fiction/fantasy style that linked them comfortably with the rest of the Marvel Universe.
>
> . . . The Norse Gods are not alien either. Days of the week are named for them. Much of the pleasure of reading Thor comics is bound up with this reappropriation of a mythology so inconspicuously buried in the vocabulary of the reader's everyday speech. (Reynolds 1992, 54–57)

Marvel's appropriation of ancient Scandinavian mythology for serialized comic book narratives is an intrinsic transnational element to Thor. Furthermore, the two narrative forms have similarities as, like comic book (not to mention film) narratives, many mythological stories involve the disruption of equilibrium and the protagonist's restoration of the status quo. For example, in one Norse legend, Thrym, chief of the giants, steals Thor's hammer Mjolnir, which leaves Asgard vulnerable. Thrym demands the goddess Freya as his bride in exchange for the hammer, and Thor disguises himself as Freya in order to recover Mjolnir and, upon doing so, restores order to Asgard. In this respect, Marvel's adaptation of Norse mythology in Thor was aided by the original's seemingly shared narrative structure.

In addition, both mythologies and comic books utilize ongoing narratives, plot points from one leading into a later one. In the case of Norse mythology, events including the death of Baldur and the punishment of Loki presage Ragnarok and the end of the world, the tale of which includes resolution of a long-running rivalry between Thor and the great serpent Jormungand, who kill each other in the final battle. Serialized comic book narratives keep readers coming back for more, and the Marvel Cinematic Universe has replicated this technique with multiple films and sequels bringing viewers back for more instalments based on popular characters. The events of *Thor* follow on from those in *Iron Man 2* (2010), and subsequently influence the narrative of *The Avengers*, *Iron Man 3* (2013), *Thor: The Dark World* (2013), *Captain America: The Winter Solider* (2014), *Guardians of the Galaxy* (2014) and *The Avengers: Age of Ultron* (2015), as well as the TV series *Agents of S.H.I.E.L.D.* (2013–), which further expands the universe established by the films. The extension of serial narrative practices from Thor's mythological source materials into the new Marvel Studio production strategies reveals the complex interactions between those origins and Thor's newest incarnation.

However, the adaptation of Norse mythology by comic book writers and media franchise producers involves significant changes to the original concepts, most obviously placing the Norse characters in twentieth and twenty-first century settings. For instance, a major Marvel storyline featured Thor being exiled to Earth and stripped of his powers, which forms the central conceit of the film *Thor* (Strom 2010). Whereas in the comic books, Thor's exile lasts for multiple issues and involves him being trapped in the body of a human, in the film Thor is simply sent to Earth and returns to Asgard after a few days. Norse iconography and images are also a major component in Marvel's adaptation practices, as evidenced by Lee's description of the Norse gods' appearances. Furthermore, Branagh has mentioned that he read *Thor* comic books as a child, because of what he saw as their European aspect:

> Of all the American comics, 'Thor' was the only one I was really familiar with from my childhood, and it intrigued me, maybe because it was a bit more European, with those Viking helmets and its basis in Norse myth. The scale was exciting, and I did love the character and the story. It had depth and gravity in addition to being an entertaining ride. (Dawtrey 2011)

Kirby's designs of Thor, described as crucial by both Lee and Branagh, are maintained in the film's production design, as the sets, costumes and props of Asgard are decorated with Norse symbols and runes.

The extras on the DVD and Blu-Ray releases of *Thor* feature production designer Bo Welch and costume designer Alexandra Byrne discussing the influence of Norse features on their contributions to the film. Additionally, in an interview before the film's release, set decorator Lauri Gaffin also describes the design of *Thor*, claiming,

> The aesthetic of Asgard is a hybrid between preexisting artwork from the comic book and extensive research conducted within the film's art dept. with regards to Norse mythology, modern architectural design and future worlds imagined. (Wilding 2011)

These aspects of *Thor*'s production emphasize the influence of the originally Scandinavian features of the character on the film adaptation of an American comic book appropriation of Norse mythology. Production discourse reveals that, though far removed from its origins, Viking cultural heritage is still present in the design of this superhero film, this transnational feature feeding into the Hollywood assembly.

Two Worlds, One Hero

The Transnational From Reception to Textual Content

As well as visual features within the *mise-en-scene*, the cast and crew of *Thor* added further transnational flavors to its discursive surround. In particular, Branagh provides *Thor* with "Britishness," as do the actors Hopkins, Hiddleston, and Elba, while Hemsworth brings "Australianness" and Skarsgård brings "Swedishness." Branagh was a major part of the film's promotion, appearing along with Hemsworth and Hopkins on the cover of the April 2011 edition of *The Hollywood Reporter*. The accompanying article constructs Branagh as a Hollywood outsider (Galloway 2011), struggling to recapture the promise of his early career and to carve out a place in Hollywood filmmaking. The article presents Branagh as a great asset who brings distinction and uniqueness to the film. The DVD and Blu-Ray releases of *Thor* also emphasize Branagh, with a commentary by the director and a featurette entitled "Our Fearless Leader," in which Anthony Hopkins states that a desire to work with Branagh was his main reason for taking the role of Odin. Marvel's emphasis of Branagh, an identifiably and emphatically non-American director, as a key figure within the production of *Thor* helps to position the film as transnational, a point that was picked up on by reviewers.

The BBC's film critic Mark Kermode describes Branagh as having "a sense of big blusterous entertainment" which is evidenced in his previous films such as *Mary Shelley's Frankenstein* (1994) and *The Magic Flute* (2006), making Branagh an ideal director for *Thor* (Kermode 2011). Other reviewers also emphasized Branagh's influence, crediting the director as handling the potentially problematic and preposterous subject matter very well: "this very intelligent and now unjustly maligned director has put his personal mark on the picture" (Bradshaw 2011). Branagh's reputation as a director of films based on Shakespeare's plays was another common point of reference in both positive and negative reviews, as when Claudia Puig writes, "It takes a director known for his Shakespearean acumen to make a spectacular summer action movie filled with epic battles and familial struggles" (2011). In one other high profile instance, Roger Ebert concurs with Puig, stating,

> The director given this project, Kenneth Branagh, once obtained funding for a magnificent 70mm version of "Hamlet." Now he makes "Thor." I wonder with a dread fear if someone in Hollywood, stuck with a movie about a Norse god, said "Get Branagh. He deals with that Shakespeare crap." (Ebert 2011)

Ebert's review is particularly telling, as his disparaging comment equates familiarity with one European narrative tradition, "Shakespeare" with another, "Norse." Ebert echoes the discourse of the new international division of cultural labor developed by Toby Miller et al. (2005, 111–72) to describe the transnational assembly of this Hollywood film. Nor is this understanding solely found in reception, as a transnational sensibility is a key conceit in the film itself.

Much of *Thor*'s plot focuses on the main character being exiled from Asgard, so the film is built on his crossing the border between Asgard and Earth. An earlier border crossing is responsible for Thor's exile, as he leads an unsanctioned incursion into Jotunheim, realm of the Frost Giants. Significantly, the Asgardians travel via the Bifrost, a bridge rather than a vessel, which spans the borders of space between the Nine Realms, just as the cast and crew crossed national borders to create the film. Border crossings permeate the film from the beginning, the opening scene taking place in the border state New Mexico, near the town of Puente Antiguo. This Hispanic name appears in supertext, as does "New Mexico," two languages immediately apparent. Jane's research team encounters Thor, who is effectively an immigrant. His presence is a mystery, and Jane's question, "where did he come from?" immediately questions Thor's origin and otherness. Border crossings continue, as the following scene takes place in Tønsberg, Norway, 965 A.D. as Odin's voiceover informs the viewer that "once, mankind accepted a simple truth: that they were not alone in this universe." These words speak against isolation, and the Norway sequence demonstrates both the dangers and advantages of transnationalism. The Frost Giants would homogenize the world into undifferentiated ice, but the warriors of Asgard, led by Odin, ensure that "humanity would not face this threat alone" (Odin), crossing onto Earth/Midgard to drive the Frost Giants back to Jotunheim.

Odin describes Asgard as a "beacon of hope," and it is tempting to view this realm, or nation, of gods and celestial warriors as America, much as the United Federation of Planets serves as a metaphor for America in the *Star Trek* franchise. But America comes under threat in *Thor*, and it takes the external aid of Asgard to save Earth again—the realm of Asgard understands the need for unity and support. Unlike America, Asgard is a monarchy, ruled by Odin with Thor as his heir, but Odin mentions that both Thor and Loki "were born to be kings." This proves a major plot point, as it is subsequently revealed that Loki is the son of Laufey, taken by Odin from the Frost Giants' stronghold in Jotunheim. Odin explains that he hoped to forge a peaceful alliance between Jotunheim and Asgard by raising Loki as his son, presumably so that Loki could become king of Jotunheim. While Asgardian monarchy is clearly "Other" to the democracy promoted in American ideology, it is not presented as oppressive or unwise—indeed Odin appears as the epitome of wisdom (an element also found in the Norse legend of the character), in contrast to Thor's initial arrogance:

> ODIN: You are a vain, greedy, cruel boy!
> THOR: And you are an old man and a fool!
> ODIN: Yes . . . I was a fool, to think you were ready. . . . you have betrayed the express command of your king. Through your arrogance and stupidity, you've opened these peaceful realms and innocent lives to the horror and desolation of war!

Part of Odin's wisdom is his commitment to peace through unity and his willingness to overlook difference. Even after Loki touches the Casket of Ancient Winters and reverts to his true Frost Giant appearance, Odin still calls him his son. Loki, however, takes an essentialist view of his identity: "no matter how much you claim to love me, you could never have a Frost Giant sitting on the throne of Asgard!" Loki's hatred of his own identity prompts him to activate the Bifrost to destroy Jotunheim and the Frost Giants. Yet, like the Frost Giants, Loki homogenizes and replicates, creating multiple illusory copies of himself. Attacking difference and creating sameness, the film suggests, is literally the product of the God of Mischief. Loki's destructiveness is based on an individualized self-loathing, which contrasts with the embrace of difference shown by Odin and learned by Thor through his experience on Earth. Even stripped of his powers on his arrival on Earth, when Thor becomes a mortal, he still possesses great strength and combat skills, as well as the knowledge of Asgard.

As noted above, movement is key to transnationalism, and both Loki and Thor move between different realms in *Thor*. This movement is physical, in that they travel between Asgard, Earth and Jotunheim, but it is also ideological, since each brings their knowledge and influence to the places to which they travel. Loki's outsider status in Asgard facilitates the climactic incursion of the Frost Giants; Thor's presence alerts SHIELD to the existence of extra-terrestrial intelligence. The transnational movement of Loki and Thor makes them *liminal*: "Liminal entities are neither here nor there; they are betwixt and between the positions assigned and arrayed by law, custom, convention, and ceremonial" (Turner 1969, 95). Liminality, the state of being between positions, is an essential feature of superheroism (Gaine 2011) that, crucially, only Thor embraces. The importance of the "TWO WORLDS" in the film's tagline is that it is Thor's time on Earth that enables him to become a hero, learning wisdom and becoming worthy of his power. Notably, the film's discourse ignores the third realm of Jotunheim, Loki's realm, in favor of a diegetic worldview that focuses on the positive connectivity shared by Earth and Asgard.

Thor's embrace of liminality is unique in the film. While Loki's origin as a Frost Giant makes him a liminal figure in Asgard, he denies and seeks to erase that part of himself by destroying the Frost Giants, prizing one identity over another. Heimdall may appear liminal, as he stands at the border between Asgard and the other realms, but crucially he never *crosses* the border, remaining squarely of Asgard, even standing aside when Sif (Jamie Alexander) and the Warriors Three travel to Earth without authorization. Thor's friends are simply Asgardians on Earth, clearly Other and outlandish to the extent that SHIELD agents describe them as "Xena, Jackie Chan, and Robin Hood," all figures out of place in twenty-first century New Mexico. Thor, however, learns the value of other peoples, liminality, and, therefore, of *heroism*. It is from the borders that superheroes can engage with society in order to defend it, yet they cannot become too involved because this compromises their heroism. Therefore, Thor must return to the borders because it is from there that he can do the most good (Gaine 2011, 119–28). Borders may be urban, such as Bruce Wayne living on the outskirts of Gotham City, or national, as argued by Anthony Peter Spanakos in relation to Iron Man and the Incredible Hulk (2011, 15–28), or even celestial, as in the case of *Thor*, but they remain crucial in contemporary superhero filmmaking.

Thor's most heroic act is sacrificing himself to the Destroyer so as to satisfy Loki: "These people are innocent; taking their lives will gain you nothing. So take mine, and end this." It is his sacrifice that finally makes him worthy of Asgardian power, which resurrects him. A range of cultural reference points are combined in Thor's resurrection. The transnational Thor occupies a liminal space between pagan (Norse) mythology and Christian imagery, between science fiction and fantasy, forming the nexus point at which those competing ideologies and aesthetics meet, and it is this combination that creates his superhero identity. Thor's willingness to defend Earth makes him capable of doing just that—and when his Asgardian physicality is fully restored, the compassion and humility Thor learned as a mortal remakes him into a (super)hero. Now he can return to Asgard and save Jotunheim, not as a king, for Odin remains in power, but as a hero, who returns to defend Earth again in *The Avengers* and *Thor: The Dark World*.

Not only are theology and mythology combined, but magic becomes intertwined with science. This is *Thor*'s most touching scene, which takes place after Thor's failure to reclaim the hammer Mjolnir, when he has been taken prisoner by the agents of SHIELD Erik extracts him from the SHIELD base, after which Thor and Jane talk atop her makeshift research station. Thor explains his understanding of the universe: "Your ancestors called it magic; you call it science. Well, I come from a place where they're one and the same." This union builds on an earlier debate between Jane, Darcy, and Erik, in which science and magic are allowed to reconcile rather than clash:

> JANE: Well, if there's an Einstein-Rosen bridge, then there's something on the other side. And advanced beings could have crossed it!
>
> ERIK: Oh, Jane.
>
> DARCY: A primitive culture like the Vikings might have worshiped them as deities.
>
> JANE: Yes! Yes, exactly. Thank you.

Just as science and magic are unified in *Thor*, so are science and social anthropology, the gap bridged by Darcy, an outsider among the physicists, a political science student who was "the only applicant" for an internship. Yet Darcy offers the social anthropological view that supports Jane's "scientific" hypothesis. The presence of Swedish actor Skarsgård, playing a Scandinavian character that was told stories of Asgard as a child, is a somewhat ham-fisted way of emphasizing the cultural background of Thor and Asgard as something non-American. Erik thereby works to bridge potential gaps in audience knowledge about Norse mythology, while acting as a helpmeet for Thor, being one of the few human characters to recognize the Norse god. In doing so, Erik is more than a transnational character; he also bears the additional burden of being a cultural interpreter, forced to translate Thor's history and to explain the modern world to his national culture's ancient god. Moreover, the stories Erik has born witness to are not simply presented as something European, but also as literally alien.

In the Puente Antiguo library, Erik finds a book entitled *Myths and Legends from Around the World*. A shot of a page depicting Thor and Mjolnir displays text in English, Danish and Icelandic. The book is a compendium of myths and legends that have traveled and survived in different cultures, speaking to audiences beyond their places of origin. This reiterates Reynolds's argument that Norse mythology lingers in contemporary culture (1992, 57), and Thor continues to resonate with audiences. The same is true of superheroes, as demonstrated by the global consumption of comic books and, subsequently, superhero films. Various authors have written on superheroes as myth. For example, Kaklamanidou has claimed,

> Superheroes have been part of societal mythology for thousands of years. ... Hercules and Achilles ... had human flaws, but they were also almost indestructible. This dichotomy between human imperfection and fantastic strength or abilities is still what defines the superhero of the 21st century. (2011, 63)

Likewise, contemporary superheroes are being constructed as the bearers of modern myth making, as when Will Brooker writes, "To insist that Batman is one thing is, finally, to ignore the fact that Batman is more than a character, more than a brand: he is a myth" (Brooker 2012, 217; see also, Housel 2008, 76). A feature of enduring and new myths is their ability to speak to different audiences, and the modern myths of superheroes have also demonstrated their enduring and transnational appeal.

Returning to Erik, not only is he a Scandanavian among Americans (having traveled to New Mexico in response to Jane's request), he knows mythology as well as physics, and he crosses other borders as well. He is familiar with SHIELD (it is implied that he knew Bruce Banner) and is able to cross into their base to extract Thor from their custody. His continual straddling of borders makes him as transnational as Thor, but crucially Erik is comfortable with this status. In Thor's transnational flux, neither of one world or another, Erik becomes a voice of wisdom. The two characters bond over competitive drinking, which can be seen as an Americanization of these non-American actors and characters, but equally can be read as a stereotypical image of Viking culture. Cinematic representations of the

Vikings often feature halls for dining and drinking, such as *How To Train Your Dragon* (2010) and *Beowulf* (2007). *Thor*'s inclusion of such a scene is another recognizably transnational feature in this global Hollywood text, and also emphasizes unity between two transnational figures. Significantly, the scene between Erik and Thor is juxtaposed with a scene that highlights difference, as the film cuts to Loki crossing the border from Asgard into Jotunheim, where he is met with hostility until he offers Laufey the chance for an aggressive incursion. Just as Thor is learning to cross the metaphorical border and accept his own otherness, so Loki seeks to provoke aggression and, ultimately, destroy the Other.

Conclusion

Despite the gaps between worlds, spanned by the Bifrost, *Thor* ultimately demonstrates connectivity. In the scene when Thor explains to Jane that magic and science are the same in Asgard, he unites his understanding of the universe with her own—her sketches and his come together as manifestations of their combined understanding. He draws the World Tree, Yggdrasil, literally joining the Nine Realms/the universe together, and this conceit appears again in the end credits. The credits sequence shows Yggdrasil as a beautiful array of gases, stars and nebulae, shimmering, celestial light that unites the cosmos. While Thor destroys the Bifrost at the film's climax, apparently severing a connection, the final scene between Thor and Heimdall suggests otherwise:

> THOR: So Earth is lost to us . . .
> HEIMDALL: No. There is always hope.

The final shot is a close-up of Thor smiling, before the credits sequence that displays Yggdrasil: the visual links created by the editing indicate that hope is found through connection. The images of Yggdrasil emphasize universalism, the importance of interconnection that has been highlighted by transnationalism between the realms/nations, a conceit that is developed further in *Thor: The Dark World*. These images encapsulate *Thor*'s theme of interconnection, the hero's acceptance of difference valorized over the xenophobia exhibited by the Frost Giants, Loki and, initially, Thor himself. While Thor at first seeks to destroy the Frost Giants, he learns the importance of accepting and respecting difference. This is shown in dramatic gestures like destroying the Bifrost in order to save Jotunheim, and smaller moments such as his promise not to break more coffee cups during his time on Earth. This embrace of difference occurs in liminal, transnational space, where the elements of different nations and worlds are combined for the sake of peace and unity. This conceit runs through both the *Thor*'s production and its diegesis, expressed in the final images of the World Tree. *Thor: The Dark World* continues the interest in border crossing and universalism, featuring a planetary convergence that centers on London but threatens the entire cosmos. Kenneth Branagh may have vacated the director's chair, replaced by Alan Taylor, but liminality, transnationalism and border crossing remain a thematic concern.

Thor highlights transnational superheroism, because of the film production's transnational elements as well as its dramatic themes of border-crossing and the unity between nations. While this can be viewed as a pernicious form of homogenization—American popular culture seeking to incorporate other cultures into an easily marketable and consumable commodity—*Thor* valorizes understanding and acceptance of difference, presenting a world where borders are made to be bridged and that, through interconnection, there is always hope.

Acknowledgments

Vincent thanks the editors for their assistance and also Amanda Dillon for originally describing *Thor* as a cultural appropriation.

Note

1. For a similar example, see Brian Ruh (2008, 138–52).

AMERICAN SUPERHEROES IN JAPANESE HANDS

Superhero Genre Hybridity as Superhero Systems Collide in *Supaidāman*

RAYNA DENISON

Superheroes are so routinely remade that the practice has become part of their genre logic: they can be killed then resurrected, or rebooted, translated, transmuted across media formats and, within US comic books, they are often multiply serialized within concurrent series as well as being continually reworked by fans (Brooker 2011; Schumaker 2011; Ndalianis 2009). Defined in part by their intertextuality and multiplicity, superheroes, and especially those emanating out of US culture, have become so broadly dispersed in so many formats as to have become at least transnational if not, at times, global in their meanings and reach. In this chapter I argue that as these US superheroes are continually changed as they travel: redubbed, edited, and culturally reframed during their global wanderings, making it difficult to maintain claims about their national status. Others have already begun to break down the superhero's identity, examining the interlaced ethnic and racial palimpsests incorporated within some superheroes (Weinstein 2006; Brown 2001), but the layering of national identities within transnationally circulating superheroes has tended to go unaknowledged (for other interventions in this area see: Vincent Gaine and Kevin Patrick, this collection).

The conflation of national identities within superheroes becomes especially crucial when examining what happens to US superheroes when they are remade abroad. Mark Rogers has argued that "comics publishers serve as "license farms" for the larger media industries" (2012, 147), and this has been as true for transnational media production as it has been for the comic book publishers nestled within larger US media conglomerates. Further, the transnational industrial ambitions of superhero copyright holders means that US-created superhero texts are not always remade in the USA; they are frequently licensed out to producers from other nations (O'Rouke and Rodrigues 2007). This chapter analyses one such nationally complex superhero text—Marvel and Japanese media producer, Tōei's, television show *Supaidāman* (*Spider-Man*, 1978–1979, Tokyo Channel 12 [TV Tokyo])—in order to think through what happens when Japan's local superhero genre collides with America's globally famous superhero, Spider-Man.

Recently, the collaborations between Spider-Man's production company, Marvel, and overseas producers have enjoyed heightened transnational visibility and flow. For example, Marvel has sold licenses to re-imagine Spider-Man within local comic book industries as far afield as India (where they partnered with Gotham Entertainment Group in 2004 to create the *Spider-Man India* comic book) and Japan (where they partnered with publishing giant Kodansha to create the *Spider-Man J* manga, 2004–2005). These have both resulted in "comics" that have subsequently been re-sold in the USA, presenting new transnational interpretations of the Spider-Man character that could be exported back to his home nation. These new Spider-Man stories have transposed this superhero into Indian and Japanese contexts, complete with name changes (Peter Parker becomes Pavitr Prabhakar in India and Shō Amanō in Japan) and a move away from Spider-Man's usual home in New York City. The opening lines of the translated *Spider-Man J* suggest how Marvel embraces and celebrates these transcultural adaptations of Spider-Man: "Each corner of the globe has its own unique take on the AMAZING SPIDER-MAN!" (2008, 3) Henry Jenkins names Marvel's practices as corporate hybridity, citing its emergence as evidence of convergence between media production cultures (2006, 114). I argue that such hybridity is not new, and that *Supaidāman* offers just one instance of an earlier period of commingled transnational superhero history, as Marvel's superhero became part of Japan's *hīrō shirīzu* (hero series) television genre.

The difficulties in conceptualizing and researching genre hybridity have been noted in relation to both film and comic book studies. Henry Jenkins has cogently argued that

> Comics are not immune to industrial pressures towards standardization and differentiation, yet these forces operate differently in a context in which a single genre dominates a medium and all other production has to define itself against, outside, in opposition to, and alongside that prevailing genre. (2008, 231)

The genre Jenkins refers to here is the "superhero genre" of comic books, which have long since informed a transmedia genre of superheroes that has continually moved between comic books and (blockbuster) films, from television shows to varied additional media formats. This US-originated superhero genre has become deeply enmeshed with global superhero cultures, and it is frequently the case, as will be shown hereafter, that local superheroes have long been responding to its conceits.

Within film studies too, Janet Staiger, Mark Jancovich, and Jason Mittell are among those who have directly questioned previous approaches that have sought to assign texts to singular genres. Staiger, questioning the "purity hypothesis" of genre studies, argues "that, historically, no justification exists to assume producers, distributors, exhibitors, or audiences saw films as being 'purely' one type of film" (2000, 70–71). Jancovich, likewise, has questioned the positioning of Hollywood studio-era filmmaking within the horror genre, noting that "different forms of horror operated" within the 1940s meaning that, as far as critics were concerned, a multiplicity of "horror genres" were contiguously operant within Hollywood in that period (2010, 48). This understanding of genres as multiple and mixed aligns with the need that Mittell cites for revisiting genres in television and film through their cultural contexts as well as texts (2001). Analyzing *Supaidāman*'s texts in relation to its contexts of production and circulation in Japan, I combine these genre studies approaches in order to question the global reach of the USA's superhero genre. I further combine these approaches with textual analysis as an aid to unpack the imagery and creativity involved in adapting *Spider-Man* for Japan and to demonstrate links between *Supaidāman*'s texts and contexts. In so doing, I will demonstrate how Marvel's Spider-Man character has long enjoyed life as a "transcreation" (Jenkins 2006, 115) that hybridizes US and other superhero cultures.

From US Superheroes to Japanese Hīrō Shirīzu

Genre Hybridity and the Rise Japan's Superhero Media Culture

Spider-Man has a long transnational history. Tōei's *Supaidāman* was, for example, not the first incarnation of Spider-Man in Japan. Previous to its adaptation into live-action Japanese television, Marvel sold another license to Kodansha for a manga drawn by Ryoichi Ikegami (1970–1971), which again localized the superhero, renaming and relocating him to Japan. This earlier Spider-Man manga was not connected to the television adaptation that followed just a few years later, indicating that Marvel's licensing of

Spider-Man was not a fully integrated, pre-planned process during this early period. Nonetheless, rather than being a one-off encounter, the licensing of *Supaidāman* on Japanese television remains a product of long-standing superhero exchanges that took place between Japan and the USA in the aftermath of World War II.

As Anne Allison has shown, Japan had its own pre-war superheroes who were popular in manga and *kami shibai,* a form of street theater involving serialized storytelling centered around colorful graphic-art illustrations (2000b, 262; 2000a, 131). However, in the immediate postwar period, and particularly as television began to be popularized within Japan, local and imported superheroes started to commingle, becoming more plentiful and popular. On the one hand, the first American superheroes were imported to Japanese television screens towards the end of the US Occupation of Japan in the mid-1950s. "The first American series to be shown on Japanese television was the Fleischer brothers' animated *Superman* in 1955" (2003, xv, originally produced in the USA 1941–1943), note Jonathan Clements and Motoko Tamamuro. But it was the 1958 broadcasts of George Reeves in the live-action *Adventures of Superman* (1952–1958) that really popularized superheroes, with *Adventures of Superman* "watched by 74.2 percent of all TV sets in Japan" (xv). Clements and Tamamuro attribute early experiments in Japanese superhero creation to the success of *Adventures of Superman,* seeing most of the 1960s and 1970s Japanese superheroes as responses to this history. In this version of the history of Japan's superheroes, therefore, it is the popularity of US superheroes in Japan that led the way to the creation of local responses to, and adaptations of, these characters.

In alternative reading, it is possible to see the rise of the Japanese superhero as part of a local set of exchanges between early television and other prominent Japanese media. Film and television special effects and manga's influence on early Japanese television programming both played significant roles in the development of the local *hīrō shirizu* genre. In the former case, cinema led the way in the creation of a home grown set of special effects technologies and techniques that became so dominant in Japanese media productions that a genre was named after them: the *tokusatsu* (special effects) genre, later spilling over from film into television. This genre famously began with the creation of *Gojira*'s (*Godzilla,* Ishiro Honda, 1954) special effects by Eiji Tsuburaya. Through Tsuburaya Productions, Eiji Tsuburaya went on to popularize and standardize practical effects techniques in Japanese film and television. His "suitmation" effects allowed actors in costumes to do battle within and destroy miniaturized city sets, in addition to utilizing a wide range of practical effects like composites, matte paintings, stunt work, and miniatures to create a sophisticated, local system of visual effects that was influenced by, but not slavishly aligned to, Hollywood's techniques.

Within the *tokusatsu* genre, most critics cite the creation of three *tokusatsu* television series as foundational to the creation of what would later become the *hīrō shirīzu*: *Urutoraman* (*Ultraman*, 1967, Tokyo Broadcasting System, made in conjunction with Tsuburaya Productions), *Kamen Raidā* (*Masked Rider*, 1971, Mainichi Broadcasting System) and *Himitsu Sentai Go Renjā* (*Secret Task Force Five Rangers*, 1975, NET) (Clements and Tamamuro 2003; Allison 2000a; *Nikkei Entertainment* 2012, 18–19) all of which pre-date Toei's *Supaidāman*. These series were huge successes at the time of airing, and have all spawned massive, multi-media franchises lasting to the present time (Clements and Tamamuro 2003; *Nikkei Entertainment* 2012, 19). In *Urutoraman* a giant cyborg superhero does battle with massive *kaijū* (monsters); whereas *Kamen Raidā* follows a cyborg hero who does battle against the terrorist organization that created him; and, in the first of what would later become the *Mighty Morphin' Power Rangers* series in the USA, *Go Renjā* are a team of five special agents battling the Black Cross Army using advanced machinery (for more information, see: Allison 2006, 94–114).

Though all notably different, each series has at its core a masked hero (or heroes) with special abilities (created through otherworldly origins, scientific tampering, or specialist training), but perhaps especially notable for their gadgets and vehicles. The uses of gadgets, costumes and/or special vehicles in each show meant that the *hīrō shirīzu* capitalized on growing links between television and the toys industry in Japan. Marusan, Bandai and other major toy producers in Japan became closely involved with the production of content, acting as sponsors and license holders for ancillary toy products based on Japanese superheroes, thereby helping to spread the characters throughout Japanese children's culture (Allison 2006). The superhero genre in Japan, consequently, was a transmedia phenomenon from its inception, working to transport superheroes from screens into the everyday lives of Japanese children.

Nowhere is this trend more clearly delineated than in the manga-inspired anime that emerged in the postwar period. Marc Steinberg has scrutinized the early experiments undertaken around Osamu Tezuka's *Tetsuwan Atomu* (*Astro* or *Atom Boy*, or *The Mighty Atom* whose initial manga ran from 1952 to 1958 and whose television anime was aired on NTV from 1963–1966), to produce "media mix" (a local form of transmedia franchising) around anime (Steinberg 2012). But manga also has a more direct influence on live-action Japanese television superheroes. One manga author, Shōtarō Ishinomori, was particularly influential early on, creating the original manga and character designs for two of the most popular Japanese *hīrō shirīzu*: *Kamen Raidā* and *Himitsu Sentai Go Renjā*. Manga, therefore, has an under-estimated significance as a source text for early Japanese superheroes, just as US comic books acted as the sources for their multi-media superhero success stories.

However, as anime became more plentiful, superhero stories are reported to have migrated across modes of production as the 1970s progressed; moving across television formats from live-action to anime, which resulted in the declining popularity of *tokusatsu* shows (*Nikkei Entertainment* 2012, 18). *Supaidāman*, which appeared on Japanese television between 1978 and 1979, came at the cusp of this shift from live-action *tokusatsu* to anime superheroes, and its production, borrowing from US comic book sources at a time of market decline, can therefore be read as an attempt to import a "spectacular" character into a waning genre.

Spider-Man in *Supaidāman*

The Localization of an American Superhero

As these multiple histories of superheroes in Japan demonstrate, *Supaidāman* was produced in a market replete with superheroes, both foreign and domestic. As a part of a local superhero genre Anne Allison tells us that Japanese

> superheroes are as strange a species as the *kaijū* [monsters]—mixtures of machinery, electricity, and bestiality. This very strangeness is also of central importance in both the text of the media story lines (on the television program, in comic books or children's magazines) and the children's merchandise that accompanies them (action figures, warrior robots). (2006, 96)

Examining Spider-Man's transformation into Supaidāman, therefore, helps to uncover what of, and how, this US superhero was transposed into Japanese culture. *Supaidāman* is an exceptional show within the *hīrō shirīzu* genre because the central characters presents both an imported superhero *and* an amalgamation of the elements made popular by previous *tokusatsu* heroes, making him multiply hybrid. Consequently, as a character, Supaidāman offers a compilation of traits worth examining for the ways he brings together the machinery, electricity, and bestiality of Allison's "strange species."

On the surface, there is very little of Marvel's Spider-Man in Supaidāman. Like the other transnational Spider-Man characters outlined above, Supaidāman was given a new origin story and a new local alter ego when he appeared on Japanese television. Takuya Yamashiro (played by Shinji Tōdō), a professional motorcycle racer, replaces photo journalist/student Peter Parker in the central role and is reimagined as the indulged (*amae*) eldest child of prominent astro-archeologist Dr. Hiroshi Yamashiro (Fuyuki Murakami). Takuya becomes Supaidāman after his father investigates a meteor crash and is killed by an invading alien force, the Iron Cross Army, replacing the "Uncle Ben" narrative from the USA while still providing the superhero's revenge-based motivation for the remainder of the series.

Supaidāman is created by Takuya's meeting with Garia (Toshiaki Nishizawa), the lone survivor of a spider planet (he is described as a *supaidā seijin*, or "spider alien" in a later episode) who saves Takuya's life by injecting him with spider extract. Garia does this after Takuya falls into the cave system in which Garia has been trapped for four hundred years, exacting a promise from Takuya that Garia will be avenged against the Iron Cross Army that killed his people. Along with the large, metallic bracelet-communicator that injects the spider extract, Garia gifts Takuya with the "Spider Protector" (his costume), the Spider Machine GP7 (a flying sports car) and, most significantly for the series, with the Marveller space ship that transforms into the giant robot, Leopardon. Both Supaidāman and Takuya Yamashiro, therefore, represent stark localizations; Japanese reimaginings of the US superhero character for a *tokusatsu* genre diegesis.

However, this surface difference belies a series of allusions and amalgamations underpinning Spider-Man's importation. A range of Japanese superhero predecessors can be read through Takuya Yamashiro and Supaidāman alike. For example, the villainous Iron Cross Army seek Supaidāman's true identity throughout the series, and despite their suspicions, they routinely overlook Takuya, branding him a fool. In Episode 14, one of their monsters declares his suspicions about Takuya, to which henchwoman Amazoness (Yukie Kagawa) dismisses the idea declaring, "That man is stupid," and in subsequent episodes Takuya is referred to simply as a "fool" (Episode 20). Supporting evidence for their conclusions is replete within the series as Takuya allows himself to be beaten up and is frequently shown running away from Iron Cross Army henchmen. Playing the fool as Takuya does throughout the series, Supaidāman's alter ego manifests a kinship with Clark Kent's attempts to hide Superman's abilities from prying eyes. This allusion is aided by the presence of Takuya's intrepid photo-journalist girlfriend, Hitomi Sakuma (Rika Miura) whose ignorance of Takuya's real identity is presented as an homage to *Superman*'s Lois Lane. Although no overt references are made to Superman in the *Supaidāman* series, the popularity of Superman in multiple comic book and television versions preceding *Supaidāman* (Allison 2006, 98) suggest compelling reasons for reading TakuyaYamashiro-Supaidāman as a variant on the Clark Kent-Superman dual identity.

Takuya's homage to Clark Kent is taken to extremes though, with Takuya framed as fiscally irresponsible and not just as clumsy and "foolish." For example, Takuya is never shown racing in the series (just practicing and noisily tuning up his motorcycle), and instead is presented as an economic drain on his family. In Episode 5 Takuya is forced to beg his elder sister, Shinko (Izumi Ōyama), for a down-payment on a motorcycle after his is wrecked in a collision with the Iron Cross Army. In this sequence, Takuya is shown on his knees while his sister, little brother and girlfriend all sit on the living furniture around him, watching as he formally requests money from Shinko, asking her to access the inheritance left by their deceased father. Played for comedy and embarrassment, this scene demonstrates Takuya's lack of economic independence and power, an embarrassment all the more redolent during the period of rapid economic growth Japan was enjoying in the late 1970s. As an economic "loser" within this period of growth, Takuya's secret identity localizes and exaggerates the comedic elements found in previous US versions of Clark Kent, while echoing Peter Parker's lack of economic power, offering a stark contrast between the infantilized Takuya and his superheroic alter ego.

However, Takuya Yamashiro's motorcycle racer identity is also highly intertextual. It parallels the Red Ranger's favored mode of transportation from the Japanese *Go Renjā* superhero series. In making Takuya a motorcycle racer, *Supaidāman* capitalizes on what was becoming a socially marginalized, but important, postwar form of transport and subculture. Unlike the *bōsōzoku* motorcycle youth gangs, who were becoming a social problem in urban Japan during this period (a gang of whom, the Skull Gang, or *Dokurotan*, appear in Episode 13; see: Standish 1998), Takuya's motorcycle offers a way of displaying the character's youthful exuberance. Further, the motorcycle riding shows off Takuya's skills and physicality in order to suggest how he comes to master Supaidāman's more complex alien technologies. In addition, giving Takuya a motorcycle also helps to differentiate between Takuya and Supaidāman's vehicles, enabling additional potential toy

1. Supaidāman poses and recites his catchphrase (Episode 18). Credit: Tōei-Marvel.

manufacturing. Therefore, the intertexts incorporated within the Takuya Yamashiro character and his props inform not just *Supaidāman*, but also its contextual surround.

The same is also true for Takuya's secret identity as Supaidāman. *Supaidāman* was a very early live-action adaptation of Spider-Man, with only a preceding cartoon (1967–1970, ABC) and some early episodes of the live-action US television version of *Spider-Man* (starring Nicholas Hammond, 1977–1979, CBS), available to guide Tōei's creative staff beyond what could be gleaned from translating *Spider-Man* comic books. It is perhaps unsurprising, therefore, that Supaidāman's characterization displays significant evidence of local and transnational inspiration and borrowing. For example, Supaidāman routinely poses and utters weekly plot summary-catchphrases before fighting his way through to the episode's main villain (see Figure 1). Steinberg traces this kind of posing back to its roots following "the success of the 1966 *Urutoraman* (*Ultraman*)," which

> introduced fixed poses into the action, effectively stilling motion at key moments in the series. These fixed poses of masked figures enabled an ease of transposition from screen to *manga* to toy to the child imitating these poses in play. (2012, 229)

In this respect, Supaidāman's performance emulates popular local *hīrō shirīzu* representations of superheroic characters as a means to compete in an increasingly crowded superhero genre on Japanese television.

In addition, Supaidāman's pre-fight poses also seem inspired by the "pause/burst/pause" fighting styles of Hong Kong cinema, which David Bordwell comments upon writing that "each set [a sequence of moves] is a series of rapid moves broken by poses" (2000, 224). Leon Hunt further connects this sort of fixed posing in *kung fu* cinema with star charisma, arguing that these moments emphasize the *qi* (or aura) of stars (Hunt 2003, 42–44). Shot from multiple, often low, angles and using slightly different poses each week, Supaidāman's costumed performance works to highlight the figure of the costumed superhero in a similar display of his fighting prowess, shifting from pose to pose in a momentary pause in action before fights begin. The "paused" moments of posing act as moments of character spectacle, with the repetition of the superhero's image from multiple camera angles signaling the character's heightened diegetic significance (see Tasker 1993 for more on the spectacle of the star body). Supaidāman's pauses-to-pose, like those undertaken by Hong Kong stars and Urotoraman, augment the "star" presence of the superhero character while invoking the intertextual chain of locally and transnationally popular genres, stars and merchandising products to which his performance style refers.

Furthermore, locally popular martial arts fads also played a significant role in the content of *Supaidāman*. For example, Aaron Gerow has discussed the incursion of pro-wrestling into Japanese media in this period, saying in relation to the *Godzilla* film series that

> the insertion of monster rasslin' into the series may have been part of an effort to elongate the franchise by borrowing the success of pro-wrestling, a sport that, under the deft promotional strategies of the star wrestler Rikidōzan, was one of the most popular media phenomena in Japan from the mid-1950s to the early 1960s. (2006, 64)

The influence of pro-wrestling is still evident in *Supaidāman*, as in the episode titled "The Tears of Samson the Pro-Wrestler" (Episode 17), which sees Samson, the younger brother of a successful pro-wrestler, turned into one of the Iron Cross Army's monsters in an attempt to achieve wrestling glory. In this instance of hybridization, *Supaidāman* takes on aspects of its Japanese cultural surround (themselves already transnational) in order to heighten the impact of its action sequences. In a similar move, Episode 39 tells of the Iron Cross Army's attempts to gather and manipulate the best fighters in Japan to fight in a "World Martial Arts Tournament" with the purpose of assassinating Supaidāman. The transnational flavor of this sequence (featuring a Japanese pro-wrestler, a Brazilian wrestler, a Japanese *kendō* expert, and a machine-monster hybrid villain) seems rather more an attempt to highlight Supaidāman's superiority over all other fighters, thereby returning attention to the special stunt system created around the central superhero by *Supaidāman*'s stunt team.

Nevertheless, this special stunt system also works to emphasize what was unambiguously imported from the US Spider-Man. It is in the "Spider Protector" (Supaidāman's superhero costume) that the series borrows most wholeheartedly from the iconicity of the US Spider-Man. The Spider Protector is a close copy of the costume worn by Nicholas Hammond, even opening across the back of Takuya Yamashiro/ Shinji Tōdō's shoulders in the same way as Hammond's suit did in the 1977 pilot film for *The Amazing Spider-Man* (directed by EW Swackhamer). Along with the costume, the *Supaidāman* producers recreated the superhero's most famous powers, especially emphasizing his "Spidey sense," which is frequently transmuted into dream-visions in *Supaidāman*.

Additionally, Garia's gifts, especially the bracelet-communicator's ability to shoot "Spider Strings" and "Spider Nets," mimic the US comic book character's web-slinging abilities. It is therefore the most recognizably iconic aspects of Spider-Man's character that most impact on *Supaidāman*'s content. Running contrary to Randy Duncan and Matthew J. Smith's claim (quoting Les Daniels), that Spider-Man is a "superhero Everyman," and that "'it is his simple humanity, rather than his exotic talent, that has won him millions of enthusiastic fans'" in Japan (2009, 240), it was precisely Spider-Man's iconic costume and superheroic abilities that were deemed recognizable enough to import. Consequently, Japan's *Supaidāman* can be seen to invert the relationship between audiences and the central character, making Supaidāman, not Takuya, the localized heart of the series.

The re-use and repetition of certain stunt and fight footage across episodes also works to produce a unique and instantly recognizable Supaidāman performance style. Toei's experiments with stunts and fighting techniques in *Supaidāman* were used to create a unique and local brand of superheroism through the repackaging of an iconic US character. Supaidāman swings and jumps between the same trees in multiple episodes, he fights Iron Cross henchmen at the same racecourse in two different episodes, he fights on the same hillside multiple times and kicks and punches villains from a spinning platform set up in the same window on two occasions. Repetitions like these, although likely to have been a cost-saving measure, helped to create consistency within Supaidāman's fighting performance style and enabled emphasis to be split between stunt work and special effects sequences creating a new variation on *hīrō shirīzu* action.

Hirofumi Koga, a member of the Japan Action Group, which provided suitmation heroes and monsters for Toei, is credited with the stunt performances of Supaidāman in costume, despite the credit sequences locating both performances in Tōdō (IMDb n.d.). Stan Lee, in an interview for the DVD release of *Supaidāman*, compliments these in-costume performances for their local idiom, saying, "They [Tōei] gave Spider-Man a certain kind of walk when he walked or ran, which was different than the way he did it in the American cartoons. . . . It was very interesting." The slightly hunched, diagonal running style that Lee liked was unique to Supaidāman's performance within the Spider-Man intertext, as was the stunt footage that involved practical effects and composited imagery.

Though these stunts were not dissimilar to those produced for the US live action television series, their production in the Japanese context, by a Japanese creative team, is a source of considerable local spectacle when viewed in conjunction with the imported superhero character. Their reuse and repetition works as a means to position certain techniques and maneuvers as dominant within the Supaidāman performance style, utilizing local techniques and systems of production to create a unique brand of superheroism. Additionally, Supaidāman was recreated with a central performance and stunt logic that worked to differentiate his movements and fighting style from the superheroes and martial artists surrounding him in the series and within Japan's wider superhero mediascape.

Re-use of stunt work and a formulaic approach to narrative ensured that *Supaidāman* contained weekly examples of spectacular imagery, particularly with respect to Supaidāman's transformations. From Takuya into Supaidāman, from Supaidāman into the driver of the Spider Machine GP7, which then became part of Marveller, which would then transform into the Leopardon robot on Supaidāman's command, these transformations repeated the same sequence of shots episode after episode. Not only does this allow Supaidāman to do battle with the Iron Cross Army's monsters (who are able to super-size at will), these transformations provide points of repeated special effects spectacle for audiences (King 2002). For example, in most episodes the GP7 is seen flying into a hatch on the lion-headed Marveller spacecraft. On the command of "Change Leopardon!" Supaidāman's spaceship would transform into a giant robot, capable of destroying the Iron Cross Army's monsters using one or a combination of his rocket-propelled shooting fists; the "Arc Turn" boomerang crest that sits, like the insignia on a samurai helmet, on Leopardon's forehead; or "Sword Vigor," a huge sword that Leopardon throws at the enemy, usually as his final move. This final move normally begins the same way: with Leopardon filmed against a black backdrop as he throws the sword, which then cuts to a composite shot sequence of that episode's giant monster exploding as the sword hits him or her. Combinations of new and repeated imagery in these sequences maintains levels of spectacle while also reinforcing a weekly formula for the special effects and action sequences, making *Supaidāman* at once spectacular and predictable in its presentation of superhero genre action.

The impetus behind these repetitions and transformations are themselves multiple. For one, these sequences involve expensive composite shots, model work and miniatures. Therefore, as with the repetitions of Supaidāman's stunt sequences, re-use and re-editing of the same footage across episodes drastically reduced costs. Like the superhero transformations in anime, too, the repetition of these transformation sequences worked to emphasize the iconography of the central character, associating him with specific action moves that could be easily copied by toy manufacturers and children alike, as Steinberg has claimed.

In this regard, repetition also helped to showcase features of the toys produced around the *Supaidāman* series by Popī, which had connections to Bandai Toys (Saffel 2007, 108–9). Radio controlled GP7 cars, Leopardon figures that came with detachable hands and Sword Vigor and several versions of Supaidāman helped the show's Japanese creators commercialize their Japanese-American content and to create feedback loops between the *Supaidāman* series and the lived experiences of its core, child audiences beyond television. In this way, *Supaidāman*'s localization extended to the creation of a new "Spider-Man" culture in a new market, formulated as a transmedia phenomenon that reached out from television into their play and collecting activities.

Moving beyond contextual pragmatics, Tom Gill's (1998) observation about the stages in the various *Renjā* series' transformation sequences is also relevant to the transformations that Supaidāman goes through. Gill contends that most *hīrō shirīzu* contain both transformations (*henshin*) and incorporations (*gattai*), as characters transform from their everyday selves into superheroes and then manipulate machines in order to fight as a team. However, unlike his *Renjā* precursors, Supaidāman is a lone, alien-human hybrid superhero. Marking this distinction, Supaidāman's "incorporations" (seen when the GP7 joins with Marveller and transforms into Leopardon) work to emphasize this superhero's alien origins and abilities.

Somewhat ironically, they act as a reminder that Supaidāman is an outsider in his diegetic universe, emphasizing that while he is humanity's last line of defense, he is also a hybridized alien-human. Beyond *Supaidāman*'s text, however, these incorporations, unlike Takuya's transformation into Supaidāman, also demonstrate the character's narrative dependence on his Japanese superhero forebears. Both Gill and Allison (2002) assert that such incorporations are more normally reserved for *hīrō shirīzu* with multiple heroes, and Clement and Tamamuro (2003) have asserted that fights between giant monsters were the preserve of *Urutoraman*. Read intertextually, therefore, the *Supaidāman* series' adoption of transformation and incorporation speaks to its generic incorporation and hybridization of pre-existing Japanese superhero iconographies.

Supaidāman, as a character, thereby palimpsests iconic facets of superhero culture from both home and abroad. He brings together bestiality (in his alien, spider hybridization), with the electricity and machinery of other *tokusatsu* series (seen in his bracelet-communicator, the GP7, and Marveller-Leopardon). By importing Spider-Man, but not Peter Parker, the character's US origins are partially jettisoned, except inasmuch as they linger in the death of Takuya's father and in the influence of other US superheroes on Takuya's secret identity. Moreover, while Supaidāman's costuming, fighting and stunts all borrow from existing, largely transnational, action forms, Supaidāman's incorporation into (and of) a range of (toy) technologies signals his hybridization of successful pre-existing domestic superhero tropes. In these ways, even the central character of the *Supaidāman* series presents a challenge to notions of a singular "superhero genre" at work in global media culture.

The "Local" World of *Supaidāman*
Themes and Villains

Beyond its central character, *Supaidāman* also incorporates a range of thematic concerns and villains that run contrary to an understanding of a "pure" superhero genre. Writing about the influence of Eiji Tsuburaya on Japanese television superheroes, Ittō Onoue, Kenta Makuta, and Naoe Kimura comment on the "Tsuburaya Method" and its emphasis on "rich themes." They claim that, in the *Ultra* series (originating from *UltraQ* 1966 and *Ultraman* 1967), "In the stories, real social problems, logical problems, are casually incorporated and, because they are made to be at the eye-level of its child viewers, they gently pose questions like, 'If it was you, what would you think?'" (Onoue et al. 2012, 30). This explains why so many of *Supaidāman*'s themes echo those facing contemporary Japan, including adult aspects of culture, such as the disenfranchised youth of the *bōsōzoku* biker gangs.

These sorts of social problems appear at different points of the series, especially in relation to the family. There are repeated stories centering on children with missing or dead parents (Episodes 18, 21, and 25) and others about adoption and orphans (Episodes 20 and 23 respectively). Nowhere is the postwar issue of broken nuclear families more obvious than in Takuya's own domestic arrangements. While the death of their father acts as a motivating force during the series, the Yamashiro family barely mention the absence of their mother. Instead, the young Yamashiro siblings raise one another, which they do thanks to Shinko's (Izumi Oyama) management of the household, and Takuya's hands-on, fatherly oversight of his younger brother.

Uniting these social problems, Episode 15, "The Promise of Our Lives," features a young boy named Junichi whose father has previously died in a car accident, and who suffers from a heart condition. Junichi's precarious health and social position lead to him being bullied at the beginning of the episode by Takuya's younger brother, Takuji. Takuya intervenes to protect Junichi, befriending the young boy as both Takuya and Supaidāman, thereby helping him to gain in confidence. Disciplining his younger brother, Takuya is also shown scolding Takuji in his sister's presence, and both reiterate the moral message of the episode, that bullying those weaker than oneself is a despicable act. While this sort of moralizing message is common throughout global children's television (Buckingham 2002), the social problems in *Supaidāman* are locally inflected ones. Though the moral of the tale is transnationally understandable, it, and others like it, are shot-through with references alluding to the perceived collapse of Japan's *ie* (extended household) system, forcing families into precarious social positions compounded by the loss of one or both parents and the absence of the traditional familial network of support. *Supaidāman*, as a result of this dominant theme, tells stories recognizable to many during the postwar recovery period in Japan, and it does so by emphasizing the suffering and victimization of Japanese youth.

In addition to the locally oriented themes of *Supaidāman*, its villains are also replete with hybridized meanings. As part of the *tokusatsu* genre, *Supaidāman* bears many hallmarks of the broader science fiction genre under whose umbrella many *tokusatsu* productions have been categorized (see: Tsutsui and Ito 2006 for Japanese examples and Bolton et al.

2. Professor Monster's (Mitsuo Andō) costume suggests localization of popular US science fiction film iconography (Episode 41). Credit: Tōei-Marvel.

2007 for more on Japanese science fiction). *Supaidāman*'s villains, from the primary series antagonist Professor Monster (Mitsuo Andō) and his glamorous army commander, Amazoness, to their monsters and henchmen, all provide Japanese variations on science fiction and US comic book idioms. Mitsuo Andō, for example, is an emphatically local, yet generically hybridized actor. Andō also played the arch-villain of *Go Renjā*, whose Black Cross Army is echoed in *Supaidāman*'s Iron Cross Army. Andō, consequently, provides a star intertext that connects *Supaidāman* to its *hīrō shirīzu* predecessors.

However, Professor Monster's costuming emphasizes the transnational science fiction and horror elements of his characterization, more than it reveals or revels in Andō's star presence. For example, a metallic-looking mask covers half of Andō's face signaling Professor Monster's alien origins. As the series progresses, Professor Monster becomes increasingly cadaverous, as *Supaidāman*'s make-up artists use green and purple contour make-up to effect a gaunt, monstrous look for the character (see Figure 2). Through these means, Professor Monster acts as a generalized conglomeration of science fiction villain tropes—cyborg, alien, mad professor among them—before ending the series by taking on the role of giant monster (*daikaijū*). More a universal amalgamation of monstrous types than a local monster, Professor Monster's Japanese identity is signaled through Andō's star intertext, but subsequently denied by his generic costuming.

3. Amazoness (Yukie Kagawa) in Wonder Woman inspired costume (Episode 19). Credit: Tōei-Marvel.

Amazoness, by contrast, is a more fully transnational character. Amazoness is consistently framed as a glamorous and powerful character, alternately wearing fashionable clothing or revealing mini-skirts and leotards (in her costume as the leader of the Iron Cross Army). However, Amazoness is more cerebral than Professor Monster's monsters and henchmen, and constantly seeks to entrap Supaidāman. This tendency is perhaps most visible in Episode 19,"The Unmapped Town of the Phantom Boy" (Figure 3) when Amazoness pretends to be a guardian goddess protecting a village of telepathically powered aliens hiding on Earth. In this episode Amazoness's costume dramatically changes.

The change is presaged by her appearance in a cave filled with ancient Japanese archaeological artifacts including prehistoric pottery and figurines. These traditional objects contrast strongly with Amazoness's newly outlandish appearance in a bright red wig fitted with a tiara-like headband that emulates the look of US superhero Wonder Woman, especially so when the red wig is later replaced with a black one. This costume transformation makes explicit what Amazoness's name suggests: an irreverent pastiche of the best-known female US superhero, Wonder Woman. Amazoness thereby offers further evidence of cultural borrowing at work in the *Supaidāman* series. Again, this borrowing runs deeper than costuming: Amazoness is one of the few antagonist characters to have a secret identity in *Supaidāman* (as magazine editor Saeko Yoshida), just as Wonder

Woman becomes Diana Prince. But it is her role as the leader of the Iron Cross Army that aligns Amazoness most closely with Diana Prince's military career in *Wonder Woman* (1975–1979, ABC and CBS). As an unacknowledged, unlicensed remake of a US superhero as a Japanese villain, Amazoness temptingly offers a way to read *Supaidāman* as a critical inflection of the US superhero genre, turning one nation's superhero into another's localized villain.

The monsters of *Supaidāman* tell a different tale of absorption and hybridization, creating chimera out of Japanese folklore and science fiction tropes. While many of *Supaidāman*'s monster antagonists are rage-filled animal-machine hybrids, others provide more complex engagements with the *kaijū* character type. In one rare example, Samson, who is turned into "Samson the Rock Man" in Episode 17, is transformed into a geological-humanoid monster. However, it is female monsters who seem to occupy the most liminal spaces between *Supaidāman*'s genre systems. Episode 10, for example, names its monster "*Hebi-onna*" in a direct reference to a local monstrous "snake woman" *yōkai* figure. *Yōkai* form the major group of Japanese folklore figures, imagined as monsters, ghosts, spirits and minor deities across their histories (Foster 2009, 126–27). In *Supaidāman*'s *yōkai* hybrids, such monsters are reformulated as science fiction amalgams created by Professor Monster's experiments.

In one particularly gruesome example, the bones of a *yōkai* cat are disinterred from a shrine and incorporated into "*Monster Bem Kaibyōjū*," or "Demon Cat Monster Bem" (Episode 8). The name refers in part to a popular Japanese monster series *Yōkai Ningen Bem* (*Humanoid Monster Bem*, 1968–69), about a monstrous protagonist who wishes to become human. However, in *Supaidāman*, the science fiction inflected *yōkai* becomes a villain requiring a spiritual response from the superhero. After the female *yōkai* cat monster kidnaps a class of young children, Supaidāman does not simply do battle with her. Instead, he goes to a shrine to perform a ritual intended to pacify the original *yōkai*. Supaidāman is pictured in several shots praying over a fire while burning a scroll with an incantation on it, effectively taking on the role of an *onmyōji* (a traditional form of wizard popularized in the Heian era; see: Miller 2008). In battling the curse of this *yōkai*-monster, therefore, Supaidāman too becomes more inflected by traditional Japanese folklore.

There are myriad other examples of monsters crossing between generic categories in *Supaidāman*, not least because marginality and social liminality are hallmarks of these kinds of hybridized creations. What monsters allow in *Supaidāman* as a series is a weekly shift in generic impulses, sometimes based on traditional folklore, and at others on science fiction, thriller or horror narratives. However, at other times, the schemes of the Iron Cross Army seem to have been motivated by merchandising, as when Professor Monster replaces a pop band with cyborgs and places a pain-inducing sonic signal into their music designed to incapacitate Supaidāman, a song that can then be repeated throughout the episode (Episode 7). *Supaidāman*'s monsters, like its other villains, are sourced from a variety of genres and put to a range of production system ends, acting as homages to a wide variety of cultural figures from Japan and abroad. Through the series' Japanese themes and its villains' multifarious manifestations, therefore, *Supaidāman*'s hybrid identity is deepened, making this version of the "superhero genre" simultaneously local and universal in its appeals to a wide range of genres.

Conclusion

Supaidāman, as series and character, offers evidence confirming the variety at work within the "superhero genre" of the 1970s. *Supaidāman* is rarely, if ever, a "pure" example of any one variant of the superhero genre, and instead is routinely a product of collisions between generic systems. These collisions can be seen in the retention of the US costume, in combination with local *kaijū* villains and heroic robots. At a deeper level too, while Supaidāman the superhero hybridizes popular US superhero traditions (combining Spider-Man and Superman), his incorporation of (and into) Japanese superhero narrative traditions suggests that the figure of the superhero was a deeply contested and transnational one even in 1970s Japan. Moreover, this trend was exaggerated within Supaidāman's monstrous antagonists, who combine everything from traditional folklore to universal science fiction tropes in their harrying of Supaidāman. This was not, however, simply a case of throwing everything into a generic blender; rather, *Supaidāman* represents a purposeful, tactical combination of local and foreign elements designed to appeal to children and families in postwar Japan.

The tactical nature of these combinations can be read most easily in their highly commodified moments; at those moments of repetition used to "transpose" Supaidāman from character into toy into playground performance. Supaidāman's poses and repeated stunts helped to ground the superhero in physical Japanese spaces, all the while displaying the character's iconic "American" attributes. There is never, therefore, just one version of Supaidāman-Spider-Man at work; like the genre surrounding him, Supaidāman always contains myriad potential meanings and his own cultural palimpsest, ready for redeployment.

What *Supaidāman* reveals, therefore, is the flexibility of the superhero genre, and the ease with which local variations on superheroes can incorporate the early US characters that once offered them inspiration. Rather than seeing superheroes and their genre as a product of US culture, therefore, *Supaidāman* requires us to reconsider the genre's national singularity. The superhero genre manifests in distinct versions around the world and at different historical moments, developing into a wide range of superhero systems that now circumnavigate the globe in close proximity.

SECTION TWO

Superheroes on World Screens

From Local Productions to Transnational Blockbusters

HEROES OF HALL H

Global Media Franchises, *Doctor Who*, and the San Diego Comic-Con as Space for the Transnational Superhero

LINCOLN GERAGHTY

Founded as the "Golden State Comic Book Convention" in 1970 at the Grant Hotel in downtown San Diego, the San Diego Comic-Con has become the premiere site for fans and global companies to meet and share in all manner of popular media, including comics, film, television, and computer games. Moving to the San Diego Convention Center in 1991, Comic-Con now attracts more than 130,000 people a year. So, from a hotel lobby hosting comic book dealers, attracting roughly three hundred die-hard collectors, the site for comics and the superhero stories contained within has changed dramatically to incorporate industry, artists, producers, celebrities, journalists, and fans. Drawing on field research and analyses of media texts and production histories, I argue that Comic-Con International (to give it its proper title) provides a space for the promotion of global entertainment brands—where traditional American comic book superheroes such as Superman or Batman now compete with other international icons such as Doctor Who to attract the interest of media executives, journalists, and the devotion of increasingly knowledgeable fans.

As a result, the San Diego Convention Center, the hotels, and the city itself become familiar places returned to every year, where fans and collectors can get spoilers, see special screenings, buy new merchandise, and meet their favorite stars for the duration of the event. For one week in July, San Diego turns from a Southern Californian family-holiday destination to an international focal point for the screen superhero. This chapter examines the increasing importance of Comic-Con as a platform for launching non-Hollywood media products in the USA and building an American fan base for them. By analyzing how BBC America has used the rebirth of the iconic British television series *Doctor Who* (Moffat 2005–) to build a brand identity, I argue that Comic-Con has changed the conceptualization of the modern-day superhero and, consequently, a traditionally American cultural trope has become transnational in perspective and adaptable for a global audience.

What this means for the actual products being launched in San Diego is that they are no longer aimed at a niche audience—they are mass-market commodities, with timeless comic book superheroes from DC and Marvel, competing with new characters from the worlds of television, film, and anime. Moreover, generations of fans collide in Comic-Con, offering producers and industry tycoons ample opportunity to market their brands and extend the shelf life of their media texts—whether in paper, electronic, television, film, or computer-game form. Stan Lee, renowned comic book writer and legendary creator of Marvel Comics' most iconic characters, says of the San Diego Comic-Con, "The thousands of convention-goers are grown-ups, adults who are interested in movies, television, DVDs, and, of course, comic books. . . . These fans are tremendously important to the comic book business, just as they are to any creative endeavor" (Lee cited in Spurlock 2011, 5). Therefore, I examine the relationships between convention space, event programming, fandom, and texts in what follows, in order to explore how Comic-Con is reshaping and expanding the meanings of the superhero in contemporary culture.

Superheroes and Time Lords

San Diego Comic-Con and Global Entertainment as Event

After moving from the Grant Hotel to the El Cortez Hotel in 1972, Comic-Con spent many years building devoted and regular attendance. San Diego offered attendees good weather for the four days in July when the convention was held and enough space to offer a mix of attractions: from dealer rooms, to autography booths, to the annual costume competition and Comic Book Expo, where retailers and publishers did business with each other. By 1979, however, the hotel space was no longer adequate, and Comic-Con moved to the Convention and Performing Arts Center (CPAC) in downtown San Diego. During the 1980s more events were added to the program: the Will Eisner Comic Industry Awards and international media such as Japanese anime became popular among fans and gained dedicated program tracks. By 1990 the convention was attracting thirteen thousand attendees, and another move in 1991 to the bigger and newly built San Diego Convention Center on the harbor allowed for more space and more opportunity to expand the daily program. The city council started to see multiple income streams beyond comics and memorabilia, and thus downtown streets and billboards were plastered well in advance of the convention, using superheroes and popular animated TV-show characters to advertise the location as well as the event. Forty-eight thousand people attended Comic-Con in 1999, and the city itself was becoming an attraction, not just the comics and people inside the convention center.[1]

At Comic-Con we see non-traditional fan spaces, such as the tourist-focused Gaslamp Quarter and Seaport Village, utilized alongside more business-oriented spaces such as hotel conference rooms and exhibit halls. An empty and blank space, or "non-place," to use Marc Augé's (1995) term for generic places, the San Diego Convention Center is reinvented for Comic-Con and temporarily becomes an active and real fan space for nostalgia, collecting, and personal interaction. Nicky Gregson and Louise Crewe, who discuss flea markets and jumble sales held in parking lots and church halls, contend that "consumption occurs in sites and spaces that are ordinary and mundane in their location and in their situation in everyday life" (2003, 2); thus the cavernous and versatile convention center, along with the city streets and buildings that surround it, are transformed into spaces that allow for multiple exchanges and mass consumption. Where all entertainment media forms converge on one city, there grows a new, albeit temporary site for superhero creation and consumption—fans and the industry rub shoulder to shoulder in a unique moment where both hold equal power. As writer and director Joss Whedon reflects,

> [Comic-Con] has definitely gotten bigger and more mainstream. The industry has figured out where the true fans are. This has created a dichotomy between the comic fans and the movies – in some cases, a bitter rift. But I believe there could be harmony between the comic book folk and movie makers. Ultimately, they just need to sit down or possibly make out. This is the kind of place Comic-Con is: It's a place where people with the same passion – whether their obsessions are similar or very, very different – come together. To make out. (Quoted in Spurlock 2011, 11)

While Whedon's view of the fan-industry relationship at Comic-Con seems a little utopic, Henry Jenkins proffers a more negative view:

> Today, one of my big ambivalences about Comic-Con is how much it now emphasizes fans as consumers rather than fans as cultural producers. . . . [It] puts the professionals in the center and the subcultural activities the conference was based on at the fringes (2012, 25).

I disagree with Jenkins's assessment of where fandom is located relative to industry at Comic-Con. For sure, consumption forms a large part of the activity that goes on in the rooms and main exhibition hall, and Hollywood studios have the biggest booths selling their latest wares. However, as I have already mentioned, the convention spills out into the city streets and other public and private buildings. Fans occupy more places and create more spaces for their activities and practices than the industry can define and control. So while the professionals are at the center of the exhibition hall and panels, advertising their own creations, fans are inside the convention meeting new fans, arranging meetings, and gathering new ideas and inspiration for creative activities and projects. Outside, fans revel in transforming San Diego into their space, daubing walls and windows with flyers and posters for fan clubs, groups, zombie walks, and activist marches. Subcultural identity and the activities that go with it are at the heart of Comic-Con, and one therefore has to reconsider what spaces constitute the convention and which geographic places act as sites for fan interaction and creativity.

Shifts in fan creativity are matched by Comic-Con's expanding, transnational vision for its event content. Comic-Con was once entirely American in its focus—DC and Marvel, US comic artists, film, and TV series dominated. But the organization has become a global nexus for all sorts of popular media and transnational texts: British science fiction, Japanese anime and computer games, Spanish and Mexican horror, Canadian superheroes, Belgian adventurers, and Danish toy companies stand side by side with established American comic icons such as Superman and major Hollywood studios such as Warner Bros. Comic-Con International, officially renamed in 1995, provides a space for the promotion of global popular-media texts, where American and international comic fans can meet, and foreign media companies compete with US conglomerates.

Comic-Con International's mission statement, also adopted in 1995, indicates a desire to both appreciate the comic book form that spawned the original convention in 1970 and expand its scope to include other kinds of popular-culture texts:

> San Diego Comic-Con International is a nonprofit educational corporation dedicated to creating awareness of, and appreciation for, comics and related popular art forms, primarily through the presentation of conventions and events that celebrate the historic and ongoing contribution of comics to art and culture. (Quoted in Sassaman and Estrada 2009, 9)

In keeping with this mission statement, other events have been initiated by Comic-Con International to support the comic arts, including the Alternative Press Expo and WonderCon—both held until recently in San Francisco but now moved to Anaheim to accommodate larger crowds.[2] Following an unsuccessful bid in 2010 from Anaheim to become the new host of Comic-Con, fans were outraged to think that San Diego might be under threat (Thompson 2010).[3]

Despite issues of space, Comic-Con International and the city of San Diego have become attractive destinations for fans and Hollywood-studio executives to promote comics and the popular arts. Moreover, the convention center was expanded in 2001, adding two new halls used to gather thousands of fans for the masquerade costume ball and to seat the same fans for the latest blockbuster movie launch. Ballroom 20, for example, can hold 4,250 people and has hosted *Star Wars* film festivals and premieres of new comic book superhero storylines. However, with the opening of Hall H in 2004, which can seat over 6,500 people, Comic-Con became able to handle the largest of blockbuster launches. Showcasing the stars and directors of some of the most popular film franchises, Hall H became a Mecca for fans eager to see sneak previews and hear hot gossip months before films premiered in cinemas:

> Comic-Con proved to be the launching pad for many popular films, especially those with their roots in comic books, such as the *X-Men* and *Spider-Man* films, *Iron Man*, *Superman Returns*, *Hellboy*, *Sin City*, *300*, *The Spirit*, and *Watchmen*, to name just a few. (Sassaman and Estrada 2009, 154)

As popular genre programming on US television continues to attract global audiences, cult TV producers have begun to utilize Hall H to launch new series and preview current ones. Seen as a "testing ground" for ensemble cast series like *Lost* (2004–2010) and *Heroes* (2006–2012), Comic-Con has became the spiritual home for many writers and actors who would regularly attend the event seeking to boost awareness of an upcoming project. As a mass media event, Comic-Con is shaping transnational US-derived programming content, presenting it to a global audience and creating a ready-made international fan base before a series has had time to finish its first season or a film has been released.

Seeking higher esteem within the Comic-Con pecking order, Hollywood studios compete to get their new film or television show into Hall H. Running from dawn to dusk, with lines for popular panels forming often days in advance, the mixed program of film launches and television-script read-throughs attracts not only thousands of fans during Comic-Con, but also the world's press, who flock to interview stars and get angles on what new things will be out in the following year. The big superhero franchises, like *The Avengers* and *Spider-Man*, start off in Hollywood but make their way through San Diego to gather momentum and hopefully set up lucrative box-office returns.

In 2010, for instance, Hall H hosted panels to launch Disney's *Tron: Legacy* (2010) and Marvel's *Captain America* (2011). In 2011, *The Twilight Saga: Breaking Dawn Part 1* (2011) and *The Adventures of Tintin* (2011)—the latter offering a rare appearance by Steven Spielberg—were joined by television hits such as *Glee* (2009–) and *Doctor Who*. In 2012 television seemingly took over, with panels for *The Big Bang Theory* (2007–) and *The Walking Dead* (2010–) proving very popular, in addition to another appearance by *Doctor Who*. In a transnational media industry, where Comic-Con is taking on greater importance in the making and breaking of new TV shows, films, and even franchises, television has taken a greater share of event spaces like Ballroom 20 and Hall H. As a result, comics and comic producers—particularly those like Marvel and DC—have to reassert their traditional authority in the same space, by building bigger and bigger booths in the main Exhibition Hall and proliferating panels in other rooms, to attract and cater to loyal comic book fans. However, while film and TV push American superhero cultures to do more to maintain their traditional presence, newer transnational superhero texts fill in the gaps, occupying more and more smaller booths in the hall and offering their fans opportunities to interact with writers and artists at a more personal level. Ironically then, while American popular television and film battle with Marvel and DC comic book superheroes for attention, more independent and transnational superhero texts still find room to establish themselves at Comic-Con.

The expansion of Hall H's program to include science-fiction television as well as the usual superhero films further signals Comic-Con's shift toward the promotion of global popular culture beyond the comic book. The fact that the BBC's *Doctor Who*, broadcast on BBC America in the USA, attracts thousands of fans dressed as Daleks and various incarnations of the Doctor suggests a global audience for this traditionally UK science-fiction television franchise. In turn, these *Doctor Who* events and fans solidify its cult reputation and appeal, but also transform central characters (in this case usually the Doctor) into international superhero icons, who sit side by side with their American cousins like Superman and Captain America.

San Diego Comic-Con and Fan Practices and Pilgrimages

If Comic-Con has become a particular place for Hollywood promotion and superhero adoration, then it is also a space for the recycling of old media and entertainment forms. Series like *Doctor Who* and comic books like *Superman* clearly have pedigrees that stretch further back into history than the convention. Old and new versions of both appear at the same time, with independent traders selling valuable original issues of *Action Comics* and toy dolls of William Hartnell, the original Doctor. In many ways Comic-Con represents the physical manifestation of Henry Jenkins's theory of "convergence culture," where the convention space allows for the search for and archiving of new forms of entertainment, and where "the flow of content across multiple media platforms" links the Internet and online gaming with older media forms such as comics, film, and television (Jenkins 2006, 2). In convergence culture, old and new media collide, and fans are able to remain loyal to favorite childhood series and characters at the same time that the very same media texts are recycled and reimagined for new audiences and new fans. Part of Comic-Con's significance for fans and contemporary entertainment industries is in bringing these histories of fandom together in one space and temporal moment, which means that it conflates fandoms or at very least compresses the experiences attendant within their usually separate cultures. As a result, it enhances the text's pleasures for multiple generations of fans and maximizes profit and profile for media companies.

John Fiske described the traditional fan convention, most famously illustrated by the *Star Trek* and *Star Wars* franchises, as a space where "cultural and economic capital come together" (1992, 43); the fans love and valuing of a text is expressed alongside their financial investment in it, represented in their purchase of expensive tickets, souvenirs, and memorabilia. Yet the traditional convention is also a site for communal nostalgia, collecting, sharing stories, and a way to bring past experiences into the present. I would argue fans are "locked into an endless cycle of re-enchantment" (Gregson and Crewe 2003, 112) with their favorite superheroes and animated television characters. Therefore, the fans traveling to San Diego Comic-Con go on a symbolic pilgrimage to a physical incarnation of an imagined community space—for an event in a space that is neutral for most of the year, but highly emotive for one week in July. The physical location draws fans while the city acts as a backdrop from which the experiences of the traveling fans are drawn and on which their memories of favorite media texts are based.

Jennifer E. Porter sees fan convention attendance as a form of physical pilgrimage in a secular context. Using the work of anthropologist Victor Turner, she argues that the pilgrimage to a shared site is a liminal journey of transformation to find *communitas*, "communal fellowship," with other fans (Porter 1999, 252). The site of fan tourism, therefore, whether specifically tied to the fictional text (a filming location or theme park ride), or a neutral and generic site (a hotel ballroom or convention center), provides "a time and space for fans to be free to explore their love of something deep and meaningful in their lives" (267). As a consequence, these atypical fan sites become important places for popular veneration.

Will Brooker describes sites of fan pilgrimages such as filming locations as "sites of play and carnival, poetry and magic" (2007, 429). Fans get joy from traveling to and existing in the same space associated with their favorite media text. This is augmented by the fact that many fans feel the same, and the location thus becomes coded as a fan space—not an ordinary space but a communal space to celebrate the text. We can tie this with John Urry's discussion of the consumption of tourism, wherein he suggests that "satisfaction is derived not from the individual act of consumption but from the fact that all sorts of other people are also consumers" of services and souvenirs they buy while traveling (1995, 131). The San Diego Convention Center, the city, and associated buildings and tourist sites become a geography of nostalgic recollection where collectors, fans, producers, artists, writers, and stars all bring new meaning and history to the popular media franchises that Hollywood continues to market there. As Svetlana Boym says of nostalgia, it "remains an intermediary between collective and individual memory. Collective memory can be seen as a playground of multiple individual recollections" (2004, 54). As such, San Diego Comic-Con is a vast playground of memories and texts, superheroes and fans. Given that it attracts fans of all ages and levels of commitment, with differing amounts of subcultural capital, it is also a site for the establishment and cementing of fan hierarchies. Giving exclusive promotional items and information for just being there, with an emphasis on insider-knowledge provision and pilgrimage, Comic-Con is a site of nostalgia for fans who attend, but also a marker of difference for fans who cannot. Matt Hills describes a similar display of fan distinction in horror-film festivals and conventions, whereby fans who attend can get to see things first or feel closer to the stars and directors. He argues that a "fan's convention/festival attendance becomes one 'authentic' marker of 'insider status,'" and thus reflects the importance of subcultural capital in the hierarchies of fandom (Hills 2010a, 99).

BBC America, *Doctor Who*, and the US Market

Given its cultural centrality for fandom, it is no surprise that BBC America now uses Comic-Con to launch and build audiences for UK programs in a crowded international television market. The network was launched on March 29, 1998, and rebranded in 2007 as part of BBC Worldwide. Distributed in association with the Discovery Network, it is available on both satellite and cable through subscription. With a New York headquarters, BBC America has had a number of American executive officers with experience working in US niche cable networks, including MTV and Comedy Central. Deriving most of its content from the BBC and other UK broadcasters means that BBC America offers an interesting mix of drama, genre programming, and documentaries, but it has also aired classic American series such as *Battlestar Galactica* (2003–2009) and *Star Trek: The Next Generation* (1987–1994). As a result, BBC America is an inherently transnational company and its presence at the San Diego Comic-Con again suggests that the convention is becoming a site for global media interaction and international promotion.

BBC America has promoted *Doctor Who* heavily on air. In 2011, to create anticipation among the American audience for the series, the network aired new episodes at the same time as the BBC in the UK. *Doctor Who*'s simultaneous broadcast followed an experiment by the BBC a year earlier, of airing episodes of the ten-part *Torchwood: Miracle Day* series in the USA before airing them in the UK. This was in part because *Miracle Day* was a co-production of the BBC and Starz (a US-based subscription channel that produced series such as *Spartacus*, 2010–2013 and *Camelot*, 2011). However, such a focus on the US market and on attracting new audiences through a presence at Comic-Con indicates that *Doctor Who* and its spin-offs are core to the BBC's international brand, targeting multiple markets and multiple audiences (Hills 2010b, 67–69). Moreover, *Doctor Who* has had a history of traveling across the Atlantic. The original series first aired in 1977 on US television, and by 1984 was being shown on 112 US stations (Cull 2006, 61–62). Following declining ratings on both sides of the Atlantic and cancellation in 1989, the franchise was reborn in the form of a 1996 television movie, again a co-production (of the BBC, Universal Studios, and Fox Television), that was broadcast in the USA a week before UK audiences could watch it (Cull 2006, 65) and was intended as a test to "gain sufficiently high North American ratings to make a future series viable" (Wright 2011, 128).

The next sign of BBC America's international success came at the 2011 San Diego Comic-Con, where the network for the first time achieved star status by holding a *Doctor Who* panel in Hall H. *Doctor Who*, *Torchwood* (2006–), *Being Human* (2008–2013), and *Bedlam* (2011–) among others, have all had popular previews, panels, and merchandise launches in San Diego, but Matt Smith's eleventh incarnation of the Doctor was the first UK TV series to be given such prime billing—something repeated in 2012 and 2013 (see Figure 4). Further, BBC America's presence at Comic-Con included panel events with the cast and creators of *Doctor Who*, BBC America's top-rated series, supported by a centrally located BBC America booth in the main exhibition hall that attracted hordes of fans and passers-by eager to purchase the latest *Doctor Who* merchandise and grab exclusive Comic-Con freebies (in 2012 fans could get a foam Dalek hat to wear around San Diego, displaying their fandom with pride!). This complex physical presence is significant because it represents the changing nature of the event, from a celebration of American superheroes to the promotion of transnational ones. While American television, film, and comic book franchises battle for space in the panel rooms, exhibit halls, and event programs, smaller transnational companies act as alternative spaces within the main space, where fans can seek out new texts and more exclusive items, and attain higher levels within hierarchies of fandom.

Moreover, being at Comic-Con in Hall H is a boon to organizers as well as to BBC America. There appears to be a reciprocal relationship whereby *Doctor Who* gains more status by being compared and billed with colossal Hollywood franchises that use Comic-Con to premiere blockbuster releases. This allows *Doctor Who* to become aligned with the USA's popular media mainstream, rather than with UK culture or even with smaller science-fiction fan cultures. As San Diego Comic-Con diversifies its market and cult audience to include international *Doctor Who* fans prepared to travel thousands of miles to get that unique convention experience, this

4. A timeless trio: Matt Smith, Jenna Coleman and Steven Moffat on the big screen in Hall H, discussing the upcoming final season for the 11th Doctor in 2013. Credit: Lincoln Geraghty.

conceptualization of *Doctor Who*'s "mainstream" presence is complicated by being the product of a set of transnational cultural exchanges and fan interactions.

The presence and popularity of *Doctor Who* at Comic-Con speaks to the wider promotional emphasis and aspiration of the franchise that existed even from its earliest moments. According to Nicholas J. Cull, right from the very beginning the BBC intended to create a series for UK television that would offer audiences a taste of popular American examples like *The Twilight Zone* (Serling, 1959–64), which was already being screened in the UK on ITV. As well as providing the "cultural model for a British science fiction serial such as *Doctor Who*," American domination of the genre provided the impetus for the BBC to strike out in 1962 and start to develop something new for the UK. By 1963 they had settled on the time travel format and began production on a Saturday evening science-fiction serial (Cull 2006, 53). In both format and storylines—many early episodes and characters were purposely given an American flavor—*Doctor Who* bore the mark of a series trying to hold its own with international competitors. By 1966 *Star Trek* had started and clearly contrasted American space opera with *Doctor Who*'s British wit and impertinence. However, while initial viewing figures and lack of success towards the end of the first series suggest that *Doctor Who* was a minor player in the US science fiction television market, its earlier presence created a footprint on which the new series, launched in 2005 and helmed by Russell T. Davies, could rebuild a loyal audience and foster a new one more attuned to contemporary television-viewing habits and global genre tastes.

Indeed, from its inception as a family TV serial based on US-style genre programming, to its contemporary manifestation as an action adventure series, *Doctor Who* has always been linked to American ideals and the US television market. John Tulloch and Manuel Alvarado's seminal study of the series stresses its dichotomous nature, aimed at being both educational and entertaining for a multi-generational audience of British youth and adults:

> *Doctor Who* sought to entertain in a 'responsible' and educative way; and also like *The Eagle* (which was the only comic allowed in many state schools of the 1950s), it drew much of its public legitimacy from the published authority of the state's educators. (Tulloch and Alvarado 1983, 40)

Concentrating on "soft" socio-cultural scientific speculation (the what if?), stories would be about "the investigation of different cultures through space and time, rather than seeking involvement with hard science" (41). Following Lord Reith's mandate for the BBC to "Inform, educate and entertain," the series was not to promote "space travel or science fiction," but drama designed "to contain not only futuristic adventures but also historical stories that could be regarded as educational and improving for its youth audience, concerning significant events in times and places visited by the main characters" (Bignell and O'Day 2004, 30). Yet in doing so, the series could not avoid borrowing from American culture with stories involving the Doctor traveling back in time to moments of American history such as the Gunfight at the OK Corral, or participating in the Space Race between the USA and Soviet Union.

As telefantasy, the series contains both real and fantasy worlds (Johnson 2005); thus, the contemporary contexts of its broadcast meant those worlds would be influenced by both British and American culture. In terms of design and costuming, scholars have argued that *Doctor Who* took on many American styles to match competition abroad. Piers Britton and Simon Barker (2003, 172–73) saw this development as a sign of *Doctor Who* accommodating designs from contemporary science-fiction films. Similarly, James Chapman acknowledges the impact that American television series *Battlestar Galactica* (1978–80) and *Buck Rogers in the 25th Century* (1979–1981) had on the BBC and its attempts to modernize the look of *Doctor Who*. Producer Graham Williams had to comply with the BBC's tight budgetary requirements and entertain an audience becoming familiar with and attracted to big-budget cinema and television from across the Atlantic (Chapman 2006, 123). As I have argued elsewhere, "The more modern-day version of the Cyberman, with the silver jumpsuit, subdivided helmet and booming deep voice, was more like Darth Vader than synthetic human" (Geraghty 2008, 92).

Doctor Who's format "places it directly in the historical lineage of British literary" science fiction (Chapman 2006, 5), in the vein of H. G. Wells's *The Time Machine* (1895), where a genius inventor travels through time and questions notions of human responsibility and endeavor. But the figure of the Doctor himself also borrows from a deeply American tradition. He is a mythic hero, akin to the Western's cowboy or the comic book's superhero. Described as "a transcendent idea" (Richards 2003, 8–9), the Doctor was an alien that acted like a human, caught between enjoying the homely comforts of Earth and exploring the dangerous universe. On the frontier the cowboy represented America's ambivalence toward nature. Caught between civilization and the wilderness, he became a messianic figure; a redemptive figure of American idealism and the monomyth (see Lawrence and Jewett 1977). The superhero, written in the pages of comic books and personified by American icons like Superman, was a contemporary vision of the cowboy hero seen in Hollywood Westerns.

For Richard Reynolds the superhero is "a highly potent cultural myth" (1992, 82) that is embedded in the American values of freedom and individualism. Often empowered with super-human abilities, they sacrifice their lives in service to others. The Doctor—who remains caught between worlds, using his great intelligence and power over technology to save those he encounters—conforms in many ways to this American trope and fits within a tradition of storytelling very familiar to American movie audiences and comic book readers. In "The Impossible Astronaut" (2011), from a recent series of *Doctor Who*, Matt Smith's Doctor even dons the iconic cowboy hat, gleefully exclaiming, "Stetsons are cool!" (Figure 5). Therefore, I would argue that the presence of *Doctor Who* at the San Diego Comic-Con, surrounded by analogous popular stories of sacrifice and heroism, does not jar with its humble roots as a British TV series. The Doctor could be described as both British in origin and American in character; thus, his international appeal as a contemporary superhero is unsurprising.

5. "Stetsons are cool!": Matt Smith as the 11th Doctor channeling John Wayne in "The Impossible Astronaut" (2011). Credit: BBC.

Doctor Who as Transnational Superhero

Doctor Who is arguably the quintessential superhero: his knowledge knows no bounds; he has the power to travel through time and space; his companions bring their own spirit, personality, and abilities to his time traveling missions; and most of all, he is driven to protect the innocent and save those in need. Following the reboot of the franchise in 2005, the Doctor is also more of a heroic, heart-throb figure—depicted as young, exuberant, and in keeping with the times, in contrast to the more fatherly and older versions seen in the original series. David Tennant's and Matt Smith's Doctors both appear more youthful, dressed in more fashionable clothes that appeal to a retro look that is popular on the UK's high streets.

As costumes hold significant semiotic meaning for the superheroes who wear them, so too does the outfit chosen by the Doctor—after regeneration, he chooses a new wardrobe to differentiate his new self from those preceding and to reflect his new personality. Each look takes on an iconic appeal: Tom Baker's scarf, Peter Davison's stick of celery, and Matt Smith's bowtie, for example. These costume changes are significant in creating difference between regenerations, but they are largely neutral in terms of national symbols and signifiers (apart from the odd Tam o'Shanter and tartan scarf worn by Baker). Thus, while the Doctor may be British in origin and tone, his outfit is devoid of the kind of nationalistic bias seen in the colors of Captain America's red, white, and blue costume. So, while the Captain is dressed as an American superhero, the Doctor is the transnational everyman not tied to any particular nation or allegiance. Yet while the individual series continue to include these quirky visual cues, scholars have argued that overall the show has become more serious in tone, having an "emotional resonance" (Newman 2005, 115) that latterly constructs the Doctor as a much more complex and conflicted hero than in previous incarnations.

While David Rafer suggests that the Doctor has always been "touched by divinity, being almost immortal" (2007, 124) like heroes from classical antiquity, Lynnette Porter argues that the new *Doctor Who* portrays him as "gray" and more fallible due to the changing nature of science fiction programming:

> Today's SF TV heroes may aspire to be ever better people and may have the best intentions, but they seldom overcome villains or monsters simply because they are on the side of Good. The dramatic tension in more recent SF series often comes from the heroes' inner turmoil and the dissonance between what they and others expect traditional heroes to be or do. (Porter 2010, 18)

So while still "godlike" in his ability to save the day and change the lives of millions (Porter 2010, 229), the Doctor is currently a more complicated superhero figure, who questions his own reasons for doing what he does and feels guilt for the things that have gone wrong or the people he could not save.

This change in the Doctor's superheroic persona has been brought about to a large extent by the new backstory given to the character by Russell T. Davies. The last of his race, he now roams time and space filling the void in his life by sporadically meddling in other people's affairs and returning to Earth. "The back story thus locates him within a particular archetype of masculinity: the traumatised war veteran… racked by guilt over his inability to prevent the destruction of the Time Lords and holds himself responsible for what happened to them" (Chapman 2006, 190). The emotional baggage that the Doctor carries is an interesting addition that allows for more involved storylines that can stretch over the course of an entire season, rather than one single episode, and is again emblematic of the changing nature of genre television and the social times in which we now live. Unconcerned for nationalistic rhetoric, which he often confronts in the form of the British military, the Doctor is entirely transnational in his outlook as he serves as savior for all humans rather than any particular nation or nationality.

Porter argues that "gray heroes working in groups, or series in search of heroes, may represent societies' growing unease with world tensions and the search for answers beyond traditional heroes" (2010, 31). But also, the ambiguity surrounding the Doctor as hero highlights wider changes to the way these kinds of stories are being told. For example, *Doctor Who* now screens in short seasons with thirteen episodes connected by an overarching theme and enemy. In the last year these shorter seasons have even been split in two to spread the series over the calendar year—responding to the US market's more seasonal programming. Rather than the typical twenty-five minute episode over four to eight parts, each episode of the new series is around fifty minutes, faster paced, and more action orientated. Thus, in the contexts of US quality television production, *Doctor Who* is again more American than British—and UK audiences are just as content with the result. Defined as "notable for their self consciousness, visual stylishness and re-imagining of established genres for a postmodern popular culture" (Chapman 2006, 185), quality television series like *Doctor Who* place a morally ambiguous figure at the center of the narrative for the very purposes of challenging the traditional notion of the television hero as physically and morally perfect.

In terms of narrative, *Doctor Who* has adopted a more American style of production, epitomized by quality television, but it has also adapted to take on more contemporary marketing and branding strategies familiar to Hollywood in the twenty-first century. Almost in direct response to how the original series died a slow death in terms of ratings decline and lack of a popular following, Russell T. Davies wanted to make the new series a brand that would attract a much wider audience and serve the dedicated fan community—of which he was a proud member. According to Sue Short, "His role in revising the series should not be underestimated, evidently adoring the show while also understanding the need to manufacture and market *Doctor Who* as a 'product'" (2011, 178). To maintain popularity beyond the BBC audience, Davies had to make the show more attractive to international audiences—America being the biggest—and take advantage of new viewing technologies such as webisodes and on-demand services to spread *Doctor Who* across multiple media platforms. Jim Leach calls this the "multiform flow of today's media environment" (2009, 95), and the series conforms to the definition of "transmedia storytelling," where "the use of multiple media" helps "to create an increasingly elaborate world" (Tryon 2008, 307) extended over the likes of DVD, TV, webisodes, graphic novels, and computer games. The BBC's webpages for the series advertise not only the upcoming series, with episodes also available on iPlayer, but have interactive games and quizzes for young fans, interviews and production information, and a wealth of information and images from the original series that serve as an intertextual link and nostalgic archive for older fans who are fully aware of the series' heritage. These webpages also have the benefit of being accessible from anywhere in the world.

Even in this environment of online branding and transmedia storytelling, the presence of BBC America at Comic-Con, with *Doctor Who* as its tentpole, proves the importance of event status in the continued popularity of genre programming and the contemporary superhero. Fans gathering together *en masse* in San Diego to attend the panel in Hall H and see the stars create a media hype that helps promote the series to an international audience and offers a springboard for the latest episodes soon to air on television. It is a viral event where attendees can tell their friends through social media and word of mouth about previews and what is in store. The convention experience, with the "insider information" gleaned there, places fan-attendees at the center of production activity, albeit for a fleeting moment.

During that moment they then can share this enthusiasm for the series beyond Comic-Con—thus making the experience more valuable, durable, and longer lasting. Comic-Con is "an economical way of producing buzz" (Coogan 2006, 6), and as such, fans are active participants in the making and remaking of *Doctor Who* as a brand for international audience consumption. However, in creating a buzz for an industry determined to market its product, fans are not just pawns as Jenkins argues. These fans are creative in the ways they engage with the industry discourses of Comic-Con, but they are also actual subcultural producers, who transform the *Doctor Who* text like the poachers described by Jenkins in his seminal work. Fans dressed in original cosplay outfits display their subcultural creativity: "Southern belles," with dresses made from cut up TARDIS costumes; female Doctors with their own sonic screwdrivers; undead Zombie Doctors that take part in a zombie walk through the city. The transnational flavor of the Doctor is also emphasized in the diverse attendees in the hall.

Conclusion

This chapter sought to analyze the importance of the San Diego Comic-Con in the global circulation of the international screen superhero, using the example of BBC America and *Doctor Who*'s presence at the convention to demonstrate how it acts as a space for the promotion and rebranding of the UK's most famous superhero export. In the history of Comic-Con, we can see an evolution of the convention space, where, in its generic nature, it allows for multiple popular-culture products to be sold and advertised, and thousands of fans to interact and engage with their favorite media texts. The convention center is both a business space and a fan place; as global entertainment industries—from US comic book publishers to Japanese anime producers—mingle with fans in a localized environment, costumed fans spill out onto the streets of San Diego, which are themselves specially dressed for the occasion. With such an environment on offer, BBC America can capitalize on its catalogue of shows with *Doctor Who* as headliner, attracting new international audiences and building a fan community loyal to its brand and specific kinds of programming. Thus, in the process, *Doctor Who* has become a recognizable international brand, and its transnational ambitions are marked through its texts' movement away from their UK history and adoption of the American format and production methods more familiar to millions of viewers across the globe.

Alongside the likes of Batman and Superman, iconic symbols of Americana ever-present at Comic-Con, the Doctor has become more of a "superhero" character in his own right. Still distinctly British in origin, he is also American in character, influenced by the changing contexts of how television heroes have been depicted on screen. More conflicted and emotional, the Doctor is a troubled superhero attractive to a young and increasingly media-savvy audience. His superheroism is all the more remarkable for the way it has been retrospectively re-cast with homages to the alien origins, costuming, and super-intelligence of traditional American superheroes, despite the Doctor's overtly British origins.

However, by fitting in with Comic-Con's conveyor belt of panels, programs, and promotions—increasingly dictated by Hollywood's promotional interests—and adapting its narrative to suit international tastes, to what extent has *Doctor Who* changed from its original form? While San Diego Comic-Con will continue to increase in international scope and size, threatening to push BBC America to the fringes like other companies, the network's continued presence will offer cult esteem and the opportunity to connect with international fans—a priceless marketing strategy in an increasingly saturated popular-media market. Just by being there, in the city and in the convention space, BBC America has become part of the fabric of Comic-Con. Gathering in Hall H with thousands of other fans gives individual *Doctor Who* fans an experience that creates an indelible memory and becomes part of how they share and present themselves as fans within the community. Comic-Con has changed *Doctor Who* and *Doctor Who* has helped to change Comic-Con; but, more importantly, by bringing *Doctor Who*'s global fans together in Comic-Con's event spaces, new fleeting, creative fan places are generated that help to extend the global reach and life of *Doctor Who*, not as a British, but as a global media franchise.

Notes

1. In discussing the Berlin Film Festival (IFB), Janet Harbord talks about the way it helps to shape the city and vice versa: "Film festivals are mixed spaces crossed by commercial interest, specialized film knowledge and tourist trajectories" (2002, 60).

2. Even the future of the San Diego Convention Center is uncertain as the space is becoming increasingly limited for the massive crowds and exhibitors who want to attend; Anaheim remains an alternative—yet unpopular—location.

3. The issue even achieved cult status by becoming a joke on *The Simpsons* in May of that year: after Lisa derides the stereotype that all fat people are jolly, Comic Book Guy retorts, "Would you be jolly if you thought Comic-Con was moving to Anaheim?" ("To Surveil with Love"). However, there has been growing support on Facebook and Twitter from some fans who want to see the event move because of the lack of convention space. A page attracting over three thousand friends on Facebook was created to convince the board of Comic-Con International to sign with Anaheim rather than re-signing with San Diego. Although this failed and Comic-Con will be in San Diego until 2016, rumors and debate continue about a move.

BLADE OF THE PHANTOM MASTER

Heroism, Gender, National Identity, and Cultural Translation in Japanese-Korean Animation

DANIEL MARTIN

South Korean animation is currently in a period of growth, as the industry reacts with cautious optimism to unprecedented success both at home and around the world. For an animation industry that has been known primarily for its technical competency rather than creative output, international collaborations, particularly with the animation industry in Japan, have proven an interesting, if problematic, route to international and domestic visibility. The most notable Japanese-Korean co-production is *Blade of the Phantom Master* (Joji Shimura and Ahn Tae-geun, 2004).[1] This animated film is based on a manga (and *manhwa*) series published simultaneously in Japan and Korea; both film and comic series offer a fantasy-action retelling of characters and stories from Korean history and folklore, in particular the iconic tale of Chunhyang. The film offers a startling remediation of the story and the character Chunhyang, as the specifically Korean aspects of the narrative and characters have been modified, with the recasting of the eponymous virtuous maiden of the original story as a superheroic, fetishized ninja warrior particularly problematic. The film uses gender and varied notions of "heroism" to both reinforce and destabilize national identity, and rewrites the Korean folktale for an international audience, drawing on the conventions of Japanese animation's characterization and narrative to create a new hybrid media for a global market. Thus, *Blade of the Phantom Master* is a revealing case of the cultural translation and transnational re-imagining of Korean literature and folklore. These varied depictions of Chunhyang as folk hero/warrior-hero reveal parallels to the superheroes of Hollywood cinema and American comic books, demonstrating a figure of female power both culturally specific and globally comprehensible.

This chapter therefore considers the representation of the female hero/superhero in Japanese-Korean animation, in the context of the international circulation of animation from both countries, and with a specific focus on the transformation of the folktale version of the character Chunhyang into *Blade of the Phantom Master*. The female protagonist is reborn, now a transnational hybrid of folk heroine and preternaturally skilled Japanese ninja warrior; in this way, she becomes a prototype for a new South Korean superhero(ine). Drawing on analysis of industrial histories of Japanese and South Korean animation, as well as promotional materials and production patterns, this chapter examines the production and circulation of the film; further, it dissects the process of adaptation from the original source material to animation, focusing on representations of gender, nationality and heroism. This analysis reveals how the demand for globalization leads to the (re-)empowerment of a Korean icon whose identity is at once hyper-visible and invisible, and a superhero who challenges, even while reinforcing, traditional gender roles.[2]

Japanese Animation in Korea and Korean Animation in Japan

The history of collaboration between animation production in Japan and Korea reveals a complex chain of influence, imitation, cultural exchange, subcontracted production, and even, perhaps, imperialism, leading to two separate yet inseparable industries. The animation industry in South Korea has long been known as a significant base of subcontracted animation: cheap labor performed by skilled professionals in support of non-Korean projects. US television cartoons from *My Little Pony* in the 1980s to *The Simpsons* and *Family Guy* more recently have been animated in South Korea. Likewise, the Japanese industry has often relied on Korea as an efficient source of quick and cost-effective "in-between" animation for both feature films and television.

One of the long-term results of the large amount of Japanese animation produced in Korea is, according to many, an adoption of a Japanese style in Korea's own animated works. John Lent and Kie-Un Yu have noted that "when Korean studios have engaged in domestic production, they have been severely criticized for imitating Japanese work" (2001, 97). Likewise, Joon-Yang Kim blames the subcontracting process for the Japanese influence on Korean animation's visual design; Kim goes as far as to describe these works as "regarded as a national disgrace" and characterizing the situation as "new imperialism in the territory of animated film" (2006, 69). In addition to the influence gained from Japanese animation through subcontracted productions, Korean animators (and audiences) were also swayed by the popularity of Japanese cartoons in Korea. By the end of the 1990s, around 90 percent of animation shown on Korean television was Japanese (Lent and Yu 2001, 98). This trend dates back even to the period when Japanese cultural imports were circulated in spite of their official ban in Korea; as Chua and Iwabuchi argue, "Japanese pop culture had been 'copied,' 'partially integrated,' 'plagiarized' and 'reproduced' into Korean products" throughout the second half of the twentieth century (2008, 3–4). Further, while Japanese productions commonly rely on Korean labor, Korean domestic animation productions have occasionally required "Japanese collaboration to iron out . . . technical wrinkles" (Lent and Yu 2001, 95).

The result is that Korean animation, especially in the 1970s and '80s, produced characters and stories that bore a striking resemblance to Japanese properties. The most significant example is *Robot Taekwon V* (Kim Cheong-gi, 1976), which, as noted by Lent and Yu (2001) and Kim (2006), virtually plagiarises the character design of *Mazinger Z* (Toei Animation, 1972–74). Yet, as I have briefly argued elsewhere, *Robot Taekwon V* is in many other ways highly original, rich in theme and symbolic value (Martin 2011). Indeed, the superheroic character Robot Taekwon V is a figure of nationalism in South Korea and reflects a variety of political values—in some instances, in direct opposition to Japan's colonialist legacy (Magnan-Park 2010). It is therefore difficult to entirely agree that Korea's animation production reflects a simple absorption of Japanese influence. Rather, the industrial and cultural impact of Japanese animation, as well as popular culture and various media from further abroad, has been the foundation for Korea's slow but significant development of a distinct domestic style.

In spite of the wide range of collaborations and economic and industrial links between these two Asian animation industries, historically there have been remarkably few true creative co-productions. There are, however, a few notable examples of Korean collaborations and co-productions, representing a small but significant trend towards adapting Korean properties for Japanese audiences. These animations tend towards action in fantasy settings, focusing on superpowered and heroic characters, often with female protagonists.

The animated feature film *Gundress* (Katsuyoshi Yatabe, 1999), for example, is regarded in Korea as a co-production with Japan. Animation Producer Joe Jo (2000) notes that the film was co-financed and co-produced with Korean company Dong-A Export, but the film was not recognized as anything other than an entirely Japanese production on its international VHS and DVD release. The film, a science fiction *mecha* (anime's "robot suit" subgenre) set in a futuristic Japan, notably includes an identifiably Korean character in its ensemble cast, meaning that some representation is achieved. Other instances of the adaptation or incorporation of Korean properties in Japanese animation are even less recognizable. The Japanese television series *Ragnarok* (directed by Toyoaki Nakajima 2002) is based on a Korean source, a fact hidden entirely by its fantasy setting and complicated chain of adaptations: the animated series is based on a Korean Massively Multiplayer Online Role Playing Game, itself based on the popular Korean *manhwa* series by Lee Myung-jin, which takes its primary inspiration from Norse mythology. Thus, the stateless setting and ethnically indistinct characters make this adaptation a success for the Korean industry in purely economic, rather than cultural, terms.

This context is important for appreciating the significance of *Blade of the Phantom Master*, the self-declared first true animation co-production between South Korea and Japan. The Korean animation industry had long sought to overcome its reputation as an uncreative hub of subcontracted animation only, and aimed to establish an international identity equal to Japanese or American animation. As Ae-Ri Yoon notes, the drive to "throw off the shackles of being a subcontractor" and establish "creative agency" has driven the industry to "unavoidable negotiations between the local and the global animation spheres" (2009, 104–5). When the significant investment in the blockbuster animation *Wonderful Days* (released in the UK and USA as *Sky Blue*, 2003) failed to achieve meaningful success either at home or abroad, the industry scaled back its ambitions and looked to international co-productions as a way to achieve more global visibility (Martin 2011). *Wonderful Days* failed precisely because it lacked an identifiable sense of Korean identity, and there was therefore a great deal at stake in both the production and reception of *Blade of the Phantom Master*.[3]

A New Era? *Blade of the Phantom Master* as a Co-Production

Like the vast majority of animation produced in Japan, *Blade of the Phantom Master* was adapted from pre-existing material. The original comic series by Youn In-wan and Yang Kyung-il was published virtually simultaneously as a manga in Japan (serialized in *Monthly Sunday Gene-X*) and as a *manhwa* in Korea (in *Young Champ*). The series has also found a wider international audience, and is translated and published in numerous other territories, including France, where publisher Pika has released all nineteen volumes under the title *Le Nouvel Angyo Onshi*. In the case of its French release, however, the series was treated entirely as a Japanese import, and its Korean origins were ignored (as evidenced in the "Pika Edition" promotional catalog listings). In spite of the popularity of the series and its eager fan following, there has been no official English-language translation, though unauthorized fan translations/scanlations are in circulation online. The film was therefore assumed to have a built-in market consisting of fans of the manga/*manhwa*, the local popularity of which (over two million volumes sold in Japan and Korea) was frequently emphasized in the film's publicity (Shin 2004; Yoon 2004).

Blade of the Phantom Master's production represented a new spirit of creative collaboration, with Korean and Japanese staff working together on multiple aspects of the production. Yet the nature of this partnership seems to reflect Korea's apparently inferior position: more than 70 percent of the production work was done by Japanese studios, and Yang Jee-hye, the president of one of the Korean animation companies involved, was publicly (and, arguably, unfairly) disparaging about the human resources and technical abilities of local studios (Kim 2004). Tellingly, Yang summarized the need for collaboration with Japan:

> The local animation industry has just passed the transition period and is still struggling to find its direction and identity, which can differentiate its works from ones by other major international animation companies. . . . So we are now trying hard to learn advanced techniques from other international animation companies and apply them to create our own works. (Kim 2004)

Blade of the Phantom Master thus embodies the Korean industry's urgent need to transform its reputation both at home and abroad, and to escape the looming shadow of Japan's cultural dominance. The film's directorial credits, too, reflect an unequal division of production. The Korean theatrical poster for the film credits Joji Shimura and Ahn Tae-geun as co-directors, as do many other Korean sources. Yet the film's Japanese credits and promotional materials credit Shimura as sole director, and the vast majority of English-language sources follow suit. Further, numerous Korean news outlets and websites also describe Shimura as the film's only director, thus making it unclear exactly how much creative input and control the film's Korean co-director really had.

Blade of the Phantom Master was produced with assistance from several Korean cultural organizations, including the Korea Creative Content Agency (KOCCA) and the Korean Cultural Center of the South Korean Embassy in Japan. The film had its world premiere in Korea in November 2004 as the opening film of the Puchon International Student Animation Festival (Suh 2004), followed by a simultaneous release later that month in cinemas nationwide in both Japan and Korea (Shin 2004). In other respects, the film's Korean aspects were far from hidden, especially on its release in Asian territories. K-pop star BoA provided a song for the film's soundtrack, and her vast popularity in Japan (far greater than in Korea) was an important selling point, ironically reflecting the way the film was targeted to a largely Japanese audience *through* its Korean elements. The film's Japanese trailer also provides a revealing example of how its Koreanness was positioned highly positively in its marketing in Japan: "Meaningless prejudices will surely be destroyed" declares the trailer; "A new era in full-scale animation collaboration between Korea and Japan!" The trailer also provides a Japanese framework for the Korean source material, by assuring audiences that the film is based on a *manhwa* "greatly admired by manga artist Takehiko Inoue" rather than citing the Korean names of the series' creators.[4] The film's defining Korean quality, rather than its creative origins, institutional support, or popular soundtrack, however, is undoubtedly the subject matter it appropriates. *Blade of the Phantom Master* takes inspiration from a variety of Korean historical figures and fictions, and focuses most prominently on an adaptation, of sorts, of the folktale and *pansori* (traditional Korean opera) *The Tale of Chunhyang*. The film's stark difference from virtually every other incarnation of the tale is one of its most significant features.[5]

The Purity of Chunhyang

Adaptations and Incarnations of a Korean Hero

The Tale of Chunhyang is one of the best known in Korea, and its origins date back to oral traditions of shamanistic ritual and music performance. The story has been told across numerous media over a period of hundreds of years, and with significant variation, yet its essential elements remain the same. Beautiful young Chunhyang, daughter of a noble lord and a *gisaeng* (an "entertainer," much like the Japanese *geisha*), is the pride of the small town of Namwon. She catches the eye of Monryong, a visiting young nobleman, and they fall deeply in love. They plan to marry, but Monryong is called back to the capital city, where he will study to become a royal commissioner. The town's new magistrate, meanwhile, is corrupt and selfish. He demands that Chunhyang "entertain" him, and when she refuses, he cruelly orders her to be beaten and imprisoned. Throughout a lengthy period of hardship and abuse, Chunhyang never capitulates, restating her loyalty to her betrothed. She is finally freed when Monryong returns to Namwon as an undercover inspector for the King, ousts the evil magistrate, and praises hunhyang's loyalty, integrity and purity.

The story is rich in symbolic meaning, and its themes are clear; as Hyangjin Lee notes, the original *pansori* version of the tale highlights the character's "loyalty to her husband" as a key theme (2000, 71). Indeed, the eponymous character represents "the ideal Confucian womanhood cultivated during the Chosŏn [Joseon] Dynasty [1392–1910]" (Lee 2000, 68). It is important to note that Chunhyang is a symbol of chastity only in the sense of her refusal to sleep with more than one man; most versions of the tale show her consummating her relationship with Monryong. The tale promotes virtue and kindness, and is highly critical of the corruption of the aristocracy; the character of Chunhyang has become a highly nationalistic symbol of the perfect Korean woman/wife. She is thus a "hero" in what she represents: the ultimate object of desire for men, and the supposed ideal figure of aspiration for women. Her unbreakable spirit, in the face of physical torture, gives the character an almost mythical, virtually superheroic, power.

Korean filmmakers and audiences have demonstrated a fascination with the story of Chunyang: Hyangjin Lee (2000) lists fourteen film adaptations of *The Tale of Chunhyang* produced in Korea between 1923 and 2000.[6] Perhaps the most widely seen and well remembered versions include Shin Sang-ok's 1961 *Seong Chunhyang*, described as a "mega-success" and arguably a prototype for the modern Korean blockbuster (Lee and Stringer 2010, 64), and Im Kwon-taek's *Chunhyang*, a film made specifically for a "global audience" that achieved significant success at international film festivals (Lee 2005,64). The enduring value of the character as a domestic cultural icon is also evident in the "Chunhyang Festival" held annually in Namwon since 1931, which includes a "Miss Chunhyang" beauty pageant and explicitly emphasizes parallels between *The Tale of Chunhyang* and Shakespeare's *Romeo and Juliet*, proudly positioning the Korean tale within the canon of the world's great love stories.

Chunhyang represents an idealized version of the romantic heroine of traditional Korean melodrama, but her role as both hero and lover also puts the tale in the canon of great superhero romances: the larger-than-life challenges and triumphs of Chunhyang and Monryong mirror such comic book couplings as Cyclops and Phoenix, whose doomed romance was caught in a cycle of female sacrifice and reincarnation; Black Panther and Storm, the latter of whom struggled with her contradictory status as both privileged royal and disenfranchised mutant; Wonder Woman and Steve Rogers, a romance tainted by the inadequacy of a fragile human man loving an invincible demi-god.

The decision to draw from this iconic story for a manga/*manhwa* series, and to use that series as the basis for a high profile international animation co-production between Korea and Japan, is understandable: the story is seen as quintessentially Korean, but its themes are universal. Further, its melodramatic and romantic content reflects the precise qualities of the "Korean wave" media that were most popular in Japan at the time. Indeed, manga and anime in Japan had turned to the story of Chunhyang earlier, most notably as the source for a *josei* (women's) manga by the artistic group CLAMP. Their *Legend of Chun Hyang* was published in 1996, and later released in English by Tokypop as a single volume in 2004. The same incarnation of the character also made several appearances in the TV series *Tsubasa: Reservoir Chronicle* (2005–2006), which adds a strong element of fantasy to the tale. Thus, *Blade of the Phantom Master*'s appropriation of this historic romantic melodrama for an action film intended to be popular in Korea, Japan, and with anime's niche market around the world, is understandable: the property is recognizable and has proven its global success in the past, and it has already demonstrated a degree of flexibility, leading the way for a superhero narrative to be grafted on to the fantastic elements already revealed by previous adaptations.

Heroics and Superheroics

Gender and Power in *Blade of the Phantom Master*

Blade of the Phantom Master takes place in a fantasy setting, the fictitious land of Jushin, and populates its world with demons, ghosts, magic, and witchcraft. In its radical retelling of *The Tale of Chunhyang*, many of the most iconic elements of the story have been discarded in order to facilitate more action, violence, and sexual objectification. Yet character names and key plot points are retained, making this adaptation a contradiction.

It is willfully irreverent and subversive, yet continues a tradition that reinvents the core aspects of the ancient tale for a specific contemporary audience. The manga/*manhwa* series falls within the *seinen* demographic, which targets older male readers, and the film "aims to attract more mature moviegoers with a rating of 15 and over" (Kim 2004). This explains why *Blade of the Phantom Master*'s transformation of the character of Chunhyang—central to the original fable but a sidekick in this film—reflects an empowerment of the character purely for the male gaze.

Representations of power, and notions of heroism more broadly, also differentiate *Blade of the Phantom Master* from other versions of *The Tale of Chunhyang*. In the original fable, Chunhyang and Monryong held to a simple belief that the powerful should not dominate the weak, and that the wealthy should not exploit the poor. They triumphed through force of will and law, with Chunhyang simply refusing to capitulate until Monryong returned with the legal power to oust the corrupt. In the animated film, neither law nor will are adequate to triumph over the forces of evil; instead, the ability to wield weapons and inflict violence are key. Monryong, for example, is a vastly different character. Rather than succeeding in his studies to become a royal commissioner, the character in this film has failed the qualifying examination three times, and given up (the academically frustrated loser, struggling to pass an important examination, is a common trope in Japanese animation). Though desperate to free his beloved, he acknowledges that he can do little through study, instead resolving to learn martial arts and use physical (rather than moral or mental) strength to conquer Byon. However, before he can even embark on this quest, he is murdered by man-eating desert-devils, his unexpected death symbolic of the pointlessness of idealism in the dystopian world presented by the film.

The protagonist, Munsu, too, is a hero of an unconventional nature: he is physically unfit (requiring an inhaler to offset asthma-like symptoms) and easily exhausted. He triumphs in battle through the use of an enchanted medallion, capable of summoning a ghostly legion of a hundred phantom soldiers to battle for him (a hyper-exaggeration of the original fable, in which the medallion of a royal inspector defeated evil purely symbolically, representing the license to carry out the law of the king). Munsu wanders the land, protecting the weak and rooting out evil, but is highly cynical and primarily self-serving, and could hardly be described as a superhero—unlike the physically and morally superior Chunhyang.

Blade of the Phantom Master ultimately recasts the character of Chunhyang as a valiant ninja warrior, skilled with a sword and the metal claw she fires from her arm. She demonstrates considerable martial skills and superhuman combat capabilities. She cuts down the phantom soldiers summoned by Munsu with little effort, in spite of their apparent invincibility, moving faster and striking harder. She also out-duels Munsu in one-to-one combat, proving herself the most physically powerful character in the entire film. She is a bodyguard, a sidekick, a highly skilled servant in need of a master (much like a *rōnin*, or masterless samurai warrior), and an embodiment of the chivalrous *bushidō* spirit. After her liberation from the clutches of Byon—which follows the startlingly unexpected death of Monryong—Chunhyang finally has true freedom from male ownership, yet instantly pledges herself to Munsu, the man who saved her. She asks to serve as his protector and companion, casting off her name and her identity as an individual by asking to be called only "Sando"—the title given to the warrior-sidekicks of royal law-enforcers like Munsu.

Chunhyang is therefore a superhero full of contradictions. She has a title but no name, and is entirely subservient to male agency. She is scolded by Munsu for failing to demonstrate utter obedience, as he commands her, "Don't hesitate, get confused, or waver. Follow my every order from now on." Sando is later taunted by an enemy who ask her, "Are you a puppet? Can't you do anything without that man's orders?" This representation of Chunhyang/Sando as almost entirely without agency, subservient to a single man, is an aspect of the original story that has occasionally been emphasized. Shin Sang-ok's 1961 version of the tale, for example, reinforces Chunhyang's "perception of her identity as an object in her husband's possession" by changing the well known line "I have a husband" to "I already have an owner" (Lee 2000, 77). Indeed, the most recent translation of the published text of *The Tale of Chunhyang* includes the comment from Monryong that "one great principle of nature [is that] everything has a master" (Shin 2010, 18). Likewise, Sando further demonstrates her passivity and lack of will through her almost complete silence: she rarely communicates verbally or otherwise, avoiding eye contact, virtually mute. This, too, is in keeping with previous adaptations, as Lee notes that Chunhyang "in the original tale and other film adaptations tends to observe carefully Confucian views on women's silence as one of their prime virtues" (2000, 79).

Chunhayng/Sando is also consistently fetishized (see Figure 6). As in the original tale, *Blade of the Phantom Master* has Chunhyang imprisoned by the evil Lord Byon as punishment for refusing his advances. Indeed, the introduction of the character of Chunhyang happens after she has already been imprisoned, skipping over her courtship with Monryong and her initial rejection of Byon. This makes the first appearance of the character problematic, in terms of identifying with her as a symbol of power

6. South Korean theatrical release poster for *Blade of the Phantom Master*. Credit: Youn In-Wan, Yang Kyung-Il / Shin Angyo Project.

and defiance. Further, the exaggerated means of her imprisonment clearly serve to fetishize the character: Chunhyang has attempted suicide, and so has been bound and gagged, supposedly to prevent further attempts at self-harm. Thus, when we first see the character, she is virtually crucified with leather, as straps and belts hold her arms out at her sides and her feet pinned together. She is naked save for underwear, and the leather straps covering (but, more importantly, revealing) her skin. Chunhyang is presented not as a "whole" person; shots linger only on parts of her body, as Byon runs his fingers over her naked flesh, from her exposed stomach and thighs to her tightly strapped, barely covered bosom. Introducing the character in this way positions her entirely and exclusively as an object of male sexual desire. She is denied a voice—literally—and there is no context or background for the character beyond her fetishized body.

As Hyangjin Lee has noted, some previous cinematic adaptations of *The Tale of Chunhyang*, too, reflect her "inferior position as an object of male desire" and indeed, the sexualization of the character is also not uncommon, as Chunhyang herself "functions as the major signifier of erotic desire in the collective imagination in a repressed society, which prohibits public discussion or display of sexual matters" (2000, 68, 71). Indeed, Im Kwon-taek's 2000 version of the tale was marketed overseas precisely on the basis of its erotic content.[7] However, *Blade of the Phantom Master* represents a departure by sexualizing Chunhyang during her imprisonment; in other versions of the tale, it is at the moment of her consensual lovemaking with Monryong that she becomes an object of erotic fixation. By skipping this narrative content, the animated film renders Chunhyang in her introduction *only* as the object of sexual desire and abuse.

A further departure from what is arguably the most sacred aspect of the original tale comes in the battle of wills between Byon and Chunhyang. Indeed, perhaps the one single constant, unifying every other version of the tale, is the central importance of Chunhyang's unbreakable spirit. She is celebrated precisely because she never capitulates, never succumbs to the unwanted desires of others. In *Blade of the Phantom Master*'s fantasy setting, however, this is circumvented by sorcery. Byon's last resort, rather than ordering Chunhyang executed as in the original folktale, is to have her hypnotized by a witch; he breaks her will and she becomes his mindless slave, robotically following his every command. Though she is soon freed from this hypnosis, she continues to wear the leather straps and bandages of her imprisonment, covering them only with an oft discarded brown robe. Her small frame and short height are frequently emphasized by contrasting her striking appearance with the much larger man she accompanies, and when they travel, she trails behind him, rather than walking at his side. In combat, the camera lingers on her body in a highly fetishistic way.

Again, this characterization appears to be a function of "fanservice" rather than a portrayal of Chunhyang as a capable hero in her own right. Her absurdly long hair is one of the iconic features of the original Chunhyang, with her unkempt locks signifying her extensive period of imprisonment. Indeed, once again, the emphasis on Chunhyang's visual beauty is a common feature of the tale; after all, Monryong falls in love with Chunhyang after a single glance, and later tells her, "You have the bearing of a fairy. You are beautiful from the front, from the side and from behind" (Shin 2010, 45), an objectification and sexualization of the character remarkably in keeping with the treatment of Sando and the division of her body into erotic portions viewed from exploitative angles.

However leeringly *Blade of the Phantom Master* may treat its female character, there is also an undoubted celebration of her power and honor. Indeed, though not unproblematic, a long tradition of female superheroes has demonstrated that sexualization in costume design does not necessarily rob characters of their power and agency: DC Comics' invincibly heroic Wonder Woman and Power Girl, and Marvel Comics' psychic warriors Emma Frost and Psylocke, to name just a few, sport iconic skin revealing costumes. Likewise, Sando may be eroticized, but she is also more moral than Munsu, functioning as his silent conscience, wordlessly urging him to do the right thing and help people in need. She is vastly more capable in combat, more valiant, more brave. She saves his life twice, at moments when he would otherwise surely have been slain. In the film's final confrontation with an evil warlock/doctor and his ninja sidekick, she defeats both. In terms of martial action, Sando is the active and dominant character, while Munsu, meanwhile, swaggers, but to little effect. This is one of the film's primary themes, in fact, and one of its truly original elements: the physical power of women and the relative weakness of men. The film's only change from the original manga was the addition of a new female character—an antagonistic ninja called Mari, a sidekick to the villain and obvious parallel to Sando—who was specifically created by director Joji Shimura to facilitate the final battle between these two superpowered women (a scene that he describes as a "highlight" of the film) (Ahn 2004). In the world of *Blade of the Phantom Master*, martial arts and chivalry is the domain of women, not men. The landscape of the new South Korean superhero film thereby positions female warriors in central roles.

A Stateless Place

Japanese, Korean and Asian Identity in *Blade of the Phantom Master*

One of the most enduring debates taking place within academic studies of Japanese animation is the extent to which it reflects a sense of Japaneseness. Some critics regard anime as essentially stateless, while others view the recognizably foreign qualities of anime as key to its international appeal. In the case of *Blade of the Phantom Master*, and its status as a co-production, there is a great deal at stake in its having a recognizable national origin, especially in terms of its Korean identity, given the ambitions of the Korean industry to establish greater visibility, and given that the story is based on one of the nation's proudest folktales.

Susan Napier invokes the Japanese word *mukokuseki* to denote the "stateless fantasyscapes" of Japan's "nonculturally specific anime style" (2005, 24). Amy Shirong Lu, likewise, argues that Japanese animation "usually does not seem Japanese" (2008, 169). Koichi Iwabuchi proposed the theory of a "cultural odor" that denotes recognizable characteristics of any media's place of origin; for him, stateless animation lacks this, removing all signs of nationality and ethnicity (2002, 27). Lu further argues that anime blurs boundaries between Caucasian and Oriental characters; through this "racial mixing and cultural blurring, anime neutralizes itself, which reflects a broader desire to enter an extra-territorial stage of development" (2008, 172). Indeed, Korean animation has achieved international circulation in the past precisely because it lacked "cultural odor" and its origin could be disguised.[8]

Animation from Asia thus typically achieves international appeal through either representation of a stateless sort of universality or an Orientalized version of cultural specificity. Sandra Annett (2011) points to the Japanese series *Cowboy Bebop* (1998–99) as an example of a culturally intricate media that finds a way to negotiate statelessness and cultural/ethnic identity.

> If this series is "stateless," then, it is not in Iwabuchi's sense of erasing ethnicity, but in Appadurai's sense of postnational diaspora: hybridity, not corporate hybridism. While nation-states have ceased to exist, ethnic, cultural and linguistic diversity has flourished and flows through the new channels of ethnoscapes and mediascapes. (2011, 179)

Blade of the Phantom Master, too, negotiates a balance between statelessness and cultural odor carefully, arriving at a hybrid representation both homogenous and culturally specific. In some moments, scenes and settings appear strongly Asian (particularly in a brief rose tinted flashback to Chunhyang and Monroyng's romance, with cherry blossoms filling the air (Figure 7); in other parts of the film, architecture and fashion is utterly indistinct, lacking any national signifiers at all. The film's fantasy setting is the primary means through which it (partially, not entirely) evokes statelessness: Jushin is a fictitious place, and its magic and demons remove it further from a recognizable reality. Lu notes that scholars tend to identify "Asian physiological characteristics" based on qualities such as darker eye color or a "yellowish tint" to their skin (2009, 170) but argues that more common is a process of "ethnic bleaching" (2008, 172) leading to a "hybrid global 'look' . . . on their faces" (182). Both Munsu and Chunhyang are presented with brown hair and blue eyes, apparently robbing them of an obviously Asian appearance; yet in other ways, the film reflects both Korean and Japanese identity as well as a homogenized representation of Asia/the Orient. Indeed, the film's aesthetic overall reflects the recognizable "anime style" that identifies its origins as Japanese at a first glance.

7. Flashback in *Blade of the Phantom Master* in which Chunhyang and Monryong say farewell and vow to reunite. Credit: Youn In-Wan, Yang Kyung-Il / Shin Angyo Project.

The film/manga/*manhwa* draws on Korean history and literature to populate almost its entire cast, weaving elements of truth and well known fiction into an entirely new story. As well as adapting *The Tale of Chunhyang*, *Blade of the Phantom Master* uses elements from numerous other sources: protagonist Munsu shares his name with a famous real royal inspector, Park Munsu, who himself has been the subject of numerous films and TV series in Korea.[9] The film's final antagonist, depicted as an evil black-winged sorcerer holding dominion over a cursed island of zombies, is named after a real doctor, Yoo Uitae, mentor to an even more celebrated historical figure in Korea's past. The visages of the phantom soldiers summoned by Munsu's enchanted medallion are also evocative of the theatrical masks of Korea's traditional performing arts. These characters and images are invoked here in entirely new ways, and the way the film plays with history is one of its most interesting and appealing qualities. However, the question remains: in spite of all these specifically Korean elements, is the film recognizable as Korean outside its immediate domestic context? *Chunhyang* is an iconic tale in Korea, known by virtually every adult in the country; yet the story is largely unknown outside East Asia, as are the other Korean elements on display.

Indeed, the film's Korean elements are overwritten in many contexts by its Japaneseness. On the international release of *Blade of the Phantom Master* on DVD in the USA (by Funimation) and Australia (by Madman) its Korean elements are entirely disguised. Though the film was simultaneously produced with both a Japanese and a Korean audio track, the Western release includes only options for English-dubbed or Japanese (with subtitles), reflecting the dominance of Japanese animation in the Western market. Language is, in fact, one of the most crucial factors in negotiating the film's Japanese and Korean elements, and the slight but highly significant difference between the two versions of the film is highly revealing. The Korean version of the film is presented entirely in the Korean language. The Japanese version, however, retains Korean-language dialogue for its brief prologue: a summary of the fall of law and order in the land of Jushin, and an explanation of the lost society that has now become dystopian chaos. Therefore, when Munsu notes that he "lost his language" with the collapse of the government, he is referring to the Korean language heard at the start of the film.

The Korean-Japanese iteration of *Blade of the Phantom Master*, therefore, arguably evokes a problematic representation of Japanese colonialism. The cultural relationship between Japan and Korea in the postcolonial period is complicated and nuanced; in terms of animation, as discussed above, the Japanese industry effectively dominated Korea's, even during the period when Japanese cultural imports were officially banned in Korea. This political bad blood was the result of Japan's colonialist policies, the abuses of which are too numerous to name, but of significance here is the Japanese desire to convert Korea's national language to Japanese. It is therefore inviting to read significance into the Japanese-language version of *Blade of the Phantom Master*, which, rather than using the national language as a stand-in for whatever tongue the fictional inhabitants of this fantasy land may use, instead clearly distinguishes between the lost language of a crumbled nation (Korea) and the widely-used tongue of the new regime, understood and spoken by all (Japanese).

These issues speak to debates acknowledged by academics in the study of Japanese and Korean cinema and media. In fact, Hyangjin Lee has noted the problematic origins of Chunhyang as a cinematic text: the first version ever produced in Korea (*The Tale of Chunhyang*, directed by Lee Myeong-woo and released in 1935) was made under colonialist rule, and its high popularity reflected a new context for the character as a representative of a subject under oppressive colonial rule. *Blade of the Phantom Master* becomes, itself, symbolic of the complex relationship between Japan and Korea: from their history of colonialism and linguistic oppression, to the trans-Asian flow of *Chunhyang* as a historical tale with contemporary relevance, to the exchanges of influence and power in their animation industries. Chunhyang-as-Sando functions as a proto-superheroic figure in this sense, too, as an element of the "colonized" culture capable of resisting the ravages of the new regime.

Conclusion

As South Korean animation strives to penetrate the Japanese market, and further its goals among the wider international audience, it will need to carefully balance the virtues of statelessness and national identity. The success of Korean-created properties in Japan means little if they aren't recognized as Korean. Yet, as suggested at the start of this chapter, Korea's cinematic animation is currently thriving precisely by appealing to local sentiments and crafting works that are genuinely distinctive, both aesthetically and thematically. *Blade of the Phantom Master* represents a failed experiment, in many ways: an iconic Korean tale rendered unrecognizable, and a Korean film whose Japaneseness was its most visible property.

In Im Kwon-taek's *Chunhyang* (2000), Monryong justifies his desire by claiming that "a hero comes with a beauty." This naïve and chauvinistic view will be subverted throughout the rest of this film, which positions Chunhyang irrefutably as the story's central hero. The most telling scene occurs in Monryong's absence, and confirms the heroism not just of Chunhyang but of maligned and ignored women like her. As Chunhyang lies beaten almost to death, with her mother tending to her wounds, one courtesan bursts into song, listing other famous *gisaeng* of Korea who sacrificed themselves in heroic acts for the good of the nation, and thus celebrates Chunhyang as a folk hero in her own lifetime.

This emphasis on Chunhyang as just one in a long line of female heroes is an impulse extended in *Blade of the Phantom Master*, in its (not unproblematic) foregrounding of female physical power and martial skill. Indeed, this kind of gendered superheroism has emerged as a minor trend in Korean-Japanese animation. Of the scant productions listed earlier, almost all focus on superpowered women at the center of violent conflicts. From the selfless, heroic "Tera Guardian" who fights with a male counterpart as a sidekick in *Kurokami* (2009) to the all-female superteam in *Gundress* and the hyper-sexualized but hyper-powerful women warriors of *Freezing* (2011), female superheroes are at the heart of Korean-created Japanese animation. Yet while Korean artists and writers continue to author popular manga series in Japan, few properties exhibit Korean qualities to the extent of *Blade of the Phantom Master*.

Chunhyang's significance is in her national identity: she is inextricably connected to Korean traditions and folklore. Yet the visibility of her national origin is sacrificed in *Blade of the Phantom Master* in favor of emphasizing the character not as a hero but as a superhero. The female warrior of the film owes a great deal to the heroic women of Japanese animation, at once empowered and sexualized. They are stronger, faster, and more powerful than men; from the sexy cyborg protagonist of *Ghost in the Shell* (1995) to the Valkyrie-like hero of TV anime *Claymore* (2007). Japanese animation, including (and especially) properties targeted specifically towards adolescent and adult males, offers a world in which female superheroes (like the morphing schoolgirl of Naoko Takeuchi's *Sailor Moon*) stand beside and fight against men, equal if not greater in their capabilities (Allison 2000). In this, Japanese animation contributes to a global narrative of female superheroism, continued in American comic books and other worldwide media, celebrating while objectifying the female hero.

Notes

1. *Blade of the Phantom Master* is sometimes known in Korea by the English-language title *New Royal Secret Commissioner*, a more direct translation of the Korean-language title *Shin Amhaengeosa*. The Japanese language title *Shin Angyo Onshi* is also used by many fans online in preference to the film's official English title.

2. This chapter originated as a conference paper presented at the 3rd Mechademia Conference on Anime, Manga and Media Theory from Japan: "World Renewal – Counterfactual Histories, Parallel Universes, and Possible Worlds," at the Korean Film Archive, Seoul, November 30, 2012.

3. *Wonderful Days* fit a trend of Korean science fiction blockbusters failing to achieve success due to a lack of national identity, a quality that has proven to be a significant box office draw for local audiences. Furthermore, on its international release as *Sky Blue*, the film failed to impress critics, as it was often compared unfavorably to Japanese animation and dismissed by reviewers in the USA and UK. For a more detailed summary, see Martin 2011.

4. Takehiko Inoue is well known in Japan and among fans of manga for his hugely popular 1990s series *Slam Dunk*, which was itself adapted into a successful animated TV series.

5. Due to variations in the romanization and translation of Korean, Chunhyang is often written as two words (Chun Hyang).

6. According to Hyangjin Lee's research, cinematic adaptations of *The Tale of Chunhyang* include two versions made during the Japanese occupation of Korea (in 1923 and 1935), nine films made in postwar South Korea (three in the 1950s, two in 1961, two in the 1970s, one in 1987, and one in 2000) and three in postwar North Korea (one in 1959

and two in the 1980s). There have been more produced since the publication of Lee's book in 2000; notable examples include the irreverent erotic comedy-melodrama *The Servant* (2010) and a modern-day reinvention of the story in the TV series *Sassy Girl Chunhyang* (aka *Delightful Girl Chunhyang*, 2005).

7. The US theatrical poster for Im's *Chunhyang* (2000) leads with a prominent quote describing the film as "exotic and erotic."

8. Korean animation such as *Gold Wing 1,2,3* (Kim Cheong-gi, 1978), *Red Hawk* (Shim Sang-il, 1995), and *Armageddon* (Lee Hyun-se, 1996) have all be circulated in English-dubbed versions with no indication in their marketing or packaging of their national origin. See Martin 2011 for a more detailed discussion.

9. The 2002 MBC TV series *Osa Park Munsu* (*Inspector Park Munsu*) is particularly well remembered.

"TU MERA SUPERMAN"

Globalization, Cultural Exchange, and the Indian Superhero

IAIN ROBERT SMITH

In 1988, director K. Ravi Shankar shot a fantasy song sequence titled "*Tu Mera Superman*" (You are my Superman) for his film *Dariya Dil* (1988), in which stars Govinda and Kimi Katkar fly together above Mumbai dressed as Superman and Spiderwoman. While the rest of the film is a relatively traditional family melodrama without any further reference to superheroism, this sequence was later detached from its original context and uploaded to YouTube under the title "Indian Superman." To date, the clip has been watched over 9.5 million times. The circulation of this sequence is part of a wider Internet phenomenon in which clips of Indian borrowings from Western popular culture circulate on YouTube framed by their national origin. These include the song "Golimar" from the Telugu film *Donga* (1985), which circulates online as "Indian Thriller"; the reworking of "I Want to Hold Your Hand" in the Hindi film *Jaanwar* (1965), which goes under the title "Indian Beatles"; and the various clips of actor N. T. Rama Rao, which refer to him simply as the "Indian Elvis." The viral popularity of these clips reflects a fascination with cultural hybridity as manifest when Western popular culture is appropriated and reworked in Indian cinema. Indeed, this is one of the ways in which popular Indian cinema circulates beyond the traditional domestic and diasporic audiences online.

However, I would contend that this circulation does not generally extend to a broader engagement with the Indian cultural context in which these films were produced. As Mark Jancovich et al. have identified, the cult reception of international cinema often relies on a celebration of films that are framed as "weird and wonderful," "but does so in a way that has no interest in the meaning of those films within the contexts of their own production" (2003, 4). Therefore, when engaging with the global dynamics of the Indian superhero,[1] it is important that we pay close attention to the specificity of the historical and social context in which these superheroes appear. Too often these forms of borrowing are celebrated merely for seeming exotic or weird, with little conception of how these texts function in relation to local traditions and conventions. Instead, this chapter will outline an approach to transnational cultural exchange that explores the diverse meanings that superheroic characters have within Indian cinema, and moves us away from the ultimately limiting conceptual framework that sees Indian superheroes as simply exotic variations on Western archetypes.

While the recent blockbuster *Krrish* (2006) was initially promoted as "India's First Super Hero," the film is actually part of a long history of attempts to engage with the superhero genre in Indian cinema from the 1960s onwards. Within the Hindi language industry alone, these have included a range of imported characters such as the unlicensed appearance of Superman in *Superman* (1960), *Return of Mr. Superman* (1960), and *Superman* (1987), and the appearance of a wide range of local heroes in films such as *Shiva Ka Insaaf* (1985), *Mr India* (1987) and *Ajooba* (1991). Furthermore, this phenomenon is not limited to Hindi cinema with the Telugu industry producing its own version of *Superman* in 1980, and the Tamil industry recently producing the local superhero blockbusters *Enthiran* (2010) and *Mugamoodi* (2012). Even the marginal cinema of Malegaon has started to feature superhero characters as captured in the documentary *Supermen of Malegaon* (2012).

As I will outline in this chapter, there has been a clear shift in the use of superheroes over this period that reflects larger shifts in the industry and its position in world cinema. By identifying tendencies in the representation of superheroes in Indian cinema, this chapter will demonstrate the significance of cultural exchange both to our understanding of these specific superheroes and to our understanding of Indian cinema more broadly. Furthermore, as Rashna Wadia Richards has observed in her work on the contemporary Bollywood remake, it is reductive to see these processes of borrowing as a simple act of reconstructing a Western text to "conform to Indian cultural practices" (2011, 342). These processes demonstrate a much more complex form of cultural hybridization that speaks to the fluctuating dynamics of receiving and sending material around the globe. Moving beyond simplistic formulations that see Indian superheroes as purely imitative and/or exotic, this chapter will therefore position the

Indian superhero as part of a transnational dialogue that has significant implications for our understanding of the globalization of popular culture.

Indian Cinema and Cultural Exchange

In his pioneering study of cultural exchange, *The Universe of the Mind*, Russian semiotician Yuri Lotman argued that national cultures develop through a dynamic process of importing and exporting texts (1990, 146). In this process, according to Lotman, we can distinguish five successive stages that a culture must go through to move from being a receiving culture to a transmitting culture. Briefly summarized, the first stage is where the imported text keeps its "strangeness" and is held in higher esteem than the local product. The second stage is where the imported text is then imitated and adapted by the local industry. In the third stage, the imported text falls out of favor and the national characteristics of the local adaptation are valued in comparison. The fourth stage is when the local text then becomes a model for others to emulate. Finally, in the fifth stage, the local text is successfully exported around the world and the receiving culture has developed into a transmitting culture. While these are positioned as successive stages, it should be noted that these stages are not mutually exclusive and are often co-present when we consider specific historical examples of this process.

What is most useful about this model is that it allows us to see imitation and adaptation as intrinsic parts within a continuum of cultural exchange. Indeed, while Lotman demonstrated this process largely through an examination of Russian literature, Tom O'Regan later utilized the model in his book *Australian National Cinema* as a way to frame and analyze Australian cinema history. The value of the model for O'Regan is that

> both the abject home culture of stage one with its cultural cringe, and the confident producing culture of stage four with its thorough indigenization of imported models are not only part of a continuum of cultural exchange but are organically interconnected. (1996, 196)

In other words, this model moves us away from the simplistic binary of original and copy, and the attendant discourses of value, to show how creativity is itself very much connected to these intertextual processes of imitation and transformation.

In this chapter, I apply this model to key appearances by superheroes within Indian cinema from 1960 to the present day and consider how we can understand this phenomenon through these five stages of cultural exchange. I want to be clear from the outset, however, that I am using this model to specifically focus on the position of the superhero in India rather than making any claims about Indian cinema shifting from being a receiving to a transmitting culture over this period. Unlike the Australian cinema that O'Regan was observing, Indian cinema was, and still is, one of the world's largest commercial film industries and very much a dominant center of film production. It makes little sense to position Indian cinema as primarily a receiving culture given that the commercial, popular cinema of India dominates the screens of South Asia and has long had a significant presence across the world with particular prominence in the Middle East, North Africa and the former Soviet Union (Govil 2007, 84).

Therefore, the model of cultural exchange exemplified by the Australian cinema discussed by Tom O'Regan cannot be easily applied to the Indian context. Whereas O'Regan notes that "Australian agents negotiate with the international cinema on a permanently unequal basis making cultural transfers much more important to Australian film production, circulation, appreciation and criticism" (1996, 195), this is not a statement that could easily be applied to the popular cinema of India. The dynamics of power are not easily comparable given that this is a country with a number of regional industries that combined have an annual film output well above that of the USA.

Nevertheless, as Tejaswini Ganti (2002), Richards (2011), Sheila Nayar (1997) and others have demonstrated, cultural transfers still play a significant role within Indian cinema. Nayar estimates that "ninety percent of the Hindi movies in production in August of 1993 were remakes" (1997, 74) with a significant proportion of the sources being from US cinema. While Indian popular cinema is hugely commercially successful, it is often disparaged by critics both at home and abroad for being derivative of Hollywood. Ravi Vasudevan, for example, has shown that the influential tradition of film criticism associated with the Calcutta Film Society of the 1950s dismissed Indian popular cinema for its "derivativeness from American cinema" (2000, 134), while Rosie Thomas notes that First World discourse on Indian popular cinema has often framed the films as "nightmarishly lengthy, second-rate copies of Hollywood trash, to be dismissed with patronizing amusement or facetious quips" (1985, 117). As we will see in the case study of the Indian superhero film, however, the adaptation of imported elements need not be seen in this negative light. Using Lotman's model of cultural exchange, I now trace the ways in which the Indian superhero was adapted and transformed in the subsequent decades into a distinctive and globally successful cultural form.

Superman Goes to India

Formats and Remakes

The early 1960s saw the establishment of two local comic book publishers—Diamond Comics in 1960, and Indrajal Comics in 1964—who both "primarily published American superhero comics such as Superman, Spider-Man, Phantom and Mandrake, often in Hindi translation" (Mathur 2010, 176). During this period, both publishers were very much focused on presenting American superheroes to the Indian public through this act of translation. According to Yuri Lotman's model, this exemplifies the transition between the first and second stages of the five-stage process. Initially, the imported cultural form is introduced into the new market and is "read in the foreign language (both in the sense of natural language and in the semiotic sense)" (Lotman 1990, 146). Yet as these texts are translated into the local language, "the codes imported along with the texts become part of the metalingual structure" (1990, 146). Moving into this second stage, it is not only the texts themselves that are being imported but also a format that could be adapted and used within the local context. In this case, the American superhero comics were not only being imported into the country, but they were serving as a model for the production of local superhero works.

Within Lotman's model, this second stage is when we tend to see a proliferation of translations, imitations, and adaptations where the imported form becomes a format for local producers to emulate. For O'Regan, this second stage is exemplified by the "huge number of concept remakes on television worldwide – when the rights for a television quiz, variety or sports show are acquired and the format is applied with small changes to accommodate local circumstance" (1996, 199). It is worth noting too that in the context of Australian cinema, O'Regan identifies a fairly strict division of labor at this stage where "the Australian is the content, the flavor, the accent and the social text, while the international provides the underlying form, values, narrative resolutions, etc." (1996, 199). When we consider this in the light of those early superhero comics from Diamond Comics and Indrajal Comics, we can see that the introduction of American superheroes soon became a model for local film producers to emulate with the international superhero providing the "underlying form" and the Indian filmmaking teams adding the local "flavor."

More specifically, it was the introduction of Superman to the Indian market that inspired a number of film producers to produce local versions of this globally popular character, taking many of the tangible elements from the source text but transposing them into an India context. The first two significant examples were the reworking of the Superman story in two Hindi films released in the same year, *Superman* (1960), directed by Mohammed Hussain and Anant Thakur, and *Return of Mr Superman* (1960), directed by Manmohan Sabir.[2] Unfortunately, *Superman* has now been lost and no copies of the film are in circulation, but *Return of Mr Superman* survives and is a variation on the familiar Superman origin story. Featuring local star Jairaj in the title role, the story opens with a farmer discovering an abandoned child, taking him home and naming him Jaikumar. Over time the boy discovers that he has a number of superpowers such as flight, super strength and X-ray vision. As he gets older, he takes a job as a newspaper reporter but, in order to use his powers to fight crime and injustice, he invents the alter ego of the costumed superhero Superman. He is then forced to keep his identity secret from his female colleague Usha who, reminiscent of Lois Lane, is infatuated with Superman.

As is clear, the film contains many of the key story beats of the Superman comic books, although it should be noted that the film is otherwise a relatively generic low-budget action melodrama typical of Indian cinema of the period (Vitali 2010) and, as is visible in Figure 8, the costume is actually quite distinct from that of the DC Superman on which the film was based. Nevertheless, the film exemplifies a strategy that a number of studios adopted in the 1960s in which they were "cannibalising narratives, genres and spectacular set pieces from Hollywood, Europe and Hong Kong" (Basu 2010, 62), yet localizing certain elements to appeal to the domestic market.

Reflecting the gap in the USA between the 1952 *Superman* TV series and Richard Donner's 1978 *Superman* film, there was a significant length of time between the two Hindi versions of the Superman story and the later Telugu *Superman* from director V. Madhusudhana Rao, which appeared in 1980. Unlike the earlier Hindi adaptations, this film diverges quite substantially from the storyline of the *Superman* comic books. Most significantly, the powers given to the hero Raja do not derive from him being an alien, but rather he is gifted these powers by the Hindu monkey god Hanuman so that he can seek revenge on the men who killed his parents. The film is therefore part of the action-revenge melodrama genre that was

8. Paidi Jairaj in *Return of Mr Superman* (1960), Credit: Manmohan Films.

popular throughout the 1980s, and, as I will demonstrate later, the shift in the sources of his powers reflects a wider trend in the Indian superhero film where superpowers are generally attributed to mythological sources rather than the quasi-scientific origins of most US superheroes.

Despite these changes and the addition of song sequences—as Tejaswini Ganti has noted, this is one of the most common ways in which adaptations are transformed to conform with the conventions of Indian cinema (2002, 282)—the film does retain many recognizable elements from its source text. Specifically, while the film diverges from the established plotlines of Superman, it does utilize the character traits and iconography of its central character. Raja has the recognizable superpowers of flight, super strength and seeming invincibility, and he also wears the recognizable blue and red Superman costume albeit with the iconic S replaced with an H for Hanuman.

Nevertheless, it was not until a 1987 Hindi film, again titled *Superman*, that Indian cinema attempted to closely replicate the adventures of the DC character. Directed by B. Gupta, this film was highly influenced by Richard Donner's 1978 US adaptation of *Superman*. The plot not only follows the recognized Superman origin story in which a baby from Krypton is sent to Earth and grows up to be a superhero, but Gupta recreates the specific plotline of the Donner film in which Superman has to defeat the villainous Verma, modeled on Lex Luthor, who has a plan to buy up cheap real estate and significantly increase its value by destroying nearby parts of the country. While there are some sequences that contain specific changes—most obviously in the addition of song numbers—the plot, characterization and iconography from Donner's film are closely recreated, albeit on a significantly lower budget. Moreover, the film actually uses appropriated footage from the special effects sequences of Donner's film, bringing it closer to the form of appropriation that was present in contemporaneous Turkish films such as *Dünyayı Kurtaran Adam* (*The Man Who Saved the World*, 1982) that I have discussed elsewhere (Smith 2008).

As we have seen in each of these examples, this stage of Lotman's process captures the moment when the imported form has become the model for local producers to emulate with varying levels of localization. It is important to note, however, the significance of Superman as being the character so often adapted in these early Indian superhero films. Although a variety of American superheroes were adapted for the comic books, it is notable that it was DC's Superman that regularly formed the basis for the films. While this is arguably because Superman was seen as a more recognizable character than his contemporaries Phantom or Mandrake, I would contend that a more nuanced explanation is that the character is particularly germane to adaptations where superpowers are attributed to mythological sources. As an alien sent down to Earth, his origin story can effectively be interwoven and hybridized with mythological stories in a way that would be more challenging with other superheroes. Indeed, as Sarah Kozloff and others have argued, the Superman story is often depicted in the USA as a Christian allegory where Superman is a Christ-like figure who has been sent to Earth as a savior (1981, 78). The character is therefore well suited for adaptations that seek to replace the quasi-scientific origin story with a spiritual explanation for his superpowers, and there is a clear correlation with the messianic figure of Superman becoming the model for these early Indian superhero films. Furthermore, as we will see in the next section, this desire to localize the superhero through India's existing mythological stories is even further emphasized in those films that eschewed American superheroes and instead attempted to create a new specifically Indian superhero.

The Rise of the "Indian" Superhero

In the third stage of Lotman's model of cultural exchange, there is a stress on national characteristics that are then valued over and above those of the imported texts. The emphasis becomes less about imitating the imported text and more about localizing the format so extensively that it reflects specifically local concerns. Furthermore, the new text is framed as an improvement such that "the culture which first relayed these texts falls out of favor and the national characteristics of the texts will be stressed" (1990, 146). As O'Regan notes, "Lotman's third stage crucially involves perceptions. It re-evaluates the home culture's product in a situation of assumed international comparison" (1996, 201). The example that O'Regan gives from Australian cinema is the *Mad Max* cycle that was highly influenced by US road movies yet was subsequently celebrated as a distinctively Australian take on the genre.

We can clearly see a similar shift develop in the mid- to late-1980s with the introduction of "original" Indian superheroes. As discussed above, the majority of the superheroes in Indian comic books of the 1960s and 1970s were Hindi translations of US characters but this began changing in 1986 when Raj Comics established itself as "The Home of Indian Superhero Comics" (Kaur 2012, 335).[3] The most iconic comic character developed in this period was Nagraj, a "snake-man" who has went on to become the longest running Indian superhero character. Partly inspired by Spider-Man, Nagraj has a number of snake-like powers such as venomous breath and the ability to shoot snakes out of his wrists. As Suchitra Mathur has observed, "By making this snake-man association the foundational feature of their first superhero, the creators of Nagraj obviously Indianized the American superhero" (2010, 181). Indeed, the character was resolutely positioned as a specifically "Indian" creation—and, most importantly, this Indian-ness was predicated on an association with the stereotype of the Indian snake-charmer.

The Indianization of the American superhero in this period, however, was not merely about incorporating local elements of Indian culture but often involved a specific Hindu-ization of the origins of the character. This is exemplified by the original Indian superhero in the 1985 film *Shiva Ka Insaaf*. The first Hindi film to be produced in 3D, *Shiva Ka Insaaf* focuses on Bhola, a young man who was given superpowers by the Hindu god Shiva so that he could avenge the murder of his parents. Adopting the name Shiva for his superheroic alter ego, Bhola subsequently wears a ring in the shape of Shiva's third eye, fights with Shiva's weapon the *trishula*, and wears a leather costume emblazoned with a *trishula*-shaped logo (Figure 9). It should be clear, therefore, that the specific Indian-ness that is being claimed for the superhero Shiva/Bhola is based on an association with the ancient mythological stories centered on Hindu gods. Nevertheless, it

9. Jackie Shroff in *Shiva Ka Insaaf* (1985), Credit: Rupam Pictures.

is important to note that this celebration of Shiva is balanced with an attempt to incorporate signifiers of the three dominant religions in India. For example, after the death of his parents, Bhola is raised by three friends of his father, named Ram, Rahim, and Robert—deliberately evoking Hinduism, Islam, and Christianity respectively. This was a common trend at the time following the earlier success of *Amar, Akbar, Anthony* (1977), a film about three brothers who were separated as children and brought up under three different religions. Despite this gesture towards inter-faith cooperation, however, the film clearly privileges the Hindu religion and this Hindu-ization of the Indian superhero exemplified by *Shiva Ka Insaaf* continued in the subsequent decades and has become one of the dominant forms of localization in the Indian superhero film.

Reflecting the third stage of Lotman's model, there is a deliberate attempt here to localize the imported text although it is worth noting that the plot still contains many of the recognizable tropes of the US superhero. Most notably, the central love triangle in *Shiva Ka Insaaf* is modeled on Superman where Bhola gets a job as a newspaper reporter to conceal his secret identity and falls in love with the Lois Lane-like Rekha, but then discovers that she is already in love with his superhero alter ego Shiva. Therefore, despite the localized origin and mythological iconography, the film is not substantially different from those earlier attempts to localize existing US superheroes, and it is significant that even in this "original" Indian superhero narrative, it is still Superman that forms the urtext that is being adapted and transformed.

However, a significant generic shift came two years later with the release of Shekhar Kapur's *Mr India* (1987). Produced a decade before Kapur made the move to Hollywood to direct lavish costume dramas such as *Elizabeth* (1998) and *Four Feathers* (2002), *Mr India* centers on an Indian everyman character, Arun Verma, who looks after a home of orphaned children and is the only man who can save the world from the villainous Mogambo. Partly modeled on the Bond villain archetype, the megalomaniacal Mogambo lives on an island base and plans to conquer India through a campaign of terror. Unlike most superheroes, Arun does not possess any intrinsic superpowers but instead wears a watch that was passed on to him by his scientist father that allows the wearer to become invisible. Using this device to enter Mogambo's fortress, he manages to confound the guards and henchmen, and defeat Mogambo in a climactic showdown. As Raminder Kaur observes, "The film essentially presents a drama between the use of techno-science in the hands of selfless and patriotic figures such as Arun and those with selfish and megalomaniac ambitions for control such as Mogambo" (2013, 291).

Kush Varia, in his guidebook to Bollywood, notes that while "on first viewing, *Mr India* may be seen as a 'copy' of Hollywood films . . . the situation is much more complicated" (2013, 24). While the film features a number of homages to Hollywood cinema, including the Bond-style villain and a cabaret number in which the heroine Seema dresses as Charlie Chaplin, *Mr India* positions its protagonist as an ordinary Indian man who is proudly standing up against the international criminal world. Written by the screenwriting duo Salim-Javed, the film features what Rachel Dwyer notes as their characteristic mix of "social issues...populism...and pastiche of, and quotes from, other Hindi films" (2005, 165). From the plotline which emphasizes the social problem of poverty in contemporary India through to the patriotism of the central character, there is a concerted attempt here to produce a superhero that is no longer seen as an imitation of a western archetype but is instead framed as a specifically "Indian" superhero.

Significantly, it is the success of *Mr India* that helps displace Superman as the primary model for the Indian superhero film. No longer beholden to the format established in US comic books, the Indian superhero films that appeared throughout the late 1980s and early 1990s were more closely modeled on the Indian everyman character from *Mr India*. It is no coincidence that when Amitabh Bachchan was looking for a comeback vehicle after his brief mid-1980s move into politics that he elected to make the Indian superhero films *Shahenshah* (1988), *Toofan* (1989), and *Ajooba* (1991). *Shahenshah*, in particular, allowed Bachchan to portray an Indian everyman character named Vijay who takes on the alter ego of Shahenshah to fight against corruption and protect the vulnerable in Indian society. While American superheroes formed the model for many of the Indian superhero films up till this period, we see in the late 1980s the emergence of a distinctive Indian model of superhero. Nevertheless, it is telling that while *Mr India* and *Shahenshah* were both successful at the box office, they were very much the exception during this brief cycle and the genre soon came to an end. Therefore, despite the emergence of the distinctly Indian superhero form in the 1980s, it is not until the mid-2000s that we see the potential of the Indian superhero film to transform the imported genre to such an extent that it becomes its own structural model and therefore reaches the fourth stage of Yuri Lotman's process of cultural exchange.

Krrish and the Global Indian Superhero

According to Lotman's model, the fourth stage in the development from a receiving to a transmitting culture is when

> the culture itself changes to a state of activity and begins rapidly to produce new texts; these new texts are based on cultural codes which in the distant past were stimulated by invasions from outside, but which now have been wholly transformed through the many asymmetrical transformations into a new and original structural model. (1990, 146)

For O'Regan (1996, 202), an example of this within Australian film and television was when the international success of *Neighbours* (1985–) meant that it became an original structure model for the soap genre to the extent that a number of other series around the world began to emulate it. In other words, this series exemplified a shift whereby the Australian soap opera was becoming a recognized genre in its own right and was no longer seen as beholden to the influence of imported formats. It is clear that the moment that this happened within the superhero genre in India was the blockbuster success of *Krrish* (2006), a film that was promoted as featuring "India's first Super Hero." Not only was the film a commercial hit across South Asia, but the film became a model for a series of Indian superhero films in the subsequent years including but not limited to *Drona* (2008), *Enthiran* (2010), *Ra.One* (2011), *Mugamoodi* (2012) and its own sequel *Krrish 3* (2013).

In order to frame *Krrish* we should first consider its prequel *Koi . . . Mil Gaya* (2003), a film that was similarly promoted as another "first" in Indian cinema—in this case, the first science fiction film—despite a long history of science fiction in Indian cinema stretching back to *Wahan Ke Log* in 1967. Moreover, *Koi . . . Mil Gaya* interweaves appropriations from American science fiction films with the ideology and iconography of Hinduism in such a way that has significance for our understanding of the later *Krrish*. Directed by Rakesh Roshan, *Koi . . . Mil Gaya* opens with a Hindu scientist named Sanjay Mehra (played by Roshan) who is attempting to contact extra terrestrial life by sending out a message containing the religious syllable "Om." Ridiculed within the scientific community for his use of religion to contact aliens—one scientist asks him, "Oh, so they believe in your religion as well?"—Sanjay receives a response from the aliens but tragically dies in a car accident before he can properly make contact. His wife, Sonia Mehra (Rekha), who was pregnant when they had the accident, gives birth to their son Rohit (Hrithik Roshan), who has been left with a brain defect caused by the crash. The film follows Rohit as he struggles with his mental handicap and develops a romantic interest in the kindly Nisha (Preity Zinta). At his lowest point, he prays to Lord Krishna for help and is astonished when his prayers are answered by the arrival of an alien spacecraft. It is carrying a blue alien creature who combines the blue skin tone of Lord Krishna and the visage of Ganesh. Rohit and the alien come to develop a close relationship and the alien is given the name of "Jadoo" (meaning "magic" in Hindi). Taking pity on Rohit's disability, Jadoo is able to grant him greatly increased strength and intelligence. This helps Rohit to build the confidence to propose to Nisha and the films ends with Jadoo returning to his home planet while Rohit and Nisha embark on a happy life together.

As this brief synopsis suggests, while the film is often described in the West as the "Bollywood *E.T.*," it is actually more like a bricolage of various different intertexts; a conglomeration of influences that include the US science fiction texts *Star Wars* (1977), *Contact* (1997), *Close Encounters of the Third Kird* (1977), *E.T.* (1982), *Back to the Future* (1985), *Flubber* (1997), *Charly* (1968), *Independence Day* (1994), and *The X Files* (1993–2002). Despite these influences, however, Jessica Langer and Dominic Alessio see the potential in the film for a challenge to Hollywood's domination of the science fiction genre: "We would argue that even if Bollywood began as an imitation of Hollywood on some level, *Koi* demonstrates that it has begun to challenge the hegemony of Western cinematic production, both economically and ideologically" (2007, 227).

This ideological challenge is most clearly manifest in the addition of religious themes to the elements borrowed from the source texts. As I described in the synopsis above, the film contains many references to the Hindu religion, from the use of the divine "Om" syllable to contact the aliens, through to Rohit's prayers to Lord Krishna for help. The success of both these actions, against the backdrop of various Western scientific failures in the film, represent what Alessio and Langer describe as a trend in contemporary Bollywood cinema in which "Hindu beliefs are deliberately challenging Western conventions by demonstrating the superiority of all things Hindu and Indian" (2007, 225). Moments such as the success of the Hindu scientist Sanjay Mehra in contacting extra terrestrial life using the "Om" signal, inverting the scientific secularism of source text *Contact*, suggest a commentary on the neglected role of religion in these Hollywood texts. While this commentary is fairly limited, not least because the specific source texts are never explicitly referenced, *Koi . . . Mil Gaya* does display the ambivalent tension between oppositional critique and mimetic reverence that is often central to these processes of transnational appropriation.

As Anustup Basu (2011), Carolyn Jess-Cooke (2009), Langer and Alessio (2007) have all argued, there is an emphasis here on reformulating the science fiction genre through an explicit process of Indianization. Indeed, for Cooke, the film's realignment of the science fiction genre with Indian religious values can be seen as "utilising the sci-fi genre as an organising structure within which to vocalize Indian identities and ideologies" (2009, 117). Moreover, it is significant that this is an explicitly Hindu reformulation of the genre that transforms the borrowed elements as part of a wider ideological strategy to affirm the importance of Hinduism in public life. What we see when we turn to the sequel *Krrish*, however, are the ways in which this film continues to vocalize a specifically Hindu ideology but balances this with a more globally inflected and hybrid vision of contemporary Indian society.

Krrish (2006) focuses on Krishna (once more played by Hritik Roshan), the son of Rohit and Nisha, who they discover has developed superpowers as a result of Jadoo's magic. To try to conceal his abilities, Krishna is brought up by his grandmother Sonia in a remote village, yet after falling in love with the visiting Priya he decides to travel to Singapore. Promising his grandmother to keep his abilities secret, he adopts the secret identity of the masked superhero Krrish (Figure 10). He soon discovers that the megalomaniacal scientist Dr. Arya, reminiscent of Mogambo in *Mr India*, is developing a supercomputer that will allow him to see into the future. Concerned by the dangers posed by such a machine, Krrish tracks down Dr. Arya at his compound and in a climactic sequence manages to defeat him using his superpowers. The film then ends with a callback to *Koi . . .*

10. Hrithik Roshan in *Krrish* (2006), Credit: Filmkraft Productions.

Mil Gaya where Rohit uses Dr. Arya's computer to contact the alien Jadoo with an "Om."

Bringing together a wide range of influences, including Hollywood superhero films, Chinese martial arts epics, and the ancient Sanskrit epics *The Mahabharata* and *The Ramayana*, *Krrish* goes further than its prequel in positioning itself as a global cultural product. While utilizing the superhero genre to vocalize local concerns, the film is itself very much a transnational production. One of the reasons that *Krrish* is so significant within the history of the Indian superhero is that it embodies a complex form of transnationalism that reflects wider shifts in Indian cinema in the twenty-first century. Part of a trend for Bollywood films to deal with the experiences of Non Resident Indians, the film was largely shot in Singapore, taking advantage of the city-state's "Film in Singapore" scheme to subsidize on-location filming costs. The crew of the film was also transnational with the Hollywood team Marc Kolbe and Craig Mumma working on the special effects, and Hong Kong action choreographer Ching Siu-Tung choreographing the action sequences.

Balanced with these international influences, the film is also grounded in the local mythological stories that underpinned *Koi . . . Mil Gaya*. As Raminder Kaur notes, "This is not simply an imitative reproduction for Indian audiences; it entails 'transcreation'—or a transnational and translational instantiation of the superhero embedded in familial and vernacular conventions of Indian film and society" (2013, 293). We should not ignore the fact that *Krrish*'s powers derive from an alien modeled on the Hindu gods Krishna and Ganesh, nor that this alien is contacted with the Hindu mantra "Om." The superhero genre is still being used here as an organizing structure through which to express an ideological position. However, unlike some of the superhero narratives that I discussed earlier in this chapter, I would argue that *Krrish* is less about Indianizing the superhero through an association with mythological stories, than it is an attempt to present a contemporary vision of India that is culturally hybrid and globally engaged. Taking us away from the notion that the Indian superhero is necessarily a localized imitation of the US superhero, or indeed that the character himself must be located within India, the film instead draws our attention to the ways in which the Indian superhero now functions in dialogue with the local and the global.

Conclusion

For Lotman, the final stage of the process of cultural exchange is when "The receiving culture, which now becomes the general center of the semiosphere, changes into a transmitting culture and issues forth a flood of texts directed to other, peripheral areas of the semiosphere" (1990, 146). The box office success of *Krrish*, becoming the second highest grossing Indian film of 2006, led to a series of superhero films in the following years. Inspired by the success of the film and its star Hrithik Roshan, Abhishek Bachchan elected to star in the 2008 fantasy superhero film *Drona* in which the protagonist was named after a royal guru in *The Mahabharata*, while Shah Rukh Khan starred in his own superhero blockbuster *Ra.One* (2011) based around an escaped videogame character. However, both films were relative box office failures and do not therefore demonstrate the continued vitality of the genre indicated in Lotman's model. To see this process more clearly, we need to turn our attention away from the Hindi industry to the Tamil industry in Southern India.

In the years following the success of *Krrish*, the Tamil industry produced the two superhero blockbusters *Enthiran* (2010) and *Mugamoodi* (2012). While *Mugamoodi* was only a moderate box office success, *Enthiran* (2010), starring the iconic South Indian star Rajinikanth, is not only one of the most successful Indian superhero films but is also one of the highest grossing Indian films of all time. (Langer 2012) The film centers on Dr. Vaseegaran, a scientist of robotics who creates an android in his own likeness named Chitti but struggles to retain control of his creation when Chitti is given the ability to experience human emotions. The most celebrated sequences in the film focus on Chitti's superhuman abilities in which he takes part in increasingly spectacular battles with the authorities tasked with taking him under control. Furthermore, clips of these sequences have become viral sensations online, demonstrating an increasing global fascination with the Indian superhero. As Jessica Langer notes, "The international success of *Enthiran* among both Indian and non-Indian overseas audiences—driven in part by viral clips of some of the film's most outlandish action sequences, posted on YouTube—provides a non-Hindi indigenous language of India with global representation" (2012, 147). As this case demonstrates, the audience for Indian superheroes is no longer limited to the traditional domestic or diasporic market but instead reaches out to a global audience online.

Moreover, the strongest indicator that the Indian superhero has reached the fifth stage in Lotman's model is the influence that these recent Indian blockbusters are having in other national industries. In neighboring Pakistan, director Umair Nasir Ali has recently announced that he is going to direct the very first Pakistani superhero film entitled *Nation Awakes*. Most significantly, Ali explains that the reasoning behind the production of the film is that "while Hollywood has *Spiderman* and *Batman* and India has *Ra.One* and *Krish*, [we] thought the work should begin on something that represents Pakistan" (quoted in Khan 2013). The Indian superhero is therefore no longer seen as primarily imitative of the US superhero, but is instead being positioned as a recognized genre in its own right, which other national industries are beginning to emulate.

What is clear from this study is that the shift in the representation of superheroes in Indian cinema since the 1960s demonstrates the significance of cultural exchange to our understanding of national cultures. Through the use of Lotman's model, I have tried to avoid replicating what Raminder Kaur describes as the "hierarchical ontology of original and copy" (2012, 330) by moving away from a formulation which sees the Indian superhero as primarily imitative, and instead using a formulation that positions the Indian superhero in a fluid dialogue with local, national and global cultural forms. Lotman's model has been particularly useful in drawing attention to the ways in which processes of importing and exporting can illuminate our understanding of cultural development over time. Ultimately, therefore, this chapter takes the position that any claims we make about the nature of superheroes in terms of national culture must rest on an engagement with these transnational processes of cultural exchange.

Notes

1. By "Indian superheroes," I am referring here to superheroes in Indian cinema rather than those superheroes who were created for comic books in the West and

identified as being ethnically Indian such as the shape-shifting Aruna who first appeared in *Batgirl Annual #1* or the mutant Indra from the *X-Men* series.

2. According to film critic Todd Stadtman, *Return of Mr Superman* was initially also named *Superman*, but after objections from the rival producer, they were forced to change the name to this alternative title.

3. It is worth noting that there were earlier attempts at producing Indian comic book superheroes in the 1970s but the popularization of this form came in the 1980s and is tied to the success of Raj Comics.

SECTION THREE

The Politics, Morality, and Socio-Cultural Impact of Superheroes on World Screens

ALTERITY IN THE GENESIS OF THE CONTEMPORARY BRITISH TV SUPERHERO

JOCHEN ECKE AND PATRICK GILL

In the first episode of the British television series *Misfits* (2009–2013), five juvenile delinquents are given preternatural powers by a freak electrical storm. The protagonists slowly discover their new abilities over the course of the pilot, and, being largely congruent with contemporary knowing audiences, instantly make surmises as to their own narrative status. Before long, the painfully shy Simon Bellamy asks, "What if we are meant to be, like, superheroes?" To which loudmouth Nathan Young replies, "You lot, superheroes? No offense, but in what kind of fucked-up world would that be allowed to happen?"

This exchange is highly self-reflexive in a number of ways and helps establish the show's attitude toward the superhero genre in these crucial first minutes—or rather, it helps establish parts of the concept behind the particular permutation of the genre that *Misfits* represents. By implication, Nathan is making it clear that, while he would not consider the rest of the group to be superhero material ("You lot, superheroes?"), he just might think himself worthy of that moniker—or at least somewhat less unworthy. The latter interpretation is the more likely, since in the world of *Misfits*, the moral integrity often associated with superheroism is practically nonexistent. The character is keenly aware of this. Nathan's remark thus drives home the fact that the status of a superhero is not an *a priori* given in *Misfits*, but a discursive object that is constantly negotiated throughout the series.

And while *Misfits* keeps raising the question of what might make a superhero and which member(s) of the group might be considered one, the superhero status itself is never granted consensually to any member of the group. Rather, the concept of the superhero itself is almost universally mocked throughout the series, mostly on similar grounds as in the quote: what happens to superhero plots, *Misfits* asks, once they take place in a society that is rigorously stratified, making it practically impossible for some youths to ascend the social ladder, adorned with superpowers or not? What if the characters in a superhero narrative behaved the way actual human beings often do, for example, selfishly and amorally? What are the consequences if the *grand récit* of a consensual morality is replaced with a postmodernist plethora of individual value systems, all inherently contingent and fluid?

In many respects, *Misfits* can thus be regarded as a performance of British identity, pitting many narrative conceits traditionally identified as quintessentially British against a supposedly stable norm of American superheroics: the class politics and highly specific social milieu evident in practically every scene especially function as markers of Britishness. In its attitude towards the superhero genre, *Misfits* is in no way the exception on British television. Historically, British treatments of the superhero have mostly been irreverent and satirical, allowing for new interpretive mappings of the genre by introducing conventions from other sorts of narrative, such as the kitchen sink drama, and productively pitting them against superhero tropes. In order to arrive at an explanation of how this stance on superheroes came about, this chapter will examine superheroes on contemporary British television as a phenomenon that can only be understood from an historical and transnational point of view. It is our contention that the superhero genre is not at all an essentially American fixture (although the discourse has certainly marked it as much), but rather a transnational phenomenon producing a multitude of generic permutations based on a similar but different experience of modernity in countries such as the UK and the USA.

In order to understand this transnational genesis of contemporary representations of the superhero on British television, we will first provide an historical overview that led to current developments in series such as *Misfits*. We will then focus on a close analysis of three current series to demonstrate how these attitudes towards the superhero manifest themselves on British television today. We contend that these performances of Britishness do not really represent a "deconstruction" or "revision" of the genre as many critics posit (for a relevant example in the comics field, see Klock 2005). Instead, we insist that the narrative strategies found in series such as *Misfits* or *No Heroics* (2008) do not at all amount to a destruction of the superhero. They are in fact anything but: the insistence on the genre's supposed shortcomings instead amounts to a reaffirmation of its capacity to represent and negotiate the present precisely because it can accommodate the criticism.

Performing Britishness

Misfits' emphasis on the discursiveness of superheroism may not seem remarkable at first glance. After all, US superhero serials such as *The Amazing Spider-Man*, to give but one example, have successfully employed the concept since at least the 1960s, when the (fictional) New York public and press greeted the eponymous superhero with an intense skepticism at best and outright hatred and persecution at worst. But the *Spider-Man* comic books very clearly indicated the limits of this discursiveness—the protagonist's heroism is only called into doubt intradiegetically, but is never seriously in question from the reader's perspective. *Misfits*, on the other hand, gives its audience any number of cues that should at the very least make them doubt some of the central assumptions of certain manifestations of the classical superhero genre: centrally, that a person would be able to behave altruistically and act within the boundaries of an easily defined consensual morality without any ulterior motives, all the time. This is not to say that the characters of *Misfits* never behave altruistically or try to act in an ethically acceptable manner, but they only do so in fits and bursts, and their moral actions are always contingent on circumstance.

Misfits thus pits two models of ethics against each other by engaging in its metafictional dialogue with the superhero genre: one static and *a priori*, the other dynamic and contingent. It thus positions itself as a superhero narrative supposedly superior to its conventional American forebears and contemporaries because of the greater complexity and ambiguity of the ethical negotiations taking place in each episode (among many other things). To be able to do so, it necessarily reduces the superhero genre to a few core traits against which it defines itself. The series thus (perhaps deliberately) misreads the genre as an ahistorical, static set of rules and conventions that has not been modified since the superheroes' beginnings in the USA of the late 1930s. This is patently untrue; if anything, the genre has always been characterized by an immense mutability. Henry Jenkins even speaks of a fundamental instability—of genres in general, and the superhero genre in particular. He notes that "there is not a moment in the history of the genre when the superhero is not under active revision" (Jenkins 2009, 29). In this sense, we might consider the ostentatious manner in which *Misfits* declares itself as other to previous (largely imaginary) manifestations of the genre as a necessary part of the constant evolution of the superhero.

In this sense, *Misfits*' attempts to position itself as a British, working class "other" to what is supposedly an exhausted and intrinsically American genre is a necessary act, especially in genre fiction. After all, formula fiction demands that—contrary to appearances—the creators constantly "make it new," ostentatiously changing or criticizing conventions, discarding or modifying tropes and tinkering with the ideological and moral assumptions that the genre is (temporarily) based on. In other words, there is a strong argument to be made that such acts of generic reframing are part and parcel of genre fiction and not necessarily linked to any national or transnational tendencies. Henry Jenkins, in his study of the superhero genre, speaks of the elasticity and malleability that all genres must necessarily possess, seeing that they are exposed to "a perpetual push and pull" through which "genre formulas are continually repositioned in relation to social, cultural, and economic contexts of production and reception" (Jenkins 2009, 19).

However, in the case of British uses of the superhero genre, there actually is such a thing as an overtly (trans-)national tradition in creating superhero stories, predicated largely on an ostentatiously constructed alterity to the American superhero mainstream.[1] This tradition can be easily traced throughout the entire history of British superhero stories, and it is clearly at work in *Misfits* too: it can be seen in the series' emphasis on class politics and working class settings and in its insistence on using regional British dialects and sociolects, but also in writer/producer Howard Overman's strategy of making superpowers the metaphorical manifestation of the protagonists' problems rather than their solution. Scottish writer Grant Morrison, a prominent member of the so-called British Invasion of American mainstream comics in the 1980s, sums up a typical attitude of British writers creating superhero fictions in the following manner:

> The relationship of Britons to the figure of the US superhero came with a great deal of antagonism. Many of us were out for revenge and powered by the insurrectionist energy of the seventeen-year-old, sneering and demanding. The critique was often barbed, and, in some cases, clearly intended to be fatal. (Morrison 2011, 187)

While Morrison is commenting on a very specific historical moment here, referencing the punk movement by implication and the state of the American comics industry at the beginning of the 1980s, there is nevertheless a case to be made that his remark bears certain hallmarks of the universal, too.

British creators have practically always felt the need (and also a certain amount of public pressure) to perform their cultural and ideological otherness when producing superhero stories. Morrison expresses this need in the following manner:

> The Americans expected us to be brilliant punks and, eager to please our masters, we sensitive, artistic boys did our best to live up to our hype. Like the Sex Pistols sneering and burning their way through 'Johnny B. Goode,' we took their favorite songs, rewrote all the lyrics, and played them on buzz saws through squalling distortion pedals. . . . Most important for me, we were encouraged to be shocking and different. (Morrison 2011, 186)

In this passage from his autobiography, Morrison seizes on the fact that the British creators' production of alterity is predicated on a dialectic relationship: the members of the British Invasion did not come up with superhero fictions of a different kind because of their essential otherness; instead, they constructed and performed their otherness in their work partly because it was expected of them, and partly because they were the products of a similar but different experience of the 1970s. It is therefore possible to speak of a transnational tradition of British superhero fictions in much the same terms that Laura Doyle defines transnational cultural processes in general. From the point of view of transnational theory, the superhero genre and its British incarnations must be seen as forms that "take shape not strictly within a single national or religious political world but rather within a horizon of historical events experienced in common and yet differentially" by different nations, in this case the United Kingdom and the USA. We must therefore analyze American and British superhero fictions "dialectically, as entities created by their agonistic entanglements with each other" (Doyle 2009, 5).

The ostentatious alterity of British superhero fictions is indeed predicated on a similar but different experience of history: world history as well as genre history; cultural history as well as the history of film, television and comics. As for the latter, there is no doubt that the British superhero genre is indelibly linked to the comic book medium. It is therefore necessary to explore this history to some extent, comparing the medium and the genre's evolution in the USA and the UK before this discussion can turn to an analysis of superheroes in British television.

A Brief History of British Superheroics

The Nineteenth and Early Twentieth Century

In both countries, comic books were a product of late nineteenth century popular culture, developing out of the pictorial practices of nineteenth century newspaper and magazine culture.[2] And while the products of both industries can be said to be largely concerned with processing and representing the experience and anxieties of modernity, it is obvious that comic book creators in the USA and the UK were facing rather different modernities. This is reflected in the heroes and heroines of the late nineteenth and early twentieth centuries' popular fictions: while "the social and political outlook of the Victorian comic was highly conservative" (Chapman 2012, 28), publishers, authors and artists nevertheless made sure that the characters and situations reflected their readers' daily lives, sometimes even allowing for the sly subversion of Victorian values, as in the case of the highly popular Ally Sloper, hero of what might be called proto-comics. The character, who made his first appearance in 1867, "represents everything that the hard-working, respectable working classes should not be"; he is "feckless, work-shy, a scrounger and a rogue." Ally Sloper prefers to make "his living as a conman"; he is "a social deviant, but his comical ineptitude makes him a safe deviant" (Chapman 2012, 20).

A more or less direct line can be drawn from the exploits of Ally Sloper to many British comic books of the twentieth century, the common denominators often being class consciousness, the desire to accurately portray social milieus (in however satirical a fashion), and—at times—the penchant for the subversion of authority, quite evident in popular periodicals such as *The Dandy* and *Beano*.[3] Paul Gravett and Peter Stanbury put it the following way:

> Class-consciousness, however it is learnt, remains fundamental to British people and to many of the comics they read in which they themselves appear. So, expensive, well-printed, educational comics such as *Eagle* (1950–69) or *Look and Learn* (1962–82) were clearly aimed at the kids, and at the parents who bought them, from the middle classes. Most of the comical weeklies, however, for a long time lower in price and print quality, mostly centered around concerns of their principal target readership, the working class. Through all kinds of signals, the characters in many of the comics, both old and contemporary.... convey assumptions about which rung they occupy on the social ladder, from Lord Snooty "slumming it" with his poor pals to Dan Dare and

> Digby's officer-and-batman working relationship. (Gravett and Stanbury 2006, 20)

What we can draw from this will be relevant to the discussion of the superheroes' TV incarnations: first of all, the class-consciousness of British comics contributed to a different kind of protagonist in British comics, a protagonist more often than not rooted in a specific social stratum; and a politics of representation much more indebted to modes of social realism.

This, then, is one historical reason why superhero comics did not really catch on in the UK at the same time as they became pervasive in the USA. To this day, the attitude that, as British comics artist Paul Grist puts it, "Some things don't travel very well," is pervasive in the British comics industry when it comes to the genre. Despite quite a bit of evidence to the contrary, the view that "the one thing that British comics have never really done is superheroes" (Grist 2011, 7) prevails, a stance which is further exemplified by the fact that the major works on the history of British comics by James Chapman and by Paul Gravett and Peter Stanbury devote either very little space to the genre (Chapman) or no space at all (Gravett and Stanbury).[4] While it may be risky to extend this thesis from one medium to the other, it nevertheless becomes apparent that British TV producers, as soon as they tackle superhero fictions, tend to modify the genre on exactly these grounds: by injecting a considerable dose of class consciousness, and by adding narrative features and premises usually associated with social realism.[5] Famously, the US superhero genre came to be inextricably linked to performances of American identity during the Second World War.[6] While there were some roughly comparable patriotic developments in British comic books (see Chapman 2012, 37–47 for details), the superhero never experienced the same fusion with national identity. Apart from the thorough identification of the genre with the USA and the very divergent histories of the American and the British comic book medium, there were rather straightforward reasons for this: while the Second World War "increased household income and reduced availability of consumer durables" in the USA and thus "boosted comic books and all forms of mass entertainment" (Gabilliet 2010, 20), the wartime economy in the UK put restrictions on new periodicals, which meant "that no new titles could be launched during the war" (Chapman 2012, 36). British superheroes were thus ideologically and historically unlikely and, on top of that, very difficult to produce from an economic and legal point of view. After the war, a British import ban on American newspapers and magazines precluded the arrival of the original American comic books until 1959 (for more, see:

Chapman 2012, 178). This is not to say that there were no British superheroes at all until the early 1960s. Characters such as Maskman or Captain Might, for the greater part highly derivative of US superhero archetypes, debuted after the Second World War. They have mostly been forgotten, though, as the quote by Paul Grist and their omission from comic book historiography shows. Their cultural impact was minuscule at best.[7]

A Brief History of British Superheroics

After World War II

What does all this entail for the British attitude toward superheroes? Most of all, it further clarifies the British perspective on the genre: for the greater part, American superhero comic books only became available to the UK public at the beginning of the so-called Silver Age, that is, at the end of the 1950s. The majority of British audiences thus never had the opportunity to identify with the characters and the genre to the extent that Americans did in the 1930s and 1940s, during traumatic times that would in no small part define American identity for decades to come. Due to the highly disposable nature of the monthly periodicals, it is also quite likely that most of the British public only had sporadic access to the Golden Age manifestations of the genre, or no access at all.

The relative inaccessibility of Golden Age comic books likely helped the aforementioned process of simplification and reduction—for British artists and writers, it was thus relatively easy to construct an essential superhero to fit their assumptions and prejudice about the genre. Consequently, British creators came to see the superhero as a historically contingent figure indelibly connected to the wartime USA and to the simplistic narratives of World War II propaganda and New Deal ideology, both grievously outdated in the midst of the Cold War and in the wake of the social revolutions that came in the 1960s. Those British comic book writers and artists growing up with Silver Age comic books were indeed to take to the superhero genre with the eyes of the historian, most likely keenly aware of their own identificatory and ideological distance.[8] The same can be said for the creators of British TV series. In this light, it is hardly surprising that a genre so bound up in American national identity would prompt British creatives to fashion counter-narratives that were to frame and perform their own otherness, and in particular their similar but different experience of twentieth century history.[9] Still, it is important to reaffirm that these markedly transnational manifestations of the genre do not amount to its destruction;

they do not even signify a British refutation of superheroes. Instead, it is helpful to think of the special relationship between British and American superhero fictions that is expressed in these works along Grant Morrison's lines:

> Now here were the proud Americans handing us their dream children, like Romans in Britain delivering their gods into the hands of the Celts for a revamp. The gray skies over Britain split. The superheroes arrived to save the day, and when the cape was dangled, we grabbed hold and were lifted into the golden clouds above the lengthening dole queues. We became known as the British Invasion. (Morrison 2011, 187f)

Morrison enacts a remarkable reversal here, for in his point of view, it was not the British artists who saved the superhero genre, but the superheroes themselves that came to their authors' and artists' rescue. Once again, this interpretation highlights the complex transnational entanglement of the genre, and it again points toward its flexibility to produce innovative and meaningful permutations even to this day—especially because at this point, it comes with the baggage of more than seventy years of history that can be tapped into at will that, in conjunction with the concerns of the present, to produce endless variations and transformations of the genre. A keen authorial awareness of the genre's potential and history has thus produced a wide range of transnational manifestations of the superhero in the British context, and continues to do so.

Superheroes on British Television

While this range of anglicized superheroes within the realm of comic books at least produced a certain number of straight-laced specimens (however unsuccessful) and while the British Invasion resulted in characters of considerable depth and complexity, the story of superheroes on British television screens can be told rather more quickly, as despite being a commonplace phenomenon, they tend to fall into easily identifiable categories. In this regard, it is perhaps most illuminating to point out that there has as yet been no British superhero drama (with the exception of *Misfits*, which will be discussed later). Rather, overt superheroes on British television screens have only ever occurred in two generic guises; namely, in comedy and in children's television. This simple generic observation may at first appear surprising, though given the different historical developments in Britain and America outlined above, it is perhaps inevitable that the veneration reserved for American superheroes in their serious incarnations (i.e. in comic books as well as film and television drama) should be thus undermined.

Regardless of the exact formats in which they appear, TV superheroes in Britain never adhere to what may be thought of as the overly simplified standard superhero recipe. Instead, they always work to undermine the status of the superhero. Sketches from *Do Not Adjust Your Set*'s "Captain Fantastic" (1967–69)[10] and *Monty Python's Flying Circus*'s "Bicycle Repair Man" (1969) to "Angel Summoner and BMX Bandit" as featured in *That Mitchell and Webb Look* (2006–2010) do not simply make fun of individual instances of superherodom—they question and undermine the very concept.

Representations of superheroes aimed at children are equally irreverent, as even the most cursory glance at a list of children's superhero shows including *Super Gran* (1985–1987), *Danger Mouse* (1981–1992), *Bananaman* (1983–1986) and *SuperTed* (1982–1986) will confirm. While this short list can only hint at the general tone with which British television tends to approach the phenomenon of superheroes, it should suffice to provide some context for a discussion of three more recent television series, *My Hero* (2000–2006), *No Heroics* and *Misfits* (2009–), which the present essay will focus on in order to illustrate how pervasive a model the ostentatiously constructed alterity to the American superhero has been, and continues to be in the world of British television.

While the choice of the pilot episodes of *My Hero*, *No Heroics*, and *Misfits* for our analysis—three series created within ten years of each other—may at first appear as one of similarity over difference, the three shows are far more different from one another, in their tone in general and in their treatment of superherodom in particular, than can be outlined in a few short paragraphs. If one were to argue that British TV never spawned superheroes to be venerated because it simply lacked the budgets to come up with convincing special effects, one would have to look no further than Paul Mendelson's *My Hero* to illustrate the point. But as will be discussed, there are a multitude of ways unrelated to the BBC's budget in which the star of *My Hero* undermines classical expectations of the superhero.

A traditional sitcom complete with laugh track, *My Hero* centers on the relationship of alien superhero Thermoman with his human love interest, Janet, in the deliberately anti-heroic setting of the town of Northolt. In contrast to this, Drew Pearce's *No Heroics* is set before a more metropolitan backdrop, even though the characters' lives seem largely restricted to quotidian settings like the pub or the corner shop. *No Heroics* does not rely on a laugh track and generally conveys a bleaker and more worldly-wise atmosphere, though it is still firmly anchored in the world of broad comedy. Howard Overman's *Misfits* is a somewhat different proposition. The only one of these three shows to be broadcast in the forty-five-minute format reserved for drama shows, *Misfits* primarily aims at holding the audience's interest in individual characters' fates over the course of several episodes and even seasons. That it also includes comedic aspects there can be no doubt, but it could be argued that this show, following a group of juvenile delinquents who suddenly find themselves imbued with preternatural powers, is the first British TV drama centering around the deeds and lives of superheroes. In how far these three shows—different though they undoubtedly are—are representative of the genesis of British TV superheroes will be discussed in the following paragraphs.

The first—and certainly most conspicuous—feature these British TV superheroes have in common is the fact that both specific superheroes and the very concept of superherodom are universally mocked within their respective series. Individual heroes are equipped with absurd superpowers or costumes, their useful superpowers are counterbalanced by outlandish impediments, or the entire world they are represented in is patently absurd. This is clearly demonstrated by George (Ardal O'Hanlon) in *My Hero*, who can only change into his superhero identity in bathrooms, thus instilling those around him with serious concern for his digestive tract. The lavatory humor is continued in one of the first exchanges of the pilot episode in which a young girl asks Janet (Emily Joyce), Thermoman's love interest, whether she would like to be Thermoman's girlfriend, only to inform her that "he could see through the door while you're on the toilet," an impracticality Janet has clearly not given much thought to thus far.

Ridiculous superhero names and costumes also serve to leave British TV superheroes in possession of as little dignity as possible. In *No Heroics*, for instance, the superhero going by the name of The Hotness (Nicholas Burns) is frequently ridiculed for his name, as is Thundermonkey (Jim Howick), whose power of summoning monkeys to come to his aid within a timeframe of just over two hours is usually met with little respect on the part of the series' other superheroes. Most common, however, is the ridicule of the very concept of superherodom by means of a representation of pedestrian, everyday aspects to be expected in a world in which superheroes are a common occurrence. Thus the opening sequence of *No Heroics* features three intertitles: A NORMAL CITY / WITH ONE SMALL DIFFERENCE / THERE ARE SUPERHEROES. The emphasis here is clearly on the normality of the city (thus there being superheroes is only considered a "small difference") and aspects of daily life create a rich tapestry of absurdity in front of which the cast's adventures are played out. For instance, the previously mentioned superhero called The Hotness is in possession of a DVD collection that includes *Some Like It Hot*, *Body Heat*, and *Cat on a Hot Tin Roof*. As The Hotness comments rather wearily, these are "heat-themed Christmas presents. No one gets bored of *that* gag!" In the society portrayed in *No Heroics*, special provisions are made for the needs of all superheroes, including a pub of their own, The Fortress, where the use of superpowers is strictly prohibited. Much of the series' humor thus stems from placing the superheroes in locations and social contexts that the genre usually scrupulously omits for very good reason: because they would inevitably show the protagonists in situations that are much closer to the audience's everyday experience where the conventions of superhero melodrama look distinctly out of place.

While *My Hero* focuses on one particular superhero rather than an entire crowd, it is made clear that superherodom—though an alien phenomenon—is not a singular occurrence and is in fact unmistakably institutionalized, as is illustrated by means of Thermoman's cousin Arnie, the erstwhile Polarman (Lou Hirsch), whose powers have been revoked by "the great and glorious Ultron Council." This thoroughly established superherodom, portrayed in both *My Hero* and *No Heroics*, provides a running commentary not only on superheroes within the given world but on comic book culture as such. The adventures of these "real" superheroes are thus constantly set against expectations of stereotypical superheroes. *No Heroics* in particular enjoys this interplay between the "real-life" experiences of superheroes and the expectations supposedly directed at them by the public and by popular culture. The single season's second episode provides the most apt example of this when it has Electroclash and She-Force visit a convention of geeks fascinated with their erstwhile exploits as all-female superhero team "Lady Trouble." It transpires that in the world of *No Heroics*, superheroes do not only act as such (more or less) in the real world—they also have comic books made of their adventures and they have fanboy admirers. What they also have is the humdrum experience of dealing with diverse hangers-on, admirers and critics.

In fact, all three series go out of their way to emphasize the quotidian and banal in the lives of the superheroes they portray. In both *My Hero* and *No Heroics* the commonplace is injected into the lives of superheroes by virtue of superheroism being a commonplace phenomenon. In *Misfits* it is already present in the characters before their transformation and refuses to leave them once they have acquired super powers. These TV series refuse to idolize their characters simply for being equipped with preternatural powers—they actively seek to illustrate the very simple assumption that where super powers are common, superheroes' lives must be equally common. If they can be relied on to offer this limited realism of thinking things through and creating worlds consistent with the basic ideas and principles on which they rest, the series may perhaps be expected to go a little further and extend this sense of relentless consistency to the portrayal of their heroes' social status.

At first, *My Hero* hardly raises any suspicions of being concerned with questions of class conflict. After all, Thermoman comes from a strange and distant planet and George Sunday, his alter ego, runs a health food shop in Northolt, which can hardly be considered a working class pursuit. In a number of ways, however, George/Thermoman is marked as an outsider struggling to fit into his Northolt surroundings. For one thing, the unmistakable Irish accent of actor Ardal O'Hanlon singles him out as a linguistic outsider and bestows on him the clichéd image of the unsophisticated intruder into polite Northolt society. In addition, his social ineptitude frequently makes him the butt of other characters' jokes or even the target of their open disdain. While the audience know that it is merely his unfamiliarity with earthly customs and etiquette that make him appear stupid and unrefined, his interlocutors, first and foremost among them the distinctly posh characters of Janet's mother (Geraldine McNulty) and Dr. Crispin (Hugh Dennis), are less forgiving in their judgment of his social skills. The superhero prototype of the alien turned immigrant is thus firmly reframed within the boundaries of the class system, allowing for new interpretive mappings and appropriations both of *My Hero* and American characters: confronted with Thermoman's comically imperfect process of assimilation, the audience might wonder just why Superman's integration into American society is portrayed as seamless, for example.

Just like *My Hero*, *No Heroics* might at first seem not to lend itself to too much social scrutiny even though it does indeed feature a very visible social divide, namely that between mere humans and superheroes. But while the main action of the series does allow the occasional intrusion of a normal human being as a victim (either to be rescued or to be taken advantage of by the series' superheroes), its focus in terms of social interaction is firmly on dealings between superheroes. Rather than presenting a homogeneous front though, the world of superheroes, like the world of our everyday experience, is presented as thoroughly stratified. This is perhaps best exemplified by life in The Fortress, the pub frequented by superheroes.

Here, superheroes compete with one another not only for success in terms of their heroic deeds but particularly for media attention. In this regard, Excelsor (Patrick Baladi) is clearly the most accomplished among them, and he usually takes his place standing by the bar, surrounded by friends and hangers-on, while the less successful main characters of the series are usually seated in a less conspicuous position, constantly having to walk past Excelsor's taunting presence. Far from egalitarian, then, the world of *No Heroics* is heavily stratified, and as in *My Hero*, the audience's sympathies are located firmly with the underdogs. This is also true of *Misfits*, whose heroes and heroines are firmly rooted in the world of disadvantage: five juvenile delinquents who cannot transcend the social standing and habits they were born into, even after acquiring superpowers.

In terms of their characters' ethics, the three shows discussed here represent a sliding scale of moral compasses. The occasional white lie aside, Thermoman will rarely do anything immoral. He may on occasion use his powers not for the greater good but to his personal advantage, as when trying (unsuccessfully) to use his memory-erasing powers on crazy neighbor Tyler. All in all, however, those few times at which he does use his powers on the innocent can be considered harmless pranks rather than morally repulsive misdeeds. In stark contrast to this, *No Heroics* features superheroes who will not hesitate to use their powers to coax, threaten or coerce averagely gifted people into doing their immoral bidding. They will stop at nothing to get recognition, sex or free goods, as in the case of Electroclash's refusal to help a corner-shop owner who is being robbed unless he promises her a supply of free cigarettes. But while wrongdoers in *No Heroics* know that they are doing wrong and are simply too cynical and jaded to care, the gang in *Misfits* seem to have very little idea of what is right and what is wrong in the first place. Or rather, they seem to inhabit a universe in which such absolute categories simply cannot exist. Admittedly, they are far less opportunistic than the selfish characters presented in *No Heroics*, but all their deeds are deliberated on pragmatically as the situation demands, rather than based on some predefined set of moral rules. This is perhaps best exemplified by their killing of various probation workers, starting with Tony in the pilot episode. However, the morally repulsive act of killing someone and burying their remains is justified by the context in which it takes place in each instance, which allows the "heroes" of *Misfits* to remain protagonists.

Conclusion

Over and over again, these series flaunt their subversion of the superhero genre's conventions, and perform their Britishness in opposition. In time, even the most central features of the superhero genre, despite the fact that some of them are left somewhat intact, thus make new interpretive mappings possible. Famously, Umberto Eco has pointed out one of the defining characteristics of classical superhero tales: their iterative nature, or the fact that after each episode, the classical superhero tale reverts back to the status quo, largely ignoring what has gone before. Characters like Superman (at least in many of their incarnations) happen

> to live in an imaginary universe in which, as opposed to ours, causal chains are not open (A provokes B, B provokes C, C provokes D, etc., *ad infinitum*) but closed (A provokes B, B provokes C, C provokes D, and D provokes A) (Eco, 18–19).

The iterative nature of Eco's classical superhero serial model is evoked in the final scene of the *Misfits* pilot when Curtis Donovan asks his fellow juvenile offenders, "So what happens now? Is this it? We're gonna be like this forever?" To which tough girl Kelly Bailey adds the question, "What if there's lots of people like us all over town?" Again, loudmouth Nathan has the definitive answer to both their questions, informing his immediate interlocutors as well as the television audience that "that kind of thing only happens in America. This will fade away. I'm telling you, by this time next week we'll all be back to the same old boring shit." Nathan's assertion works on several levels, and on some of them it could not be more wrong. His optimistic prediction on the waning of his fellow delinquents' preternatural powers in a week's time is also an extra-diegetic message to the television audience to hold out for the following week's episode. By that time, as characters as well as audience will discover, none of his new friends' powers will have faded away.

However, *Misfits*, too, will embrace the superhero genre's penchant for iterative narratives to a certain extent, at least in the sense that the series will always be about young offenders with superpowers who struggle with their social position but never quite manage to overcome their problems and move up the social ladder. The status quo to which the series invariably reverts is thus not characterized by a restoration of order and an affirmation of conservative value systems. Instead, the protagonists of *Misfits* will indeed "be back to the same old shit," but only in that their lives as superheroes will not free them of their conventional routines and problems. They will still be looked upon and act as working class juvenile offenders, they will not all of a sudden discover an unambiguous morality to adhere to, and they will forever continue to rephrase the question of what it means to be in possession of preternatural powers. In this sense, too, the series prompts its audience to reflect on the superhero genre and its conventions, and to appropriate the series as a British other—simply by putting one of the genre's central conventions into a different context.

However, while the above characteristics of these three TV series and the undermining of the status of the superhero inherent in them will inevitably be seen as typically British in and of themselves, they should not be thought of as culturally insular and cannot ever be considered in isolation from other global phenomena. If anything, what is quintessentially British about these series and their heroes is in fact a reaction—a response to a deliberately simplified perception of the US superhero genre, where heroism is universally admired, heroes have strict moral codes, and where it is not who you are but what you do that matters. That response consists of a perpetual performance of cultural alterity encompassing the constant renegotiation of the role and status of British TV superheroes and their inability to transcend everyday lives full of boring routines, inescapable social stratification and irresolvable moral dilemmas.

Notes

1. For further information on British attitudes toward the superhero, see for example Anja Müller-Wood (2010), Karin Kukkonen (2010), Ben Little (2010), and Jochen Ecke (2013). Chris Murray's (2010) essay "Signals from Airstrip One: The British Invasion of American Mainstream Comics" is equally valuable.

2. For accounts of developments in the USA, see, for example, *Outcault: Die Erfindung des Comic* (2010) by Jens Balzer and Lambert Wiesing, as well as *Of Comics and Men* by Jean-Paul Gabilliet (2010), and Robert C. Harvey's *Children of the Yellow Kid* (1999). British comics history is summed up in James Chapman's *British Comics: A Cultural History* (2012) and Paul Gravett and Peter Stanbury's *Great British Comics* (2006).

3. For further information on DC Thomson properties such as *The Dandy* and *Beano*, see Chapman 2012, 33.

4. Grist is well aware that this view is somewhat reductive, though, especially in light of the fact, as he writes himself, that "many of the most highly regarded writers and artists working for American comics (by which I mean superhero comics) actually come from the British isles" (Grist 2011, 7).

5. To give but one example: Howard Overman, the creator of *Misfits*, notes in an interview that he wanted to create "a very British take on the superhero genre" featuring

"unlikely heroes" who are "more likely to be arrested" than cheered by the general public. He clearly links his concept to class politics, stating that he wanted to do a series about "the middle England attitude towards teenagers . . . and the whole demonization thing and hoodies and antisocial behavior" (Overman "Misfits").

6. See Wright (2001) and Gabilliet (2010) for accounts of the superhero genre during WWII.

7. Only the most dedicated of fans seem aware of such early examples of British superheroes. Fan projects such as the website *internationalhero.co.uk* remain the only available sources that document the characters' existence.

8. This is not to say that they did not actively enjoy Silver Age superhero books; on the contrary, many cite the great influence that, for example, the Marvel books such as *The Fantastic Four* had on them. Famous British comic writer Alan Moore, for example, states that he "became a Marvel zombie" in the 1960s, which "was an enjoyable thing to be up 'til about 1968" (Moore "Guy Lawley and Steve Whitaker," 27). In this respect, it is important to point out that the historical perspective is not germane to British creators. In fact, the Silver Age books were often intensely self-reflexive, incorporating and commenting on the genre's history almost constantly.

9. Drew Pearce, creator of the superhero sitcom *No Heroics*, notes in an interview that he wanted to create "a very British take" on the superhero, with a special emphasis on representing the pedestrian aspects of everyday life, which the genre habitually chooses not to depict: "the funny is in the mundanity for me," Pearce underlines ("Drew Pearce Interview" 2013).

10. The actor portraying Captain Fantastic, David Jason, deserves an honorable mention in the context of British TV superheroes, having gone on to voice Danger Mouse and various other characters in the eponymous animated series of the 1980s and having famously donned a Batman costume in the role of Del Boy in the first of three 1996 Christmas specials of the long running sitcom classic *Only Fools and Horses*.

FIGHTING FOR TRUTH, JUSTICE, AND THE ISLAMIC WAY

The 99, Global Superheroes for the Post-9/11 World

RACHEL MIZSEI-WARD

The 99 are a group of superheroes created by Naif Al-Mutawa from the Teshkeel Media Group with the deliberate intention of reframing the discourse surrounding Islam in the aftermath of 9/11 (Aslam 2011; Fattah 2006; Goyal 2009; Karoub and Moore 2011; Kesting 2007). These superheroes were also intended to create positive role models for children in the Middle East, and to present a version of moderate Islam that stands in opposition to the representations of Islamic fundamentalism more commonly depicted in American popular culture (Al-Mutawa 2009a; Al Mutawa 2010; Broadway 2011; Charlene 2009; Fattah 2006; Goyal 2009; Kesting 2007; Khouri 2010). Although inspired by moderate Islamic theology, the 99 are designed to embody universal values such as strength and compassion (Agon 2012; Goellner 2009; Jayoush 2011; Karoub and Moore 2011; Kesting 2007; Khouri 2010; "The 99 Muslim Animation Series to Be in Around 100 Million American Homes from October," 2012). This chapter will discuss this Kuwaiti superhero franchise and its reception in the United States, particularly the fierce opposition to Islamic superheroes emanating from US-based anti-Islamic bloggers. The central argument of this chapter is that *The 99* is an attempt to communicate about Islamic values with America and Americans using the popular US form of the superhero.

It was this attempt to communicate that was perceived by US bloggers as fundamentally threatening to American values. I will argue that the central drive behind *The 99* was broadly similar to that seen in other US superhero groups, and that many of the issues that the bloggers raised are also highly relevant to US superheroes in general. For example, each superhero in *The 99* comes from a different country, and they embody many different ethnicities to create a global team who work together to help people (Agon 2012; Al-Mutawa 2009b; Charlene 2009; Fattah 2006). The concept of a multi-ethnic, transnational superhero taskforce is nothing new in American comics. The X-Men became multi-ethnic in 1975 with their Kenyan, German, Canadian, and Soviet characters, while *Stormwatch* (1993–) from Wildstorm Comics features a United Nations taskforce made up of international superheroes. However, superheroes in the Middle East are for the most part a recent phenomenon, including Lebanese superhero *Malaak, Angel of Peace* (2007–) and the subject of this chapter, *The 99* (2006–).

Like the majority of American superhero stories, *The 99* has been written with backstories explaining its characters' powers. Naif Al-Mutawa, their creator, derived their superpowers from Islamic theology. The Qur'an describes ninety-nine names and attributes for Allah. Each superhero in *The 99* is based on one of these ninety-nine attributes, and their superhero names are derived from the Arabic used in the Qur'an for the attributes. The superheroes (and supervillains) in *The 99* get their powers from ninety-nine mystical gems called Noor Stones, whose creation is aligned with historical events. The Noor Stones in *The 99* were created during the Siege of Baghdad in 1258, when the great Islamic library Dar al-Hikmah was destroyed by the Mongols. The librarians of Dar al-Hikmah created a magical potion to help save the wisdom contained in the library, and the gems absorbed this knowledge. This origin story for the heroes' superpowers carefully integrates Islamic history, incorporating both the Abbasid Caliphate (now Iraq) and Al-Andalus (now Spain), along with positive representations of Muslims as custodians of wisdom. This is an interesting attempt by members of one culture to communicate to another by using the other's own cultural tropes. Despite the religious elements and use of Islamic history, Islam is not specifically mentioned in *The 99*, and many of the characters are not Muslim and do not come from Islamic countries. This clearly international perspective has helped what began as a localized comic book to expand into a global transmedia franchise that includes translated comics, merchandising, a theme park in Kuwait, a cartoon program, and a film that edits together several episodes of the cartoon program called *The 99 Unbound* (2011). The cartoon is of particular interest, having been successfully distributed in Australia, India, Ireland, the Middle East, Southeast Asia, and Turkey (Topsfield 2011). The funding for the cartoon was provided by Middle Eastern investment companies, including the Islamic Unicorn Investment Bank (Aslam 2011; "Unicorn Joins Teskeel to Fund Comics Publisher" 2006; Coker 2008). Funding from this sharia-compliant bank "implicitly blessed the cartoon" (Coker 2008), and made it acceptable in certain Islamic countries, in particular Saudi Arabia. Unicorn Investment Bank also "has the right of final approval of all content published by Teshkeel" (Aslam 2011).

In terms of production, *The 99* cartoon is aimed at children, being adapted from the comic books using computer-generated animation. Both the cartoon and the comic are surrounded by a discourse of quality, with publicity frequently emphasizing the use of established writers and artists who have worked on well-known Western products, and who are for the most part from the United States, rather than the Middle East (Fattah 2006; Kesting 2007; Coker 2008; Goellner 2009). However, the cartoon has not been globally successful, having been rejected by television stations in the USA and the UK. I will examine the responses to *The 99* by US political bloggers in order to examine the discourses that led to these rejections. Commentary on *The 99* from American political blogs appears to have had a great deal of influence over how the cartoon was received in America. These criticisms from a small number of right-wing American bloggers led Hasbro's cable television station, the Hub, to drop the show from its Autumn 2010 line-up, in part because of concerns that companies would no longer buy advertising slots when the show was on air (Topsfield 2011).[1]

The Politics of Blogging and *The 99's* Islamic Origins

Dissecting the online responses to *The 99* among bloggers requires discourse analysis. Bloggers, and their reaction to *The 99*, are interesting because the bloggers are small in number, but influential. It also means that a blog's output on a particular issue can be easily studied, because blogging tools normally collate all items on the same issue into a single page using tags. In 2005, Dautrich and Barnes found that only 7 percent of the American population read blogs (2005, 9). This low figure gives the impression that blogs should have little impact in setting political agendas, yet their influence comes from their elite readership rather than their numbers. "A key reason [blogs] are important is that journalists and opinion leaders are readers of blogs" (Farrell and Drezner 2008, 17). Dautrich and Barnes's research went on to show that 83 percent of journalists read blogs, and "55% reported that they use[d] them to support the work that they do in writing news" (2005b, 10, and Farrell and Drezner 2008, 23). These figures mean that blogs can and do have a disproportionate effect on the opinions of those who frame national and international debate. Farrell and Drezner argue that

> blogs therefore affect political debate by affecting the content of media reportage and commentary about politics. Just as the media can provide a collective interpretive frame for politicians, blogs can create a menu of interpretive frames for the media to appropriate. (2008, 21)

Bloggers can be from both the right- and left-wings of the political spectrum and may be organized into larger co-operative groups such as the *Daily Kos* or *Huffington Post*. Equally, they can be broadly apolitical and concentrate on specialist subjects such as the environment. Much of the discussion of *The 99* occurred on right-wing blogs, rather than left-wing ones. Interestingly, the left-wing blogs more or less ignored the issue, except to take note of the right-wing commentary. In the case of *The 99*, the contents of blogs were quoted in news stories amplifying the agenda that these bloggers set, which was in turn reflected in the blogs' creating a circle of intensifying and repeating opinion. This repetition was enough to shape debates about *The 99* and affect how it was aired in the USA. It is typical for "blogs [to] interact with each other continuously, linking back and forth, disseminating interesting stories, arguments and points of view" (Farrell and Drezner 2008, 17). This is demonstrated in the blogger debate surrounding *The 99*.

Different right-wing bloggers posted links to each other's articles, ensuring greater readership for one another and fueling the right-wing discussion of *The 99*. This was combined with links to and quotes from these right-wing blogs being published on more moderate blogs, with the aim of demolishing the arguments. The net effect was that the debate was led by the right-wing blogs, with the moderate bloggers starting to respond from a defensive position. These debates have much to tell us about the US right wing's lingering distrust of Muslims, and are made all the more compelling because they swirled around a cartoon text that had yet to be broadcast on US television, forcing the bloggers to move beyond textual analysis and reveal their underlying prejudices. The discussion of *The 99* therefore tells us more about how Muslims are seen by the US right wing than it does about the cartoon.

It is relevant, then, to consider the longstanding stereotypes of Arab characters in Hollywood films, because these affect how Islam is perceived in the West. Although not all Arabs are Muslim, and globally only a fifth of Muslims are in Arab countries, assumptions are frequently made in Hollywood films that the terms "Arab" and "Muslim" are interchangeable. Shaheen argues that in the majority of Hollywood films, "Arabs are brute murderers, sleazy rapists, religious fanatics, oil-rich dimwits, and abusers of women" (2003, 172), while "women in the Arab world are seen as 'bosomy belly dancers' or 'mute and submissive.'" (Marrison 2004) These authors argue that such stereotypes affect how a product such as *The 99*, created in an Arab country with Arab heroes, will be received by political extremists in America. Furthermore, Shaheen suggests that "by and large, every Arab is a terrorist and every Muslim an extremist" (quoted in Curtiss and Hanley 2001). Although extreme, these positions reflect the vitriol with which Arab representations were met in the wake of 9/11. Consequently, I refer to them hereafter to assert the lingering discourses of fear and prejudice found in the writing of right-wing bloggers.

Akbar Ahmed puts forward a similar argument to Shaheen, but applied to Islam, rather than Arab characters:

> Major Hollywood blockbusters . . . have perpetuated an "Islam equals terrorism" image. Films such as these have conditioned the American public to expect the worst from a civilization depicted as "terrorist," "fundamentalist" and "fanatic." (Ahmed 2002, 73)

Shaheen argues that just as American popular culture depicts Arabs as terrorists, it similarly depicts Muslims as terrorists. This is probably an overstatement of a temporary phenomenon in filmmaking that uses Muslim characters as stock villains. Such stock villains change over time and are chosen to match contemporary concerns rather than being a considered piece of deliberate propaganda.

However, using a group as a stock villain can have an impact, particularly when it is used as shorthand for describing a minority group who are easy to identify. It can be argued that part of the reason for the lack of acceptance of *The 99* in America is that Muslim superheroes are uncommon in American comics. Muslim characters that have been introduced to American comic books have not been universally well received. Marvel led the way in 1994 with the female superhero M in *Uncanny X-Men*, and after 9/11 further Muslim superheroes were incorporated into both DC and Marvel line-ups, but these have had limited success. For example, the superheroine Dust was introduced into Marvel's *New X-Men* in 2002. The character is clearly identified as Muslim in the comics, and she occasionally wears traditional niqab dress. Axel Alonso, the editor-in-chief of Marvel, stated the company's position as: "I don't view a Muslim superhero as avant-garde. . . . Muslims comprise approximately 23% of the world's population, and we like our comics to reflect the world in its diversity" (quoted in Karoub and Moore 2011). DC introduced its own Muslim superhero in 2010 to the Batman universe. The character, Bilal Asselah, or Nightrunner, is a French-Algerian free runner who acts as a vigilante in Paris. He is recruited by Bruce Wayne (Batman) to be part of a global Batman franchise, Batman Incorporated, which aims to fight crime across the world (Higgins and McCarthy 2012).

As with *The 99*, the character Nightrunner was poorly received by American conservative bloggers. *Newsweek Pakistan* summarized the reaction:

> When Batman tapped Nightrunner, a French Muslim youth, as his delegate in France, all hell broke loose. Some French and American right-wingers voiced fears that Bruce Wayne, the American billionaire who moonlights as Batman, could be double-crossed and blown up in a suicide attack for trusting the wrong people. Never mind that both characters are fictional. (Aslam 2011)

Newsweek Pakistan suggests that right-wing commentators have made the assumption that Muslims should be automatically assumed to be untrustworthy and that suicide bombing is a typical Muslim activity. The American right-wing blogger Warner Todd Huston complained, "Apparently Batman couldn't find any actual Frenchman to be the 'French savior' (2010), while Avi Green similarly complained, "Bruce Wayne goes to France where he hires not a genuine French boy or girl with a real sense of justice, but rather, an 'oppressed' minority who adheres to the Religion of Peace" (2010). Here the criticisms appear to be that Nightrunner, by being both Muslim and an immigrant, is not authentically French.

However, this is problematic when we consider that Algeria had been under French rule since 1830, and a department of France until 1962. Colonial ties do not end when colonies become independent nations. As a former French colonial state, Algeria continues to have close connections with France. Nightrunner speaks both French and Arabic, and the character describes himself as a French citizen who has lived his entire life in Paris (Higgins and McCarthy 2012). His version of Paris is not that of "the city of light" but rather the areas of low-income housing in *les banlieues*. These aspects of Nightrunner's biography are ignored by the bloggers, who see his religion before his citizenship and assume that as a Muslim he cannot also be French. These examples of American reaction to US-created Muslim superheroes suggest that the reaction to *The 99* that this chapter concentrates on is not anomalous.[2]

Superheroines in Hijab

Myra MacDonald argues that

> the capacity of images of the veiled Muslim female body to provoke intense reactions, both from Muslims and non-Muslims, and to eclipse Muslim women's own diversity of voice and self-definition, raises significant issues for feminist debate. (2006, 7)

For the female characters in *The 99*, questions of women's choice became crucial to blogger reception. Some of the female Muslim characters wear hijab and some do not, suggesting a diversity of practice and viewpoint for the characters. In addition, there are different kinds of hijab depicted, showing that the writers acknowledge significant regional differences in this cultural practice around the world. The use of hijab in the depiction of these female characters caused a lot of discussion among commentators in the blogosphere. The response was strong and often highly critical of the inclusion of these characters.

Since 9/11 the hijab has become one of the most important visual signifiers of Islam. In particular, it is frequently used to frame Western discussions surrounding the human rights of Muslim women. The concept of hijab revolves around ideas of modest dress. However, there are wide regional variations in what is considered to constitute "modest dress," and this can be based on cultural rather than religious norms, as well as personal choice.[3] Abu-Lughod argues, "We must take care not to reduce the diverse situations and attitudes of millions of Muslim women to a single item of clothing" (2002, 786). However, for many bloggers this is precisely what they do, as the hijab is not seen as an item of clothing, but rather as a symbol of women's oppression.

Three of *The 99*'s female superheroes wear different versions of the hijab: Samda the Invulnerable, Mujiba the Responder, and Batina the Hidden. These three characters all come from Islamic countries where the hijab is common. Samda the Invulnerable is an eight-year-old from Libya named Aisha. Her name is particularly significant when considered from an Islamic perspective. Aisha is the name of Muhammad's "most beloved" wife, and a common Islamic name for girls. Further, according to tradition Muhammad married Aisha when she was nine, a child, and similar in age to Samda. Samda is depicted wearing the hijab, or headscarf, and the character's profile on *The 99*'s website states that "she dresses in a stylish hijab *of her own choosing*" (my emphasis). This is important because

11. *The 99* cartoon's depiction of Batina the Hidden, hijabi superheroine from Yemen. Credit: Teshkeel Media Group.

there is frequently a discourse in the West surrounding the hijab that argues for "the reductive interpretation of veiling as the quintessential sign of women's unfreedom" (Abu Lughod 2002, 786). It is interesting that Samda, as an eight year old, may be considered too young to make a choice to wear the hijab, but she is not—apparently—too young to be a superhero. Equally, it must be considered that the hijab that Samda wears is described as "stylish." This moves the hijab on from being simply a utilitarian item of clothing, or a religious signifier, to being also a fashion statement. The second character in hijab is Mujiba the Responder, who is a nineteen-year-old dyslexic geology student from Malaysia named Dayana. However, the most controversial of the women in hijab is Betina the Hidden.

Unlike Samda the Invulnerable and Mujiba the Responder, Betina wears a niqab, which covers not only her hair, but also her face, leaving only her eyes visible (see Figure 11). Betina the Hidden's backstory is underdeveloped, but we do know that she runs a superhero retreat in the Himalayas, and comes from the Yemen. However, this lack of information and her costume fit well with her superpowers, which allow her to blend into the background and become almost invisible. Invisibility is a common power among superhero characters and covers both male and female characters. Examples include the Invisible Man from *The League of Extraordinary Gentlemen*, the Invisible Kid from *Legion of Super-Heroes*, Martian Manhunter from the Justice League of America, and the Invisible Woman from the Fantastic Four. Despite this wide usage of invisibility in comic books, the invisible superheroine remains problematic. The Invisible Woman is frequently sidelined in Fantastic Four narratives, while Betina's invisibility, in combination with her niqab, make her superpower disempowering, allowing her to fade into the background. However, her role at the superhero retreat nuances this. The retreat cares for superheroes who can not control their powers and need help and guidance to return to society. Although seemingly invisible, Betina is performing the essential task of nurturing and caring for her superheroic colleagues. Her invisibility shields them from those who might want to hurt them.

Among the bloggers Andrea Peyser, writing for the *New York Post*, was particularly critical of *The 99* regarding gender and representation. Her blog appears to have shaped the debates surrounding *The 99* cartoon and was frequently quoted in other blogs. These blogs either supported Peyser's Islamaphobic stance (Geller 2011; Seidl 2010), or quoted her in order to create outrage among those who did not support her position (Nolan 2010; Khouri 2010; Schindler 2011; Merica 2011). Peyser wrote:

> Hide your face and grab the kids. Coming soon to a TV in your child's bedroom is a posse of righteous, *Sharia*-compliant Muslim superheroes—including one who fights crime hidden head-to-toe by a burqa. These Islamic butt-kickers are ready to bring truth, justice and indoctrination to impressionable Western minds. (2010)

The central drive of the blog is that any form of information on Islam that is delivered in a popular medium must also be indoctrination.

Peyser quotes from a self-confessed "mom-of-two" in her blog to establish that there is widespread support for her viewpoint. Peyser's own status as a parent is used as a way to show authority and confirm that her opinion is valuable. The quote says:

> I have no problem with Muslim superheroes, but lose the burqa. A female superhero should not wear a symbol of subservience to men. It's also completely impractical when fighting bad guys. (2010)

What is interesting is that this contains two separate arguments. The first is that the burqa is a symbol of subservience to men to Peyser, but as we have noted, this is at best contentious and is more likely to be an issue for the viewer than the authors of *The 99*.

The other side of the argument is that practicality should be part of the superhero outfit. Although there has been a trend towards more realistic superheroes, as typified by Christopher Nolan's Batman trilogy, there is still a disparity between male and female characters' costumes. For example, in *The Dark Knight Rises* (2012), Batman's costume uses body armor and flat boots, while Selina Kyle wears a skin-tight cat-suit with high stiletto heels. However realistic the film or comic book claims to be, the majority of American superheroines are expected to fight crime in tight, revealing clothes and high heels. It seems contradictory to complain about the practicality of a superhero costume that incorporates a burqa when the typical American superheroine's costume is no more practical. It may simply be that the burqa is always considered un-American, unlike superheroine costumes, and the argument of practicality is simply there to justify a position that has already been taken.

Pamela Geller's criticisms of Batina the Hidden follow on from Peyser's comments:

> It is mainstreaming the institutionalized oppression of women under sharia, as exemplified by the burqa-wearing superhero. One would think that the male superheroes would have superpowers strong enough to be able to control themselves without the women having to don cloth coffins. (2011)

This statement expresses a common argument that hijab exists to conceal women's out-of-control sexuality because men cannot be expected to resist it. However, it can be argued that it is in American superhero comics that women's sexuality is depicted as out of control. Superheroines are scantily clad in sexually revealing costumes, with poses that emphasize their breasts and bottoms. This is in stark contrast to the superheroes who, although usually heavily muscled, represent a masculine power fantasy for male readers, rather than an erotic fantasy.

Geller may have a point that some narratives in American comics written for mature audiences suggest that it is the male superheroes who cannot control their lust. For example, the Comedian attempts to rape Sally Jupiter in Alan Moore's *Watchmen* (1986–1987), while in Garth Ennis's *The*

Boys (2006–2012), the superhero group the Seven expects a new superheroine, Starlight, to perform oral sex for temporary membership in the group. Geller is quite incorrect though in this case, where the superheroines of the 99, by comparison to Sally Jupiter or Starlight, are modestly dressed, well-educated, and shown to be vital members of the team and present because of their competence rather than their sexual availability.

The masking of superheroes becomes bound up in these blogs with the idea of hijab being used to "hide" women's identities. The general dislike of Batina the Hidden, and her "burqa" as expressed in these blogs, becomes quite odd when considered in the context of other superhero costumes. Superheroes in comics have a long tradition of being masked to conceal their real identity, starting with the Phantom (see Kevin Patrick's chapter in this collection), and encompassing numerous popular characters such as Batman and Spiderman. This trope can also be seen in pulp era characters such as Zorro and the Shadow. Why has Batina's niqab, which is effectively a mask, become problematic when popular American superheroes Batman and Spiderman cover their faces so they are similarly unrecognizable? In her blog Andrea Pesyer writes:

> Wonder Woman-style cleavage has been banned from the ladies [of *The 99*]. And, in this faith-based cartoon, hair-hiding head scarves are mandatory for five characters, not including burqa babe Batina the Hidden. (2010)

For Geller, "'The veil' becomes an all-encompassing symbol of repression" (MacDonald 2006, 8), and the sexualized American superheroine is by implication preferable to the modestly clad and competent Muslim woman. She also emphasizes the idea that the clothes for the female characters of *The 99* are forced on them ("banned" and "mandatory"), rather than being a reflection of their culture and personal beliefs.

Phyllis Chesler's problem with the superheroines in hijab is that they are unsuitable role models for children:

> We have specifically religious Islamic figures, including face-veiled women, being introduced to our children in the West as alternative heroes and role models. There is something disturbing about this picture. (2010)

However, she does not specify why it is disturbing to see women in hijab represented in children's media. There is also a clear resistance to the concept of Muslim role models, implying that they are unsuitable for Western children. This suggests that Muslims fall into the category of "other," and denies that "alternative role models" may be valuable for those who feel similarly othered. Most of the bloggers do not seem to recognize that only some of the characters in *The 99* are Muslim, and find it difficult to find a place for Muslims in popular media.

The focus on the hijab is interesting in that it emphasizes a small group within the overall female population of *The 99*'s characters. Simply put, not all of the female superheroes in *The 99* wear hijab. Part of this reflects the global nature of the characters. Not all the characters are Muslims, nor do they all come from countries where hijab is habitually practiced. For example, Wijad the Loving from the Philippines, Mumita the Destroyer from Portugal, and Hadya the Guide who lives in London but originates from Pakistan, do not wear hijab. Of these characters that do not wear hijab, Noora the Light's lack of hijab is represented as a deliberate statement and as an intentional choice made by the character. Noora is an eighteen-year-old university student called Dana from the United Arab Emirates. In the United Arab Emirates hijab is prevalent, so it is fair to expect that Noora might choose to wear hijab. Noora discovers her Noor Stone while being held captive by kidnappers, in a similar manner to Iron Man, and uses it to escape when her father will not pay the ransom. After her superpowered escape and subsequent invitation to join the 99, Noora has to convince her father that superheroism is a valid path. In choosing not to analyze Noora, the bloggers purposefully overstate the significance of hijab-wearing superheroines in *The 99*.

In *The 99* the hijab is presented as a choice that the characters make on an individual level; some choose to wear hijab for cultural or personal reasons and some do not. What is important is that the choice of dress is considered by the creators of *The 99*, and this varied depiction of female characters represents part of the attempt to communicate the Middle East and its various sorts of identity to the readers. Even though the comic is Islamic, there is no emphasis on the religious implications or otherwise of the hijab. Instead these depictions act to complicate the way that Islamic women are understood, and the potential feminist stance of women choosing to define who they are, on their own terms. However, all these varied images of womanhood are automatically combined by the American right-wing bloggers with already circulating negative representations of Islamic women. This is also the case for sharia law, which I will consider in relation to how its negative perception in America affected US reception of *The 99*.

Sharia Superheroes

Sharia, like the hijab, is one of the most divisive aspects of contemporary Islamic practice. It is the term for Islamic law derived from the Qur'an and a book called the Sunna, which compiles a series of quotes and actions of Muhammad. It is a form of traditional religious law that is interpreted in different ways by Islamic scholars according to religious school, local culture, and tradition (Mallat 2012). The connection between *The 99* and sharia is mentioned by a few right-wing bloggers as being an important reason to reject the cartoon program. However, some more moderate bloggers perceive *The 99*'s connection to sharia as something that can be compared to the religious background of America's Golden Age superheroes.

The funding for *The 99* is provided by a sharia-compliant investment bank which looks for religiously acceptable opportunities in which to invest. Although this funding has been beneficial for *The 99*, contributing towards further product development and expansion in new territories, it has been perceived negatively by some bloggers. For example, Pamela Geller argued that

> a sharia board approved *The 99*, and sharia in all its mainstream and traditional forms calls for the subjugation of non-Muslims and the denial of basic rights to them under the rule of Islamic law. I don't consider that an acceptable level of "moderation" or "toleration." (2011)

For Geller the connection to sharia makes *The 99* unacceptable because of her perception of what sharia law must mean. This denies (or Geller is unaware of) the vast differences in interpretation that occur across different Islamic countries and different sects of Islam regarding sharia law.

While Geller is arguing against a version of Islam, and sharia, that is intolerant and curtails human rights, Peyser puts forward a view that suggests sharia is an insidious danger to children:

> They're taking advantage of the fact that in every middle-class household, Mom and Dad are working their asses off. . . . They know the kids are watching TV or on the Internet. So maybe sharia becomes OK. It's a game. It gradually becomes more and more in their lives. (2010)

Here sharia is something children need to be protected from. This quote suggests a particular way that children's television is being viewed—by children on their own, without any input from their parents who are busy working. Peyser's narrative appears to be that cunning Muslims are taking advantage of this situation to force an Islamic agenda on children who do not know any better.

More moderate websites were able to see similarities between *The 99* and established American superheroes. Both Khouri on *Comics Alliance* and Karoub and Moore on *Huffington Post* note that the superheroes in *The 99* have very similar ethical backgrounds to superheroes like Superman and Batman:

> *The 99's* connection to Islamic law seems tenuous at best. The reality is that Superman himself operates in a way that would be very agreeable by most mainstream interpretations of sharia, and it is with pronounced irony that conservative Americans, particularly those in favor of living life like we're all Boy Scouts, react so hatefully towards Muslims, who are truly their allies in this regard. (Khouri 2010)

Khouri argues that the conservative nature of *The 99* should make it popular with conservative America because there are more similarities than differences in their politics. Here the position of the right-wing bloggers is being challenged by the liberal press, who suggest that US cultural conservatives have much in common with their Muslim counterparts. Similarly, Karoub and Moore argue:

> Basically, *The 99* is based on Quranic archetypes, the same way that Batman and Superman are based on Judeo-Christian and Biblical archetypes. And just like Batman and Superman are secular story lines, so too are the 99. (2011)

The stories of Superman and *The 99* being secular rather than religious is significant in this quotation. Karoub and Moore attest that *The 99* does not argue for a particular set of religious laws, rather the central narrative remains the traditional superhero desire to help those in trouble and provide a role model towards good behavior. It is interesting to note that the bloggers were arguing against values that are traditionally those of the most iconic American characters—that of being good citizens—while at the same time presenting the argument that they were attempting to defend those values. While the right-wing bloggers are writing in opposition to sharia, they are ironically also criticizing many of the ideological traits at the heart of popular US superheroes.

Bloggers as the New Supervillains

The creator of *The 99*, Naif Al-Mutawa, gave several interviews about the effect bloggers had on *The 99*, in particular the way that the show had been dropped by Hasbro. For example, Isaac Solotaroff, the director of a documentary about Al-Mutawa and *The 99*, *Wham! Bam! Islam* (2011), "said he attended a planning meeting with the Hub in March and said he has no doubt that blog pressure has delayed U.S. distribution" (Schroeder 2011). Al-Mutawa has also noted that "one of the comments on the blogs that ended up delaying us was someone who warned that we can't let the Muslims brainwash our children like the Mexicans did with `Dora the Explorer.'" (Karoub and Moore 2011) This idea that *The 99* cartoon show would brainwash children has been explored in this chapter's quotations from right-wing blogs.

However, the concern over the Latina character *Dora the Explorer* further reflects right-wing concerns over demographic change in America. Demographic projections suggest that by 2050 Hispanics will make up 29 percent of the American population, while white people will be shifting towards minority status at 47 percent of the population (Passel and Cohn 2008). Even *The 99*'s director, therefore, claims that race is a major concern for white right-wing groups, and that the cultural and ethnic differences implied by *Dora the Explorer* and *The 99* are problematic for them. The positive portrayal of Latino and Middle Eastern characters is a problem for American right-wing blogs; any kind of otherness of race, religion, or political thinking is considered inherently un-American. All of this is despite these groups being long present parts of the American "melting pot." Al-Mutawa "see[s this reaction] as an illustration of this country's deep ambivalence—and sometimes suspicion or outright hostility—to Islam" (Schroeder 2011). This hostility to Islam is further demonstrated in the reaction to Barack Obama's Presidential Summit on Entrepreneurship.

In April 2010 Barack Obama referenced Naif Al-Mutawa and *The 99* in his speech at the Presidential Summit on Entrepreneurship. Obama stated, "His comic books have captured the imagination of so many young people with superheroes who embody the teachings and tolerance of Islam" (*President Obama Gives Naif Al-Mutawa and THE 99 A Shout Out* 2010). Although this was positive recognition from the American President, it appears to have had negative consequences for both Obama and Naif Al-Mutawa. Al-Mutawa discusses this in the British edition of the technology magazine *Wired*:

> Bloggers labelled us "Obama's Trojan horse" that had been created to teach sharia law to America's children. With the help of the accelerant of lies, the new "truth" of *The 99* spread like wildfire among the anti-Obama and Islamophobic blogs, none having seen so much as a frame of the animation they were vilifying. It didn't matter that the world recognised our great potential. All that mattered was that I was a Muslim and the president liked what we were doing. A handful of people used threats and lies to delay the broadcast of *The 99* in America. (2012)

For *The 99* Obama's support was a disadvantage, because those who disliked Obama were frequently also Islamaphobic. However, what is most significant is that these right-wing gatekeepers wielded power sufficient to shape the spectrum of US discourse at this time, connecting Islamophobic fears across the board: from an animated TV show to the country's President.

The 99 had become caught up in a wider political smear campaign taking place in 2010, when there was growing confusion among Americans over Obama's religion, with 18 percent believing he was a Muslim, a statistic that increased to 34 percent among conservative Republicans (Pew Research Center 2010). Obama's support of projects such as *The 99* was seen by some as just one more piece of evidence that Obama was a Muslim. For the right-wing blogs, therefore, the support of President Obama for *The 99* was evidence that *The 99* was inherently un-American, because President Obama was inherently un-American. In this respect, at least, in the radical political echo chamber of right-wing blogs, a view that would normally be considered extremist outside of the Internet became normalized. *The 99*, consequently, was not just denied traditional television broadcasting because of its own content, but also because it became associated with a wider debate of racial intolerance circulating in the USA at the time.

Conclusion

In examining the right-wing criticism of *The 99*, it is clear that there was a broad range of responses to the cartoon, and also to the issues raised by the right-wing bloggers. For the most part, the left-wing blogs were broadly accepting or neutral about the cartoon, while critical of the right-wing bloggers. This was part of a cycle of feedback between the two groups, in which *The 99* caused a lot of controversy among American right-wing bloggers, and then left-wing bloggers criticized the controversy, but not the cartoon. The right-wing bloggers' distress over a children's cartoon suggests that *The 99* was, to an extent, successful at highlighting the lack of balanced representation of Islamic cultures on American television. Although these bloggers were a small group of individuals, US broadcasters were sensitive to their criticisms and caved under their pressure. The right-wing bloggers were broadly successful in their aim of censoring the cartoon; their impassioned response meant that the television program was not aired in the USA until 2012, and even then it was on Netflix rather than a traditional television station. This was then only a temporary victory for the right-wing bloggers, and it did not affect the cartoon's reception in other English speaking countries. Initially, however, these bloggers were quite successful in agitating against the cartoon. This is particularly important as despite their criticisms of the "Islamic" content, these bloggers were commenting on the program without ever having seen an episode.

The right-wing response to *The 99* may be an aberration. Since *The 99* controversy another Islamic superhero cartoon, *Burka Avenger*,[4] has been released without significant discussion from American bloggers. This is despite the fact that the cartoon is made in Pakistan and features a titular character who is both Muslim and wears a burka as her superhero costume. Instead, the character's costume has been criticized by Western-educated Pakistanis who feel that the burka "cannot be used as a tool of empowerment" (Ehrlich 2013). The creator of the cartoon, Haroon, rejects this, arguing, "She wears a burka not because she is oppressed, she wears it because she chooses it to hide her identity the way superheroes do" (quoted in Saeed 2013). The other side to this is that in the scenes set during the character's daily life, Jiya (the Burka Avenger) wears a shalwar kameez, not a burka, and does not cover her hair. Just as in *The 99*, the importance of education is highlighted. Jiya works as a teacher in a girls' school and uses books and pens as weapons when acting as the Burka Avenger.[5] Her villainous opponents are a Taliban leader and a corrupt local official who in the first episode try to shut down the girls' school where she works. The cartoon was shown in the summer of 2013 in Pakistan and attempts are being made by Bollywood studios to option the intellectual property for a live-action film ("'Burka Avenger' May Get a Bollywood Remake" 2013). The lack of interest from right-wing bloggers suggests that they may have moved on from their concerns about Islam, prevalent in 2010 and 2011, to other worries. In addition, although the show has a wide Internet and smart-phone presence, it has only been aired in Pakistan and has not yet tried to penetrate the US market.

As this chapter has demonstrated, blogs can affect public debate around popular entertainment. The attempt by Teshkeel Media to distribute *The 99* in USA has been the problem for the bloggers rather than the existence of the show. This was further compounded by the show's depiction of a variety of different representations of Muslim women. Finally, it should also be noted that, despite the right-wing bloggers' concerns over the hijab and sharia law, *The 99* is politically and culturally conservative. As Khouri states, "From all appearances, *The 99* is about as subversive as baseball and mom's apple pie" (2010). This makes *The 99* similar to popular US superheroes such as the Avengers, Batman, and Superman.

As a product, Naif Al-Mutawa intended *The 99* to have global appeal, which would advance a set of positive role models, particularly of women, for viewing children. At the same time, *The 99* was created to advance an alternative view of Islam to counteract the discourse of Muslims, and particularly Arabs, as terrorists after 9/11. Part of this alternative view was to show the clothing and customs of the Middle East in a positive light. *The 99* represents an attempt by the Middle East to communicate the idea that Muslims and Arabs are good citizens of the world using forms and language that are derived from the American superhero. Responses to this attempted communiqué show how potentially successful it was as right-wing bloggers fought to resist its messages. Significantly, the criticisms of American bloggers have not stopped the spread of *The 99* brand in other territories. In 2011 the comic book had a global circulation of one million copies, while the brand makes most of its profits through merchandising that puts the characters on back-to-school bags and lunchboxes (Aslam 2011). As it finally reaches America via Netflix, *The 99* continues in its attempt to emulate the success of America's global superhero brands.

Notes

1. The first season of *The 99* was finally aired in America in Autumn 2012 on Netflix.

2. There are further examples of Muslim characters in specialist comic imprints, including the mature lines Vertigo and Wildstorm, both of which are owned by DC Comics. Examples include Aisha, a violent female character from Afghanistan in *The Losers* (2003–2006) and Habib Ben Hassan, the Doctor, a superhero from *The Authority* (1999–) whose origins are as a Palestinian suicide bomber. A film adaptation of *The Losers* in 2010 changed the character of Aisha radically, making the character American with South American roots, and omitting her religion completely. Much of the character's violence was removed to make the film more "PG-13 friendly" (Marshall 2010). However it is not clear why her religion was ignored. Specialist comics imprints

can publish a greater variety of Muslim characters; however, both *The Losers* and *The Authority* have limited audiences, and little effect on the content of mainstream titles.

3. It is important to note that ideas about modest dress and the covering of women's hair are not unique to Islam. For example, orthodox Jewish communities practice *tzniut* which requires modest dress and hair covering for women.

4. http://www.burkaavenger.com/

5. It is interesting to note that the Pakistani teenager Malala Yousafzai, who was shot by the Taliban for campaigning for girls' education, said "Pens and books are the weapons that defeat terrorism," in her speech at the opening of a new library in Birmingham ("Malala Yousafzai Opens New Birmingham Library" 2013).

THE CONTEMPORARY INCARNATION OF THAI SUPERHERO *INSEE DAENG*

A Divided Figure in a Divided Nation

MARY J. AINSLIE

Since its rapid growth from 1997 onwards, with the success of such films as *2499 Antapan Krong Muang* (*Daeng Birley and the Young Gangsters*, 1997) and *Nang Nak* (1999), contemporary Thai film has continued to thrive as popular entertainment in both urban and rural areas. In the guise of epic heritage productions, popular romance dramas, slapstick comedies, and ever-popular horror films, New Thai cinema[1] promoted a hegemonic unifying vision of the nation that neatly side-stepped the growing internal strife of a period when Thailand's decades of economic growth had imploded in the Asian economic crisis of 1997. Amidst this turmoil of shattered dreams, abandoned half-built skyscrapers, and a plunging stock market, many Thai productions not surprisingly offered a nostalgic depiction of the nation and its people that championed abstract notions such as tradition and conformity. Such nationalistic representations included the affirmation of a pure and traditional "Thainess" through delving into and representing pre-modern history and particularly the monarchy (*Suriyothai*, 2001; *Tawipob/The Siam Renaissance*, 2004), nationalistic conflicts against Thailand's immediate neighbors (*Bang Rajan*, 2000), the figure of the hardworking rural peasant as a bastion of national purity, and the creation of an "other" onto which to project the negative qualities that must run counter to this notion of "Thainess" (*Zee-Oui* 2004 and *Laa-Thaa-Phii/Ghost Game*, 2006).

Marshaling such discourses, this chapter will conduct a critical analysis of the 2010 Thai superhero film *Insee Daeng* (*The Red Eagle*), which was the remake and re-launch of a series of 1960s films built around this character. The film depicts a superhero figure fighting corrupt government officials and their shadowy underworld in 2013 Bangkok. Through close textual analysis of the film itself, plus an overview of the wider context in which it was produced and released, it will indicate that, while the film and the reincarnation of its central figure appears very much in keeping with the conservative ideological agenda of New Thai cinema, the "extreme" nature of its central figure and its depiction of Bangkok can be considered quite progressive in its attitudes and approaches during a very divided period of political turmoil.

The Contemporary "New Thai" Superhero

In the contemporary context, institutions are pulled between the competing forces of hierarchical and unequal contemporary Thailand, with its radical social, ethnic, and cultural divisions. While cities such as Bangkok have grown enormously and spectacularly since the 1980s boom, life in the outer provinces and the villages within them remains vastly different, as rice farming continues to be a main source of income and village life is radically different from that of urban Bangkokian elites. To add to this social inequality, contemporary Thailand has also been increasingly divided by political turmoil, a state that arguably began with the removal of the democratically elected Prime Minister Thaksin Shinawatra in a bloodless military coup in September 2006 and was followed by a refusal to hold democratic elections for several years after.

A millionaire media mogul and entrepreneur, Thaksin's enormous popularity came from policies that directly targeted the rural poor. As a relatively new figure who was apart from traditional aristocratic Thai elites, Thaksin was arguably the first political figure to realize this potential vote and tap into the disgruntled and ignored lower classes, who were suffering from Thailand's economic crisis in 1997. This control over and access to Thailand's resources and his monopoly over electoral odds threatened older royalist elites and the opposition Democrat Party. Various street demonstrations called for the forcible removal of Thaksin by the monarchy and eventually the military staged a coup in September 2006 and the courts "dissolved TRT and barred over 100 of its leaders from politics" (Glassman 2010, 767). The Democrat party therefore formed a government in 2008 without winning any elections (768). The Red Shirt movement[2] (a street movement that is largely associated with poorer provincial areas and lower class workers) was formed as a response to this and, at times, its actions have been unfocused and violent. Their demands are also unclear, and at times seem to represent little beyond an attempt to bring down the government and an anger at the vast inequality experienced by provincial (particularly Northeastern) Thais. Likewise the oppositional Yellow Shirts who demonstrated against Thaksin (who are associated with urban Bangkokian middle class Thais) have also called several demonstrations and occupations and have clashed with the Red Shirts, resulting in deaths on both sides and widespread destruction.

In the midst of the turmoil and confusion caused by such extreme social divisions, any close analysis of Thai film serves to indicate the many diverse political, social, and economic forces that entertainment products are pulled between in the vastly differing and diverse nation of contemporary Thailand. While big-budget lavish productions work to uphold urban hegemony and elite discourses of conformity, others embrace lower class provincial village life, mobilizing the staple visceral tropes of slapstick comedy, toilet humor, and even (at times) fairly graphic horror.

Close analysis of the superhero figure within such texts offers an indication of the immense flexibility of such a figure in the New Thai industry. The righteous individualistic hero is a character that appears to pepper contemporary New Thai productions, and these many diverse incarnations indicate a figure able to both uphold and challenge the conservative hegemony of contemporary Thai nationalism and its elite-sponsored agenda. Films such as *Ong-Bak* (2003), *Khon Fai Bin* (*Dynamite Warrior*, 2006), *Chocolate* (2008), *Ma Noot Lhek Lai* (*Mercury Man*, 2006), and *Khun Krabii Hiiroh* (*Sars Wars*, 2004) all deploy heroic figures who adhere to all the hallmarks of a superhero (or, rarely, heroine, in the case of *Chocolate*) and display the familiar characteristics of an outsider and/or emotionally distant figure who enters a community, resolves its conflicts, and restores the status quo (Ndalianis 2007, 3) through the familiar traits of preternatural physical prowess, fantastical acrobatic sequences, and other super-human abilities.

Certainly, it is the high-grossing *Ong-Bak* franchise that seems to most successfully deploy such a figure in the resolute Muay Thai boxing hero Ting. In keeping with the conservative agenda of an industry that rose out of the ashes of the economic crisis, Ting serves to champion nationalistic notions of "Thainess" in the face of perceived outside threats, so giving substance to the ideological myths that permeate contemporary Thai society at this moment (Ndalianis 2007, 3). In this case, the "Society," of which the skilled yet modest Ting is a part, is clearly marked as the innocent upcountry way of life and its simplistic peasant villagers. When their tranquility is threatened by the encroaching gang-warfare of money-grabbing

Bangkokian crime-lords, who steal and then attempt to trade their sacred statue, Ting becomes a symbol of traditional "Thainess" in his commitment to both retrieve the statue for the village and his refusal to entertain any financial or other material rewards for doing so. Indeed, Ting displays this superhero quality of "implicit goodness" in his selfless protection of society and vulnerable individuals without any personal benefit (Peaslee 2007, 38). Journeying to the center of the metropolis and his Westernized friends (who have changed their names and renounced all connection to the traditional village), he must remind urban Thailand (now full of foreigners and crime-lords) of its true nature through his commitment to his village's cause and his super-human prowess at Muay-Thai boxing.

While such a narrative may at first appear to champion lower class rural Thailand through its superhero character and story that sees him triumph over the corruption of rich urban Bangkok, Ting's depiction and his actions rather marks an adherence to the conservative and nationalist ideology of "localism," a discourse propagated by elites after the economic crisis.[3] Despite its supposed championing of the neglected rural poor and their unfair treatment under the previous capitalist expansion, Kevin Hewison (1999) criticizes such a response as a profoundly conservative and reactionary discourse that does not tackle the unfair and growing gap between rich and poor in Thailand. Instead he regards it as "negative, reactionary, and a dangerous mix of populism and nationalism" (Hewison 1999, 11) which idealizes the rural scenario while simultaneously ignoring and denying the exploitive nature of such conservative and patriarchal hierarchies that feed into profoundly right-wing discourses of "nationalism and chauvinism" (12). While initially appearing to challenge injustice and criminality, the selfless nature of the heroic character Ting is in fact an attempt to preserve an unfair and unequal society, one that does not challenge the living conditions of rural peasant Thailand but rather preserves it as something noble and desirable, particularly through his refusal to be seduced by the trappings of urban modernity.

However, not all New Thai heroes adhere to such a conservative ideological position. Rather than seeking to uphold the unfair and unequal status-quo, other superheroes appear to celebrate this lower class context and even rejoice in the chaotic diversity the country now finds itself in, indicating that the superhero figure in New Thai cinema is one that can potentially cross the various ethnic, linguistic and economic divisions with which the nation grapples. Mobilizing the staple lower class entertainment traits such as slapstick comedy and toilet humor, films such *Khon Fai Bin* (*Dynamite Warrior*, 2006) and *Khun Krabii Hiiroh* (*Sars Wars*, 2004) become much more complex in their superhero's relationship to the nationalist and elite discourses of New Thai cinema. In *Khon Fai Bin*, the central character Siang is a Robin Hood-type figure in the Northeast[4] who protects rural farmers from local elites who try to kill their buffalos in order to force them to buy tractors. While he is arguably again protecting the villagers from "progress" and exploitation, unlike Ting his celebration of (and situation within) the myths, legends and cultural practices of the Northeastern Thai region (known as Isaan) becomes an engagement from within this dynamic community and context rather than a passive depiction of its supposed "purity" and innocent spirituality. The masked Siang rides to the rescue on a rocket and fights among the silk looms of Isaan, mobilizing a *mise-en-scene* familiar to the marginalized Northeast and its cultural festivals and myths. Likewise, the many slapstick sequences coupled with evil wizards and the hero impossibly flying to the attack on rockets ensure that this film and its central figure begins to have much in common with the visceral nature of films enjoyed by lower class Thai viewers in previous decades and indeed becomes possibly the most socially progressive of these superhero incarnations.

Insee Daeng: A Superhero for the Lower Classes?

It is in light of such depictions that we must consider the recent superhero film *Insee Daeng* (*The Red Eagle*). The 2010 *Insee Daeng* film and its central figure are a significant text in the contemporary Thai industry for a number of reasons. These include its close relationship to recent political events as well as its unusual status as an adaptation of a superhero figure from previous decades of Thai film, both elements that offer an interesting case study as to how diverse social developments can affect the incarnation of the superhero figure. The film seems to follow similar conservative discourses to those found in *Ong-Bak* and, similarly, it also, at first glance, initially appears to offer a damning indictment of Thai elites through the emphasis placed on the damage caused to Thai society by rabid corruption among authority figures. However, close reading indicates that the film becomes far more complex than these nationalist discourses, and when we take into account its politically and stylistically progressive director as well as its depiction of Thailand, a much more intricate message soon becomes apparent, one that raises far more questions than answers.

This 2010 production was originally one of the most anticipated Thai films of the decade. It was director Wisit Sasanatieng's first film for four years and was an eagerly awaited addition from the filmmaker who had previously made the highly regarded *Fa Thalai Chon* (*Tears of the Black Tiger*, 2000), *Mah Nakorn* (*Citizen Dog*, 2004) and *Ben Choo Gap Phii* (*The Unseeable*, 2006) as well as had involvement in the previously mentioned *Nang Nak* and *Daeng Birley*, both of which were significant texts in kick-starting the contemporary New Thai industry. The choice of Wisit as the director to potentially resurrect what had been a major franchise and very successful series of films in the postwar era of Thai film (and a figure who was still a very recognizable superhero) was bold and inventive and publicity was correspondingly significant. The film tells the story of a vigilante former soldier called Rom who disguises himself as a figure known as Insee Daeng (Red Eagle) and is killing the crime lords and corrupt politicians of Bangkok. It begins in 2010 Bangkok, with a party leader and NGO activist standing for election by campaigning against corruption and against the building of a nuclear power plant in Chumphon province that will damage the livelihoods of the local town and its fishermen. The film moves forward to the near-future of 2013 and illustrates how the now-elected Prime Minister has gone back on his promises and given permission for the nuclear power station to be built on a beach in Chumphon. What is more he is now ordering government forces to attack and demoralize the demonstrators and is revealed to be a member of the sinister crime syndicate, the Matulee, whose members Insee Daeng is trying to destroy.

Similarly to *Ong-Bak* and the New Thai discourses, *Insee Daeng*'s superhero figure also seems to function as a conservative defender of traditional Thai "values," but one that could not be more different from the Muay-Thai village boy Ting and his provincial background. The sword-fighting, gun-wielding Insee Daeng is a superhero in the tradition of the gadget-wielding stoic billionaire Bruce Wayne/Batman, and one who also appears to have much in common with the latest brooding Christopher Nolan incarnation. While not appearing to possess actual supernatural qualities like Spider-Man or Superman, the 2010 incarnation of Insee Daeng is nevertheless a masked crime-fighter with an impressive array of weapons, a formidable motorbike, unmatched prowess with a sword and a shadowy past that constantly returns to torture him both mentally and physically. Bangkok, meanwhile, is a Gotham-inspired, shadowy world of corruption and extreme violence where gangs of shooters destroy property and kill innocents, one that is controlled by a mysterious masked order of gangsters and politicians known as the Matulee.

While notions of traditional "Thainess" do not appear to take precedence in this limited metallic palette and its urban *mise-en-scene*, there is still a clear narrative that depicts a rural way of life being threatened by the dreaded "progress" of modernity, a theme that initially places the text and its hero firmly within the discourse of *Ong-Bak* and the New Thai industry. The modern world and its "progress" is represented by illegal drugs, nuclear power stations and corrupt politicians pandering to foreign business interests at the expense of Thai workers. The film's narrative for instance, follows a group of workers in Chumphon who, together with a Non-Governmental Organization (NGO), are attempting to block plans to build a nuclear power station. While they have ensured the election of a former NGO activist Direk Damrongpapra as Prime Minister, he has now abandoned them to side with foreign interests and states that the provinces must make sacrifices for the good of the nation. One particularly memorable scene involves a long shot of an idyllic beach that is now destroyed by a nuclear power station built with assistance from the corrupt Prime Minister. A fisherman who opposed it is later beaten to death by a group of thugs for stalling progress. Again, in a similar way to the localism of *Ong-Bak*, modern ways are not wanted and are depicted as un-Thai.

However, while such a depiction in *Insee Daeng* does appear open to the localist aesthetic that runs through *Ong-Bak*, this depiction does not entirely adhere to the idealized Thailand of such contemporary productions. Further analysis indicates that the film and its superhero figure may not be as simplistic as they immediately appear. Indeed, the depiction of Thailand in the film indicates a significant level of internal critique that implicates politicians, organized crime and foreign investors in a vast conspiracy to exploit provincial Thailand and the lower-classes. In the scenes set in 2013, Direk has rejected the masses who voted for him and Chumphon and its people are now irreparably damaged. Pictures depict him shaking hands with Barack Obama and he is quick to capitulate to American business interests, with one foreign investor revealing that they actually financed his election campaign so that he would remain controlled by their interests. After investors dictate their agenda, flashback scenes accompanied by soft piano music follow and Direk is depicted before his election in the middle of the people, protesting with them with his fiancée by his side.

This is a major difference to the depiction of "Thainess" in *Ong-Bak*, where the village is represented as a passive, sparsely populated, simplistic scenario rather than through the collective action of angry workers with placards. Direk's speech to his former girlfriend Wassana however indicates that for all his marching he has now sold out the lower classes. The rural provinces must work to feed urban Bangkok, demonstrating a clear exploitation of rural areas. When Wassana argues that the poor have been forced to make too many sacrifices (she mentioned dams and mines) and reminds him of his promises, he simply states that he is a politician, perhaps implying that it is in the very nature of Thai politicians to lie and cheat, whatever their previous activist credentials.

The Absence of Idealized "Thainess"?

While this depiction of urban Bangkok as inherently corrupt and exploitive may seem to have much in common with the conservative discourses of the New Thai industry, the film nevertheless appears to reject Hewison's corresponding localist discourses in its depiction of Thailand and "Thainess" itself. Instead, the "extreme" nature of the text appears to offer a critique of the conservative depictions common in the New Thai industry. There is no idealized image of simplistic rural Thailand that we see in *Nang Nak* or *Ong-Bak*. While *Insee Daeng* may be clear about what is undesirable and ultimately not "Thai," it appears much more unclear about what actually does constitute "Thainess." Far from the conservative unity that is suggested as a solution in *Ong-Bak*, in the dystopian world of *Insee Daeng* Thailand is fragmented and bleak: there is no form of unity and community has been utterly destroyed. Few characters express any concern for their country or fellow citizens and indeed they kill and exploit almost to a random degree. While its emphasis on spectacle over narrative as a source of stimulation may certainly be in keeping with the history of the Thai film form, such "numbers" are nevertheless instances of extreme violence (rather than the narratively meaningless slapstick comedy or drawn-out romantic sequences that are so familiar in Thai film). In one scene the heroine is attacked by a group of punk-looking motorcyclists for little reason other than fun.

In the world of *Insee Daeng*, therefore, Thailand hardly seems worth defending: the staple depictions of idealized rural poverty or the aristocratic spiritual Buddhist realm and its monarch are absent. Instead a chaotic, corrupt and thoroughly barbaric world now reigns. Its extreme depiction of 2013 Bangkok is a dystopian neo-noir metallic cityscape of violent crime, drug deals, murders, police sirens screaming down streets and heavy *chiaroscuro*, a society in which, as one "expert" states in the opening, no one is doing anything good. The rolling hills and luscious paddy fields of rural Thailand are absent, as are the idyllic beaches and playful elephants that pepper both internal and external representations of Thailand. Instead, the film's opening is a sequence of unattractive mobile low angle shots that depict generic and uninspiring skyscrapers and office blocks beneath overcast clouds, with an extremely limited, almost monochromatic, grey palette.

Insee Daeng's style is correspondingly high concept and owes much to director Wisit Sasanatieng's unique approach to filmmaking. The film's action sequences are deliberately excessive to the extent that they quickly drift into the fantastical realm and become a deliberate homage to the excessive and histrionic film style of earlier eras of Thai cinema, particularly the immediate postwar era of filmmaking when (for various economic, political and industrial reasons) Thai filmmakers used silent 16mm film with live dubbers to great success. This is something that Wisit also embraced in his previous productions such as *Fa Thalai Chon* and *Mah Nakorn*, both of which achieved great success on international festival screens.

Along with such internal historical references, the highly stylized and limited yet saturated palette also appears to reference various globally prominent texts, including various Bond films and nods to *Blade Runner* (1982) and comic book/graphic novel adaptations such as *Sin City* (2005), *Watchmen* (2009) and *V for Vendetta* (2005). Indeed, *Insee Daeng* is a highly stylized action-packed and incredibly violent film, and one that seems very obviously constructed with its possible export in mind. As the prominent Thai cinema blogger Wise Kwai states, it is "perhaps the most Hollywood-like movie yet made by the Thai film industry" (2010). The title sequence is a James Bond-esque opening with slow-moving extreme close up shots of Insee Daeng's infamous red mask, set to a brooding dark soundtrack in a minor key that is similar to "typical" Bond themes such as *Tomorrow Never Dies* or *Golden Eye*. Throughout the film the cinematography and editing too is a collage of short takes and fast moving mobile cameras, with the criminals, police and ultimately the viewer unable to catch the lightning-fast superhero in their gaze. One sequence, a fight between Insee Daeng and the Matulee's Darth Maul-esque Black Devil, lasts for almost a full fifteen minutes and takes place on rooftops, on top of a giant screen on a skyscraper, in a department store and in a lift shaft, with Black Devil continuing to emerge yet again after every apparent defeat.

An "Extreme" Superhero

Within this nihilistic, detached domain, Insee Daeng himself is a correspondingly aloof and monosyllabic hero. In such a damaged world of extreme violence and corruption, the film seems to suggest that only a similarly damaged individual may offer a solution, indeed, the beginning comments from "experts" on Thai TV state that Thai society is in need of a true hero who can solve this crisis. They mention that heroes have already come along (a clear reference to the campaigner Direk as a former champion of the people before he became Prime Minister) but have turned out to be crooks.

The message here is rather more complex than that embodied by heroes such as Ting and Siang, and the figure of Insee Daeng begins to invite much closer scrutiny as a contemporary Thai text. Previous superhero figures and their texts adhere to Ndalianis's statement on standard superhero characteristics that

> occupying a space outside culture, the super/hero often serves the function of mediator figure that enters the community in crisis with the aim of resolving its conflicts and restoring the *status quo*. (2007, 3)

However, the "status quo" in *Insee Daeng* is one of extreme corruption and violence in which everything is controlled by the Matulee, a situation that is not desirable or worth preserving. If, as Ndalianis states, "The super/hero is a concrete manifestation of an abstract concept that speaks of the struggle of civilization to survive and maintain order in a world that threatens to be overcome with chaos" (2007, 3), then Rom/Insee Daeng appears to be seeking the very destruction of this world, as it has descended too far into chaos and seems to be beyond rescuing.

In this way, Rom and his alter ego *Insee Daeng* appears to take much inspiration from Christopher Nolan's recent incarnation of Batman. However, while these texts are stylistically very similar (with their brooding, tortured, aloof hero, limited palette of dark metallic colors and copious amounts of *chiaroscuro*), they contain very different ideological messages. Like Batman, Insee Daeng could be the individual needed to right the wrongs of contemporary Thailand, however, unlike Batman, his progressive nature comes from his desire to destroy such a damaged and unequal system, not preserve it. Instead of restoring order through protecting idyllic "Thainess," this hero's only goal seems to be the destruction of such a society, implying that the idyll of localism is merely a fantasy and cannot exist in the country as it currently stands in its unequal and exploitive state: Thailand needs to be changed, radically.

The figure of Rom/Insee Daeng is therefore as extreme as the text itself. As a character he belies the conventional positive attributes of the superhero figure and is difficult to sympathize with as a hero. Due to his extreme actions and brooding, aloof persona, he appears to lack the "implicit goodness" (Peaslee 2007, 38) that Peaslee recognizes as accompanying such superhero figures and their actions. He becomes much more of a vigilante figure in keeping with similar contemporary Hollywood productions such as *Watchmen* and *V for Vendetta*, a stark difference to the previous postwar filmic incarnations that the character is taken from. He lives in the warehouse of a cold storage facility that is more akin to a Bond villain's lair than a superhero's cave and indeed seems inspired by Jigsaw's hide-out from the *Saw* franchise with its grimy *mise-en-scene*, monochromatic palette and mountains of ice, while the wall is covered in black and white photographs of politicians with knives sticking out of them. His distanced love interest Wassana believes he is "addicted to pain" and, likewise, as Insee Daeng he engages in extreme violence, killing his enemies mercilessly even when they are beaten, actions that detach him from the conventional forces for good.

In his quest to destroy this "extreme" society Rom/Insee Daeng slays countless political and criminal figures in acts of barbaric vigilantism in which the viewer is spared no gruesome detail. In an opening fight sequence that sets the tone for an astonishingly violent film, Insee Daeng shoots the kneecap of a drug dealer then slices off his hand and shoves cocaine down his throat. Graphic sounds and close-up shots detail the barbarity of his actions. Likewise, Insee Daeng decapitates gangsters and beats up a crime lord in the bathroom, smashing his face against a urinal so that he spits out teeth. Possibly his most shocking action is the murder and mutilation of a corrupt senator who is also a pedophile, leaving a sinister message for police in the bed in which he leaves the senator's body. Consequently, "implicit goodness" is difficult to identify in this depiction, and the implication seems to be that Bangkok has become so "bad" that only extreme actions that work to completely destroy such a society can now be a force for good.

Indeed, in these actions the Insee Daeng character is very much outside the law, again problematizing his status as a superhero and distancing him very far from the postwar film series. The superhero figure is one that traditionally exists in various ways alongside the social forces of cohesion and authority (such as the police, the government etc.), and is one that exhibits what Peaslee calls a "common-sense approach" to maintaining order that often goes beyond the official authorities and their rules and means. Nevertheless one clear trope of the superhero is the degree to which they move alongside and not simply outside bureaucratic forces (Peaslee 2007, 41). Insee Daeng seems to be an extreme example of this "common-sense approach," but is clearly "outside" rather than "alongside" the police and has taken the law completely into his own hands as vigilante justice demands. However, in the crime-ridden world of contemporary Bangkok such actions are implied to be appropriate as the "law" is revealed to be heavily entwined within the controls of the Matulee, suggesting that it too must be destroyed. The police even attempt to protect the various victims from the wrath of Insee Daeng, such is this chaotic and barbaric world that Thailand now finds itself in. Instead of working alongside Insee Daeng, the police are "the servants of politicians" and even Lt Chart, the officer in charge of pursuing the hero, wonders at his relegation to serving and protecting corrupt politicians rather catching criminals. The extent of this corruption is finally revealed in the ending, which indicates close cooperation between the crime lords, politicians and the police. The police are merely another branch of corruption and in this seedy drug-addled world of 2013 Bangkok it appears that no one can be trusted.

Such confusion is also present in Rom himself, who, while he works to destroy particular figures, is never overtly clear about what he is fighting for (apart from the supposed complete destruction of the status quo). For instance, when he gruesomely murders the corrupt senator who is also a pedophile, there is no account of him saving the children who have been abused (although he does save Wassana, his love interest, who seems to constitute his only human connection in the entire film). One motivation for Insee Daeng's actions is his revenge against a system that exploited and almost killed him as a soldier, but this "system" is vague and many of those he targets are not obviously connected to his own treatment. Such a motivation is highly significant however, as unlike the spiritual rural outsider Ting in *Ong-Bak*, Rom/Insee Daeng is heavily embedded within this world of extreme violence (he is also addicted to morphine from a previous injury) and is very much a product of this chaotic and unfocused world of corruption, drugs and violence.

The actions of this damaged figure therefore become a potentially progressive reading of the exploited lower class soldiers who inevitably serve in the nation's armed forces, many of whom are conscripted via lottery and lack the funds to bribe their way out. Rom is a slave to his tortured past, which torments him in sepia flashbacks of a Vietnam-esque jungle scenario comparable to *First Blood* (1982) or *Jacob's Ladder* (1990) and depicts an attempt by government forces to kill him and wipe out all evidence of his mission "Operation Pali." The "Thainess" that existed before is revealed to have sent Rom to his nightmare through using him as a soldier and then attempting to discard and destroy him, and while he may be "surviving" there is little suggested way out for this detached and damaged hero. As a victim of this status quo therefore, Rom is located firmly within this environment and works to destroy it.

The cloaked Black Devil who the Matulee send to destroy Insee Daeng is likewise revealed to be another traumatized veteran from the jungle, and has even been working within the police as a means to find Insee Daeng and revenge himself. In a fascinating twist, Black Devil was one of the original Government soldiers who were sent to kill Rom in the jungle, but instead Black Devil ended up with half his head sliced off. Donning a metal scalp he now becomes even more of an extreme figure than Insee Daeng, and accuses Rom of turning him into just such a monster. Such a depiction also challenges the conventional connection between superheroes and supervillains, who often seem to function as the inverse of the heroes and so serve to further emphasize the "implicit goodness" and stable dependability of those they battle, seen in figures such as The Joker from *Batman*. However, in contrast to such a relationship, Black Devil appears to be Insee Daeng's equal in every way and is similarly extreme and psychologically damaged. His horrific nature instead seems to suggest that while the damaged Rom may be an indirect result of government control, the direct influence on loyal servants of this system is far worse, furthering the need for the complete destruction of such a system.

The Wider Context of *Insee Daeng*'s Superheroism

Insee Daeng's attitude towards and depiction of contemporary Bangkok also begins to mirror the recent tumultuous and oppressive political events within the country as well as the corresponding resurgence of the various (and at times violent) social movements to counter such anti-democratic actions. *Insee Daeng*'s implication that Thailand has already descended into a chaos from which it cannot recover is an assertion that seems motivated by the ongoing saga of inequality and exploitation that infuses the contemporary age. Like the Matulee organization, Thailand is controlled by powerful rich elites who work towards their own ends and have little concern for democracy, a state that appears to warrant the hero's destructive and unclear aims.

Indeed, *Insee Daeng*'s production and release occurred during and immediately after the particularly tumultuous period in Thai politics when Thailand was (and still is) becoming increasingly polarized, an era that some left-wing scholars even describe as constituting an all-out "class war"

(Ungpakorn 2009, 83).[5] The destruction of the democratic process by the 2006 military coup and the subsequent chaotic and violent episodes from the various protest groups adds weight to Insee Daeng's desire for the extreme destruction of such a violent and corrupt society. Likewise, the film also appears to critique the totalitarian elements of deposed Prime Minister (and supposed "champion of the masses") Thaksin Shinawatra, who, while he may have championed the rural poor as a means to stay in power, most certainly did not have their best interests at heart and engaged in rabid corruption and human rights abuses that lost him potential support from foreign NGOs after his undemocratic removal. The figure of Prime Minister Direk in *Insee Daeng* could easily function as a thinly veiled reference to Thaksin and the misplaced adulation he received. For instance, the opening of *Insee Daeng* depicts a rally at which Direk is speaking, while cheering workers form his audience. Behind him is a Chairman Mao-like depiction of a huge billboard with his face enlarged to extreme proportions, a scene that is reminiscent of the mass rallies called by Thaksin and the adulation from his supporters towards a figure who, ultimately, would certainly serve his own interests first.

This interpretation is also in keeping with the director Wisit Sasanatieng's well known left-wing political sympathies. While like many Thai public figures, Sasanatieng keeps such opinions quite quiet, he is well known to sympathize with the Red Shirts as a potential lower class movement that works against anti-democratic forces and regularly posts such opinions on his Facebook page (which is registered under an assumed name). This desire to champion the rural poor is also very much in evidence in the focus that so many of Wisit's films place on lower class Thailand and its previous eras of Thai film. *Fa Thalai Chon*, *Mah Nakorn* and *Ben Choo Gap Phii* were personal projects that he remained very much in control of, and each details figures from lower class rural Thailand who exist under an unfair and exploitive system. The desired destruction of the corrupt Thai status quo in *Insee Daeng* as well as the tragic past of its abused hero can be added to such sympathies.

The Re-appropriation of a Superhero

Such a reading is actually in stark contrast to the original Insee Daeng figure and the postwar films that the 2010 version is based on. The figure of Insee Daeng was originally from a series of films produced throughout the 1960s and '70s, which were in turn adaptations of popular novels. The hero himself was also born within and continued to grow alongside the strong and significant right-wing anti-communist discourses that engulfed Thailand throughout the 1950s and '60s in what Richard Ruth refers to as the "American era" due to the vast influx of American culture during this period (Ruth 2011). Such collaboration against leftist discourse was very much in line with the strong anti-communist state rhetoric promoted by the Thai government who sought to counter the encroach of communism in Southeast Asia after World War Two by positioning it as a dangerous external "other" in direct opposition to a nationalistically concerned and vehemently promoted "Thainess" (Winichakul 1994, 170).

The original Insee Daeng films, and in particular the final incarnation *Insee Thong* (1970) (when the hero is incarnated as the Golden Eagle, rather than the Red Eagle) are firmly positioned within and function as part of this state-sponsored agenda, as did many Thai films released during this time. *Insee Thong* in particular follows a strong nationalist rhetoric. It tells the story of the heroic defeat of the Red Bamboo gang (and its leader Bakin) that is trying to overthrow the Thai government in a similar way to the rhetoric peddled about the communist threat during this time. The "Red Bamboo" gang appears to be a very thinly veiled reference to communist insurgents and Vietnamese communist revolutionary leader Ho Chi Min himself (to whom Bakin bears a resemblance). Indeed, the film "others" its supervillain Bakin, through both his Vietnamese/Chinese appearance and sneaky abilities that include hypnotizing his opponents and causing them to see him in three images. Likewise, Insee Daeng's dramatic color switch from red to gold also underlines the perceived communist threat, implying that red is not even safe as a color, as the hero is forced to change when an imposter adopts the Red Eagle persona. The climax of the film takes place on an island where, together with the Thai military and police, Insee Thong defeats the gang and their leader, flying off into the sunset while hanging from a helicopter (a stunt which famously killed the lead actor Mitr Chaibancha when he lost his grip and fell).

Such a reading may therefore suggest that as a depiction that lies far outside such state-sponsored discourses, the 2010 incarnation is a socially and politically progressive adaptation of this superhero, despite his amoral and nihilistic qualities. However, there are many factors that problematize such an interpretation. For instance, the focus on an individual as an agent for change (rather than the mass movements that have been so significant in struggles against anti-democratic actions) places Thai citizens in a rather passive and helpless position that belies the formidable strength of the Red and Yellow Shirt movements, both of which have been significant actors in this saga. There is also a significant condemning of collective action, which is not deemed to be ultimately positive or effective. Such a depiction is easily recognizable in the motorcycle gang who threaten Rom/Insee Daeng's love interest (the NGO activist Wassana), in an exaggerated action sequence in which the hero single-handedly obliterates the entire gang by (among other means) decapitating, burning, and crashing into them before sweeping Wassana off to ride into the sunset.

A similar rejection of any potential mass and lower class agency can also be seen in the casting of the 2010 production's lead actor Ananda Everingham as the Insee Daeng character. Ananda's conventional good looks are a product of his half-Australian parentage. While the 1960s hero Mitr Chaibancha was undoubtedly popular due to his above-average height and broad shoulders (which many said made him look like the Hollywood movie stars that Thailand was bombarded by), he is nevertheless distinctly Thai. His dark skin and lower class origins ensured a popularity that was firmly embedded in his resonance with lower class Thais and indeed many of the 16mm productions he is famous for were located deep within a rural, rather than urban, context, in which his character rode into a village, saved its inhabitants from a particular threat, and married a local girl. Despite Mitr's character often embodying the new and jazzy Americanized modernity (represented when he travels around the country or even abroad), he is nevertheless a distinctly Thai hero and one starkly different from the star image of Ananda which is also connected to the highly problematic lauding of "whiteness" in the contemporary age.

Indeed, the choice of the half-Western light-skinned Ananda to play this culturally significant and very recognizable superhero reflects the normalizing of an obsession with white skin that emerges from a discourse cultivated by global corporations, who feed off of a legacy of colonial-based inequality by associating "whiteness" with modernity. Persaud calls this "an ideology of modernity based on a hierarchy of skin color, with 'whiteness' at the top and 'darkness' at the bottom" (2005, 216–17). In particular, the prominence of these affluent *luk kruengs* (literally half-children) as models and actors in Thailand is an indication that "white plus something is now in demand," something that Persaud makes explicit as "not an innocent desire and demand for whiteness, but a passionate flight, a mass migration, from all possible signs of 'darkness'" (2005, 219). The reincarnation of the Insee Daeng figure, therefore, becomes a part of this flight, as though contemporary Thailand can no longer conceive of its modern superheroes as dark skinned individuals.

Conclusion

The contemporary production *Insee Daeng* and its superhero figure occupy a contradictory and problematic position in keeping with the current impasse of contemporary Thailand. The text calls for the destruction of such an unequal and chaotic society yet does not posit any solution for its rebuilding or reforming. However, the film is in many ways a progressive text within the conservative discourses of the New Thai film industry. This can be seen in the left-wing politics of its director, the abstract high-concept style of filmmaking as well as the many competing discourses of contemporary Thailand which the film exists within as both a blockbuster product of a conservative industry and the adaptation of a previous figure. These combine together to produce a film whose message and figure is starkly different from the staple tropes of conservative localism found in productions such as *Ong-Bak*. Indeed while this chapter has also touched on the problems and issues within the depiction, there is still much to laud about the film as a welcome break from the dominant discourses of contemporary Thailand.

However, it is inevitably also important to note that the remake of *Insee-Daeng* was a commercial failure upon its release and was widely panned by critics and audiences alike. The movie was not a success and promptly put an end to the franchise that was intended to have been built around the re-launch of this superhero. Such failure can likely be put down to a convoluted narrative as well as its "extreme" depiction and high concept film style, as well as possibly the use of a performer whose star image tends to be associated with overly emotional and romantic figures rather than detached action heroes. Its drastic movement away from the depiction and discourses of its original postwar incarnation, with the loss of the hero's original "inherent goodness" and heroic cooperation alongside the police and armed forces, may also have lost many potential viewers who had initially been intrigued by the publicity that was largely based on the resurrection of such a character. While *Insee Daeng* may therefore have intended to embrace lower class Thailand and its struggles, its attempted ingenuity appears to have removed the text far beyond the preferences of its desired viewers.

Most significantly, the discontinuation of this franchise also removed any possibility of a clear ending to the film. In the final scene, Rom/Insee Daeng is depicted riding off on his motorbike to save Wassana and the demonstrators in Chumphon under the staple "to be continued..." text, setting up a cliff-hanger ending for the sequel that filmmakers had evidently expected. To deny this ending now completely removes any solution that this superhero may present for the problems of contemporary Thailand, unwittingly continuing the stalemate and social division that Thai citizens now find themselves in.

Notes

1. This term is somewhat misleading, however. Chaiworaporn and Knee note that despite the enormous boom in filmmaking, "this is not to claim that there was suddenly a clear-cut "new Thai cinema" movement at that moment" (Chaiworaporn and Knee 2006, 60).

2. There are continuing discussions about the extent to which it remains affiliated to (and even controlled by) Thaksin and whether its supporters can be considered to be an autonomous working class movement.

3. This promotes nostalgia for a purer and simpler time, one encapsulated within the image of the pre-modern impoverished hardworking and sacrificing peasant. Localism functioned as a means to deflect attention from the elites and their business interests that had ultimately caused such devastation and also fostered a degree of nationalistic social control over a disillusioned and suffering population. It is a conservative discourse that "does not provide the robust alternative analysis required of a critique of neo-liberal globalization" (Hewison 1999, 11).

4. This is the most impoverished part of Thailand, whose inhabitants are much darker skinned and speak a dialogue closer to Laos than Thai (which are linguistically very similar). Indeed, historically much of the area was originally part of Laos and its inhabitants are of Laos ethnicity, with older citizens still referring to themselves as Laos rather than Thai. Much scholarly analysis has focused on the "Thaification" of this region during the post-war era, with many arguing that this constituted a form of oppression through the suppression of local culture in favor of promoting a nationalism based on central-Thailand identity as a means to consolidate the nation.

5. While such claims do carry much weight, they are also deeply suspect due to the complicated and contradictory make-up of these various social movements.

BIBLIOGRAPHY

Abu-Lughod, Lila. "Do Muslim Women Really Need Saving? Anthropological Reflections on Cultural Relativism and Its Others." *American Anthropologist* 104, no. 3 (2002): 783–790. doi: 10.1525/aa.2002.104.3.783.

Agon, Camille. "Islamic Superheroes Going Global." *Time*, August 5, 2008. http://www.time.com/time/world/article/0,8599,1828732,00.html.

Ahmed, Akbar. "Hello, Hollywood: Your Images Affect Muslims Everywhere." *New Perspectives Quarterly* 19, no. 2 (2002): 73–75. doi: 10.1111/0893-7850.00500.

Ahn, In-Yong. "Interview with Shin Amhaeng Osa Director Shimura Joji." *Yonhap News*, November 17, 2004. http://news.naver.com/main/read.nhn?mode=LSD&mid=sec&sid1=102&oid=001&aid= 0000824179.

Al-Mutawa, Naif. "Why I Based Superheroes on Islam." *BBC*, July 2, 2009a. http://news.bbc.co.uk/1/hi/world/middle_east/8127699.stm.

———. "Guest Voices: Concentration Camps and Comic Books." *Washington Post*. July 17, 2009b. http://newsweek.washingtonpost.com/onfaith/guestvoices/2009/07/concentration_camps_and_comic_books.html.

———. "Islam-Inspired Comic Superheroes Fight for Peace." *CNN International*, August 22, 2010. http://edition.cnn.com/2010/OPINION/08/22/al-mutawa.islamic.superheroes/?hpt=C2.

———. "How Bloggers Brought Down Superheroes." *Wired UK*, March 12, 2012. http://www.wired.co.uk/magazine/archive/2012/04/ideas-bank/naif-a-al-mutawa.

Alessio, Dominic, and Jessica Langer. "Nationalism and Postcolonialism in Indian Science Fiction: Bollywood's *Koi Mil Gaya* (2003)." *New Cinemas: Journal of Contemporary Film* 5, no. 3 (2007): 217–29.

Allison, Anne. "Can Popular Culture Go Global? How Japanese 'Scouts' and 'Rangers' Fare in the US." In *A Century of Popular Culture in Japan*. Edited by Douglas Slaymaker, 127–53. Lewiston: The Edwin Mellen Press, 2000a.

———. *Millennial Monsters: Japanese Toys and the Global Imagination*. Berkeley: University of California Press, 2006.

———. "Sailor Moon: Japanese Superheroes for Global Girls." In *Japan Pop! Inside the World of Japanese Popular Culture*. Edited by Timothy J. Craig, 259–78. Armonk, New York: ME Sharp, 2000b.

Altman, Rick. "A Semantic/Syntactic Approach to Genre." *Cinema Journal* 23, no. 3 (Spring 1984): 6–18.

Amazing Spider-Man. Directed by E.W. Swackhamer, 1977.

AMPAS database. Accessed September 4, 2013. http://awardsdatabase.oscars.org/ampas_awards/DisplayMain.jsp?curTime=1378247551602.

Annett, Sandra. "Imagining Transcultural Fandom: Animation and Global Media Communities." *Transcultural Studies* 2 (2011): 164–88. doi: 10.11588/ts.2011.2.9060.

Aslam, Jahanzeb. "New Age, New Heroes." *Newsweek Pakistan*. April 18, 2011. http://www.newsweekpakistan.com/features/299.

Augé, Marc. *Non-Places: Introduction to an Anthropology of Supermodernity*. Translated by John Howe. London: Verso, 1995.

The Australian Woman's Mirror. "The Phantom." *The Australian Woman's Mirror* 12, no. 41, September 1, 1936: 49.

Balzer, Jens and Lambert Wiesing. *Outcault: Die Erfindung des Comic*. Bochum and Essen: Christian A. Bachmann Verlag, 2010.

Barker, Martin, and Kate Brooks. *Knowing Audiences: Judge Dredd, Its Fans, Friends and Foes*. Luton: University of Luton Press, 1998.

Barnes, Brooks. "Soft Pedal Captain America Overseas? Hollywood Says No." *New York Times: Media Decoder*. July 3, 2011. http://mediadecoder.blogs.nytimes.com/2011/07/03/soft-pedal-captain-america-overseas-hollywood-says-no/.

Basu, Anustup. *Bollywood in the Age of New Media*. Edinburgh: Edinburgh University Press, 2010.

———. "The Eternal Return and Overcoming 'Cape Fear': Science, Sensation, Superman and Hindu Nationalism in Recent Hindi Cinema." *South Asian History and Culture* 2, no. 4 (2011): 557–71.

Beaty, Bart. "The Fighting Civil Servant: Making Sense of the Canadian Superhero." *American Review of Canadian Studies* 36, no. 3 (2006): 427–39. doi: 10.1080/02722010609481401.

Beck, Chris. "On the Couch: Simon Wincer." *The Age* (Melbourne), September 7, 1996, 4. Saturday Extra.

Benjamin, Lesley. "Fan on the Street: Ian Jack." *David Anthony Kraft's Comics Interview* 4 (ca. 1985): 71, 73–75.

Berry, Chris. "'What's Big About the Big Film?': De-Westernizing the Blockbuster in Korea and China." In *Movie Blockbusters*. Edited by Julian Stringer, 217–29. London: Routledge, 2003.

Bignell, Jonathan, and Andrew O'Day. *Terry Nation*. Manchester: Manchester University Press, 2004.

Bolton, Christopher, Istvan Csicsery-Ronay, Jr., and Takayuki Tastsumi, eds. *Robot Ghosts and Wired Dreams: Japanese Science Fiction from Origins to Anime*. Minneapolis: University of Minnesota Press, 2007.

Bordwell, David. *Planet Hong Kong: Popular Cinema and the Art of Entertainment*. Cambridge, Massachusetts: Harvard University Press, 2003.

Box Office Mojo. "1996 Domestic Grosses." *Box Office Mojo*. http://www.boxofficemojo.com/yearly/chart/?yr=1996&p=.htm.

Box Office Mojo. www.boxofficemojo.com.

Boym, Svetlana. *The Future of Nostalgia*. New York: Basic Books, 2001.

Bradshaw, Peter. Review of *Thor*. *The Guardian* (Manchester), April 28, 2011, http://www.theguardian.com/film/2011/apr/28/thor-review.

Britton, Piers D., and Simon J. Barker. *Reading Between Designs: Visual Imagery and the Generation of Meaning in the Avengers, the Prisoner, and Doctor Who*. Austin, Texas: University of Texas Press, 2003.

Broadway, Kenneth. "NYFF 2011: 'The 99 Unbound' Introduces an Intellectually Ambitious Comic Universe." *Sound On Sight*, October 1, 2011. http://www.soundonsight.org/nyff-2011-the-99-unbound/.

Brooker, Will. "Batman: One Life, Many Faces." In *Adaptations: From Text to Screen, Screen to Text*. Edited by Deborah Cartmell and Imelda Whelehan, 185–98. London: Routledge, 1999.

———. *Batman Unmasked: Analyzing a Cultural Icon*. New York: Continuum, 2001.

———. "Everywhere and Nowhere: Vancouver, Fan Pilgrimage and the Urban Imaginary." *International Journal of Cultural Studies* 10, no. 4 (2007): 423–44. doi: 10.1177/1367877907083078.

———. *Hunting the Dark Knight: Twenty-first Century Batman*. London: IB Tauris, 2012.

Brown, Jeffrey. *Black Superheroes, Milestone Comics and Their Fans*. Jackson: University of Mississippi Press, 2001.

Brown, Phil. "Phantom Fans Are Unmasked." *The Sun* (Brisbane), April 8, 1988, 25–26.

"'Burka Avenger' May Get a Bollywood Remake." *India West*, August 19, 2013. http://www.indiawest.com/news/12977--burka-avenger-may-get-a-bollywood-remake.html.

Busch, Anita M. "'Gump' Primes Pump, but Par Plays It Safe." *Variety* 356, no. 8, September 1, 1994, 19–25.

Cavill, Henry. Interview with Simon Mayo. *BBC* podcast, June 14, 2013. http://downloads.bbc.co.uk/podcasts/fivelive/kermode/kermode_20130614-0941a.mp3.

Chaiworaporn, Anchalee, and Adam Knee. "Thailand: Revival in an Age of Globalization." In *Contemporary Asian Cinema*. Edited by Anne Tereska Ciecko, 58–70. New York: Berg, 2006.

Chapman, James. *British Comics: A Cultural History*. London: Reaktion, 2012.

———. *Inside the TARDIS: The Worlds of Doctor Who*. London: IB Tauris, 2006.

Cheshire, Godfrey. Review of *The Phantom*. *Variety* 363, no. 6, June 10–16, 1996, 40, 47.

Chesler, Phyllis. "A Disturbing Double Standard." *FoxNews.com*, October 13, 2010. http://www.foxnews.com/opinion/2010/10/13/phyllis-chesler-muslim-superhero-role-models-islamic-jihad-muhammed-allah-god/.

Chiang, Chin-Yun. *Theorizing Ambivalence in Ang Lee's Transnational Cinema*. New York: Peter Lang Publishing, 2012.

Child, Ben. "*Thor*: Kenneth Branagh's Film Looks the Wrong Kind of Weird." *The Guardian* (Manchester), July 29, 2010. http://www.theguardian.com/film/filmblog/2010/jul/29/kenneth-branagh-thor.

Chua, Beng Huat, and Koichi Iwabuchi, eds. *East Asian Pop Culture: Analysing the Korean Wave*. Hong Kong: Hong Kong University Press, 2008.

Clark, Philip. "Now, Ghost Who Goes Walkabout." *Sydney Morning Herald*, March 21, 1988, 3.

Clayfield, Matthew. "Ghost to Walk Among Us Again." *The Australian*, December 16, 2008. http://www.theaustralian.com.au/news/arts/ghost-to-walk-among-us-again/story-e6frg8n6-1111118325871.

Clements, Jonathan, and Motoko Tamamuro. *The Dorama Encyclopedia*. Berkeley: Stone Bridge Press, 2003.

Coker, Margaret. "Kuwaiti Entrepreneur Hopes to Create the Next Pokémon." *Wall Street Journal*, November 25, 2008. http://online.wsj.com/article/SB122757193882554759.html.

Comingsoon.net. "Update: A Sequel to The Phantom in the Works." *Comingsoon.net*, December 16, 2008. http://www.comingsoon.net/news/movienews.php?id=51313. Accessed: 20/04/2012.

Coogan, Peter. "The Definition of the Superhero." In *Super/Heroes: From Hercules to Superman*. Edited by Wendy Haslem, Angela Ndalianis, and C. J. Mackie, 21–36. Washington: New Academic Publishing, 2007.

———. *Superhero: The Secret Origin of a Genre*. Austin, Texas: MonkeyBrain Books, 2006.

Cook, Frank. "Pygmies Small Comfort to Mrs Diana Phantom." *Daily Mirror* (Sydney), May 16, 1978, 12.

Creed, Barbara. "The Plot Who Walks, Slowly." *The Age* (Melbourne), September 26, 1996.

Cull, Nicholas J. "Tardis at the OK Corral: Doctor Who and the USA." In *British Science Fiction Television: A Hitchhiker's Guide*. Edited by John R. Cook and Peter Wright, 52–70. London: IB Tauris, 2006.

Curtiss, Richard H., and Delinda C. Hanley. "Dr. Jack Shaheen Discusses Reel Bad Arabs: How Hollywood Vilifies a People." *Washington Report on Middle East Affairs*. July, 2001. http://www.wrmea.com/component/content/article/227/3788-dr-jack-shaheen-discusses-reel-bad-arabs-how-hollywood-vilifies-a-people.html.

Dautrich, K., and C. Barnes. "Freedom of the Press Survey: General Population." 2005a. http://importance.corante.com/archives/UCONN_DPP_Survey_GenPop.pdf.

———. "Freedom of the Press Survey: Journalists." 2005b. http://importance.corante.com/archives/UCONN_DPP_Survey_Journalists.pdf.

Davis, Charles H., and James Nadler. "International Television Co-productions and the Cultural Discount: the Case of *Family Biz*, a Comedy." 2009, 1–24. http://www.ryerson.ca/~c5davis/publications/Nadler%20-%20Davis%t20-%20International%20Television%20Coproduction%20v7%20-%2012%20May%202010.pdf.

Davis, Victoria. Letter to the editor. *The Phantom* 1126, (1996): 33. Sydney: Frew Publications.

Dawtrey, Adam. "Branagh: Titan of Stage, Screen, Tube." *Variety*, November 27, 2011. http://variety.com/2011/film/news/branagh-titan-of-stage-screen-tube-1118046404/.

Diffrient, David Scott. "From *Three Godfathers* to *Tokyo Godfathers*: Signifying Social Change in a Transnational Context." In *East Asian Cinemas: Exploring Transnational*

Connections on Film. Edited by Leon Hunt and Leung Wing-Fai, 153–61. London: IB Tauris, 2008.

Doyle, Laura. "Toward a Philosophy of Transnationalism." *The Journal of Transnational American Studies* 1, (2009): 1–29. http://escholarship.org/uc/item/9vr1k8hk.

Duncan, Randy, and Matthew J. Smith. *The Power of Comics: History, Form, Culture*. New York: Bloomsbury, 2009.

Dwyer, Rachel. *100 Bollywood Films*. London: BFI, 2005.

Ebert, Roger. Review of *Thor*. *rogerebert.com*, May 10, 2011. http://www.rogerebert.com/reviews/thor-2011.

Ecke, Jochen. "Warren Ellis: Performing the Transnational Author in the American Comics Mainstream." In *Transnational Perspectives on Graphic Novels: Comics at the Crossroads*. Edited by Daniel Stein, Christina Meyer, and Shane Denson. London and New York: Continuum, 2013.

Eco, Umberto. "The Myth of Superman." Translated by Natalie Chilton. *Diacritics* 1, (1972): 14–22.

Edwardson, Ryan. "The Many Lives of Captain Canuck: Nationalism, Culture, and the Creation of a Canadian Comic Book Superhero." *The Journal of Popular Culture* 37, no. 2 (2003): 184–201. doi: 10.1111/1540-5931.00063

Ehrlich, Richard S. "The Burka Avenger, a Female Muslim Education Superhero." *MuslimVillage.com*. August 19, 2013. http://muslimvillage.com/2013/08/19/42521/the-burka-avenger-a-female-muslim-education-superhero/.

"Episode One." *Misfits*, E4. Written by Howard Overman, directed by Tom Green, aired November 12, 2009.

Ezra, Elizabeth, and Terry Rowden. "General Introduction: What is Transnational Cinema?" In *Transnational Cinema: The Film Reader*. Edited by Elizabeth Ezra and Terry Rowden, 1–14. London: Routledge, 2006.

Falk, Lee, and Sy Barry. "Captain Amazon—Pirate Queen." *The Phantom* 958, Sydney: Frew Publications.

———. "The Name." *The Phantom* 972, 1991 [September 9, 1979–December 9, 1979], 254–68. Sydney: Frew Publications.

Falk, Lee, and Ray Moore. "The Phantom." Originally titled "The Singh Brotherhood." *The Phantom* 1, *Bulletin Newspaper* (Sidney), 1938, 5 and 7.

———. "The Singh Brotherhood" The *Phantom: The Complete Newspaper Dailies, Volume One, 1936–1937*, 15–128. Neshannock, PA: Hermes Press, 2010 [February 17, 1936–November 07, 1936].

Farrell, Henry, and Daniel W. Drezner. "The Power and Politics of Blogs." *Public Choice* 134, (2008): 15–30. doi: 10.1007/s11127-007-9198-1.

Fattah, Hassan M. "Comics to Battle for Truth, Justice and the Islamic Way." *The New York Times*, January 22, 2006. International / Middle East section. http://www.nytimes.com/2006/01/22/international/middleeast/22comics.html.

Fingeroth, Danny. *Disguised as Clark Kent: Jews, Comics, and the Creation of the Superhero*. New York: Continuum, 2007.

Fiske, John. "The Cultural Economy of Fandom." In *The Adoring Audience: Fan Culture and Popular Media*. Edited by Lisa A. Lewis, 30–49. London: Routledge, 1992.

Fleischer Brothers. *Adventures of Superman*, 1941–43.

Foster, Michael Dylan. *Pandemonium and Parade: Japanese Monsters and the Culture of Yōkai*. Berkeley, California: University of California Press, 2009.

Frew Publications. "Paramount's 'The Phantom': Coming Soon to a Theatre Near You!" *The Phantom* 1134, 40–41. Sydney: Frew Publications, 1996.

Furlong, Rob. Letter to the editor. *The Phantom* 1151 (1996): 34. Sydney: Frew Publications.

Gabilliet, Jean-Paul. *Of Comics and Men: A Cultural History of American Comic Books*. Jackson: University of Mississippi Press, 2010.

Gaine, Vincent M. "Captain 'America'?." *Superheroes on Screen*, September 2, 2011. http://superheroesonscreen.blogspot.co.uk/2011/09/captain-america.html.

———. "Genre and Supher-Heroism: Batman in the New Millennium." In *The 21st Century Superhero: Essays on Gender, Genre and Globalization in Film*. Edited by Richard J. Gray and Betty Kaklamanidou, 111–28. Jefferson, North Carolina: McFarland and Company, 2011.

Galloway, Stephen. "Kenneth Branagh on *Thor*: 'Commercial Gods Will Have to Decide Whether It's a Success.'" *The Hollywood Reporter*, April 13, 2011. http://www.hollywoodreporter.com/news/kenneth-branagh-thor-commercial-gods-177988.

Galt, Rosalind, and Karl Schoonover, eds. *Global Art Cinema: New Theories and Histories*. Oxford: Oxford University Press, 2010.

Ganti, Tejaswini. "'And Yet My Heart Is Still Indian': The Bombay Film Industry and the (H)indianization of Hollywood." In *Media Worlds: Anthropology on New Terrain*. Edited by Faye D. Ginsburg, Lila Abu-Lughod, and Brian Larkin, 281–300. Berkeley: University of California Press, 2002.

Gardiner, Peter. "The Phantom Unmasked! Is Marriage Killing off the Man Who Cannot Die?" *Queensland Times*, March 18, 1982.

Geller, Pamela. "86 'The 99.'" *Atlas Shrugs*. October 5, 2011. http://atlasshrugs2000.typepad.com/atlas_shrugs/2011/10/86-the-99.html.

Geraghty, Lincoln. "From Balaclavas to Jumpsuits: The Multiple Histories and Identities of Doctor Who's Cybermen." *Atlantis: A Journal of the Spanish Association for Anglo-American Studies* 30, no. 1 (2008): 85–100. http://www.jstor.org/stable/41055308.

———. ed., *The* Smallville *Chronicles: Critical Essays on the Television Series*. Lanham: Scarecrow Press, 2011.

Gerow, Aaron. "Wrestling with Godzilla: Intertextuality, Childish Spectatorship, and the National Body." In *In Godzilla's Footsteps: Japanese Pop Culture Icons on the Global Stage*. Edited by William M. Tsutsui and Michiko Ito, 63–81. New York: Palgrave MacMillan, 2006.

Gill, Tom. "Transformational Magic: Some Japanese Super-Heroes and Monsters." In *The Worlds of Japanese Popular Culture: Gender, Shifting Boundaries and Global Cultures*. Edited by D. P. Martinez, 33–55. Cambridge: Cambridge University Press, 1998.

Glassman, Jim. "Commentary." *Environment and Planning A* 42, no. 4 (2010): 765–70. doi: 10.1068/a42443.

Goellner, Caleb. "The JLA To Unite With 'The 99' In Middle East Crossover." *Comics Alliance*, July 2, 2009. http://www.comicsalliance.com/2009/07/02/the-jla-to-unite-with-the-99-in-middle-east-crossover/.

Goldsmith, Ben, and Tom O'Regan. *Cinema Cities, Media Cities: The Contemporary International Studio Complex* (Screen Industry, Culture and Policy Research Series). Sydney: Australian Film Commission, 2003.

Goldsmith, Ben, Susan Ward, and Tom O'Regan. *Local Hollywood: Global Film Production and the Gold Coast.* St. Lucia: University of Queensland Press, 2010.

Gordon, Ian, Mark Jancovich, and Ian McAllister, eds. *Film and Comic Books.* Jackson: University of Mississippi Press, 2007.

Govil, Nitin. "Bollywood and the Frictions of Global Mobility." In *Media on the Move: Global Flow and Contra-Flow.* Edited by Daya Thussu. London: Routledge, 2007. 76–88.

Govil, Nitin, Richard Maxwell, John McMurrin, Toby Miller, and Ting Wang. *Global Hollywood 2.* London: British Film Institute, 2005.

Goyal, Malini. "A New League of Superheroes." *Forbes India Magazine*, September 8, 2009. http://forbesindia.com/article/briefing/a-new-league-of-superheroes/3672/1?id=3672&pg=1.

Gravett, Paul. *Graphic Novels: Stories to Change Your Life.* London: Aurum, 2005.

Gravett, Paul, and Peter Stanbury. *Great British Comics: Celebrating a Century of Ripping Yarns and Wizard Wheezes.* London: Aurum, 2006.

Gray, Richard J. and Betty Kaklamanidou. "Introduction." In *The 21st Century Superhero: Essays on Gender, Genre and Globalization in Film.* Edited by Richard J. Gray and Betty Kaklamanidou, 1–13. Jefferson, North Carolina: McFarland and Company, 2011.

Green, Avi. "Detective Comics Annual 12: Batman Hires an Islamist." *The Astute Bloggers*, December 15, 2010. http://astuteblogger.blogspot.co.uk/2010/12/detective-comics-annual-12-batman-hires.html.

Gregson, Nicky and Louise Crewe. *Second-Hand Cultures.* Oxford: Berg, 2003.

Grist, Paul. *Jack Staff: Everything Used to Be Black and White.* Berkeley: Image Comics, 2011.

Groves, Don. "Village Roadshow Solid Thanks to Roc." *Variety* 357, no. 12, January 23–29, (1995), 58 and 64.

Hammond, Philip. "Delving into the Skull Caves." *The Courier-Mail* (Brisbane), February 14, 2006.

Harbord, Janet. *Film Cultures.* London: Sage, 2002.

Harvey, Robert C. *Children of the Yellow Kid: The Evolution of the American Comic Strip.* Seattle: University of Washington Press, 1999.

Haslem, Wendy, Angela Ndalianis, and Chris Mackie. eds. *Super/Heroes: From Hercules to Superman.* Washington: New Academia Publishing, 2007.

Hassler-Forest, Dan. *Capitalist Superheroes: Caped Crusaders in the Neo-Liberal Age.* Alresford: Zero Books, 2012.

Hauman, Glenn. "White Power Group Calls for Boycott of 'Thor' Over Casting of Idris Elba." *Comicmix*, December 19, 2010. http://www.comicmix.com/news/2010/12/19/white-power-group-calls-for-boycott-of-thor-over-casting-of-idris-elba/.

Heer, Jeet. "POW! BLAM! ZOWIE! Eh? A New Book Unearths the Hidden Curiosities of Canadian Comic Book Art." *Literary Review of Canada*, June 2007. http://reviewcanada.ca/reviews/2007/06/01/pow-blam-zowie-eh/.

Henderson, John. "State of the Club—A Report by the President." *Jungle Beat: The Official Newsletter of the Phantom Club* 9 (1986): 14.

Herd, Nick. *Chasing the Runaways: Foreign Film Production and Film Studio Development in Australia, 1988–2002.* Strawberry Hills, New South Wales: Currency House/Surry Hills, New South Wales: The Australian Writers' Foundation, 2004.

Hewison, Kevin. *After the Asian Crisis: Challenges to Globalization.* New South Wales: University of New England, 1999.

Higbee, Will, and Song Hwee Lim. "Concepts of Transnational Cinema: Towards a Critical Transnationalism in Film Studies." *Transnational Cinemas* 1, no.1 (2010), 7–21. doi 10.1386/trac.1.1.37/1

Higgins, Kyle, and Trevor McCarthy. "The Nightrunner." In *Batman: Gates of Gotham*, by Kyle Higgins and Trevor McCarthy. New York: DC Comics, 2012.

Higson, Andrew. "The Concept of National Cinema." *Screen* 30, no. 4 (1989): 36–46. doi: 10.1093/screen/30.4.36

———. "The Limiting Imagination of National Cinema." In *Cinema and Nation.* Edited by Mette Hjort and Scott Mackenzie, 63–74. London: Routledge, 2000. Reproduced in *Transnational Cinema: The Film Reader.* Edited by Elizabeth Ezra and Terry Rowden, 15–26. London: Routledge, 2006.

Hill, John, and Pamela Church Gibson, eds. *World Cinema: Critical Approaches.* Oxford: Oxford University Press, 2000.

Hills, Matt. "Attending Horror Film Festivals and Conventions: Liveness, Subcultural Capital and 'Flesh-and-Blood Genre Communities.'" In *Horror Zone: The Cultural Experience of Contemporary Horror Cinema.* Edited by Ian Conrich, 87–101. London: IB Tauris, 2010a.

———. *Triumph of a Time Lord: Regenerating Doctor Who in the Twenty-First Century.* London: IB Tauris, 2010b.

Himitsu Sentai Go Renjā [*Secret Task Force Five Rangers*]. NET, 1975.

Hindes, Andrew. "B.O. Boom: More May be Less." *Variety* 363, no. 10, June 15–21, 1996: 7, 10.

"Hīrō Shirīzu no Rekishi to Genzai." [The History and Present of Hero Series.] *Nikkei Entertainment!* 181, April 2012, 18–19.

The Hollywood Reporter. www.hollywoodreporter.com

Hoskins, Colin, and Rolf Mirus. "Reasons for the US Dominance of the International Trade in Television Programmes." *Media, Culture and Society* 10 (1988): 499–504. doi:10.1177/016344388010004006

Housel, Rebecca. "Myth, Morality and the Women of the X-Men." In *Superheroes and Philosophy*. Edited by Tom Morris and Matt Morris, 75–88. Chicago and La Salle, IL: Open Court, 2008.

Hughes, Jamie A. "'Who Watches the Watchmen?': Ideology and 'Real World' Superheroes." *The Journal of Popular Culture* 39, no. 4 (2006): 546–57. DOI: 10.1111/j.1540-5931.2006.00278.x

Hunt, Leon. *Kung Fu Cult Masters: From Bruce Lee to Crouching Tiger*. London: Wallflower Press, 2003.

Hunt, Leon and Leung Wing-Fai. "Introduction." In *East Asian Cinemas: Exploring Transnational Connections on Film*. Edited by Leon Hunt and Leung Wing-Fai, 1–13. London: IB Tauris, 2008.

Huston, Warner Todd. "Batman's Politically Correct European Vacation." *Publius Forum*. December 23, 2010. http://www.publiusforum.com/2010/12/23/batmans-politically-correct-european-vacation/.

Ikegami, Ryoichi. *Supaidāman*. Kodansha. 1970–71.

International Heroes. An International Catalogue of Superheroes. www.internationalheroes.co.uk.

Internet Movie Database. http://www.imdb.com.

Iwabuchi, Koichi. *Recentering Globalization: Popular Culture and Japanese Transnationalism*. Durham, North Carolina: Duke University Press, 2002.

Jacques, Bruce. "Australians Snare Phantom." *Australian Business*, March 23, 1988, 24–25.

Jancovich, Mark. "'Two Ways of Looking': The Critical Reception of 1940s Horror." *Cinema Journal* 49, no. 3 (2010): 45–66. doi: 10.1353/cj.0.0213.

Jancovich, Mark, Antonio Lázaro Reboll, Julian Stringer, and Andy Willis. "Introduction." In *Defining Cult Movies*. Edited by Mark Jancovich, Antonio Lázaro Reboll, Julian Stringer and Andy Willis, 1–13. Manchester: Manchester University Press, 2003.

Jayoush, Kinda. "Muslim Comic Book Is 'the Antidote to Bin Laden.'" *The National*, October 14, 2011. http://www.thenational.ae/arts-culture/books/muslim-comic-book-is-the-antidote-to-bin-laden.

Jenkins, Henry. *Convergence Culture: Where Old and New Media Collide*. New York: New York University Press, 2006.

———. "'Just Men in Tights': Rewriting Silver Age Comics in an Era of Multiplicity." In *The Shifting Definitions of Genre: Essays on Labeling Films, Television Shows and Media*. Edited by Lincoln Geraghty and Mark Jancovich. 229–43. Jefferson: McFarland, 2008.

———. "'Just Men in Tights': Rewriting Silver Age Comics in an Era of Multiplicity." In *The Contemporary Comic Book Superhero*. Edited by Angela Ndalianis, 16–43. NY and London: Routledge, 2009.

———. "Superpowered Fans: The Many Worlds of San Diego's Comic-Con." *Boom: A Journal of California* 2, no. 2 (2012): 22–36. http://www.jstor.org/stable/10.1525/boom.2012.2.2.22.

Jess-Cooke, Caroly. *Film Sequels: Theory and Practice from Hollywood to Bollywood*. Edinburgh: Edinburgh University Press, 2009.

Jewett, Robert, and John Shelton Lawrence. *The American Monomyth*. Garden City, New York: Anchor Press, 1977.

Jo, Joe. "Overseas Marketing Suggestions for the Korean Animation Industry." *Animation World Magazine* 4, no. 12, 2000. http://www.awn.com/mag/issue4.12/4.12pages/jokorea.php3.

Johnson, Catherine. *Telefantasy*. London: BFI, 2005.

Jones, Garrett. "The Ghost Who Walks is Stepping Out." *Sunday Telegraph* (Sydney), March 2, 1986, 130–31.

Jungle Beat. "Recent Phantom Publicity." *Jungle Beat: The Official Newsletter of the Phantom Club* 12, 1987, 8.

Kahn, Joseph P. "The Original Cape Crusader Lee Falk, Father of the Comic-Strip Superhero is a Truro Legend, Too." [Boston Globe, July 10, 1996], *Lee Falk, Storyteller*, 297–300. Stockholm: GML Förlag/Scandinavian Chapter of the Lee Falk Memorial Bengali Explorers Club, 2011.

Kaklamanidou, Betty. "The Mythos of Patriarchy in the X-Men Films." In *The 21st Century Superhero: Essays on Gender, Genre and Globalization in Film*. Edited by Richard J. Gray and Betty Kaklamanidou, 61–74. Jefferson, North Carolina: McFarland and Company, 2011.

Karoub, Jeff, and Matt Moore. "'The 99,' Naif Al-Mutawa's Muslim Comic Series, Aims To Break Through In US." *Huffington Post*, October 12, 2011. http://www.huffingtonpost.com/2011/10/12/the-99-naif-al-mutawa-comic-book_n_1006660.html.

Kaur, Raminder. "Atomic Comics: Parabolic Mimesis and the Graphic Fictions of Science." *International Journal of Cultural Studies* 15, no. 4 (2012): 329–47.

———. "The Fictions of Science and Cinema in India." In *Routledge Handbook of Indian Cinemas*. Edited by K. Moti Gokulsing and Wimal Dissanayake, 282–96. London: Routledge, 2013.

Kennedy, Buzz. "Phantom of the Uproar." *Sunday Telegraph* (Sydney), June 8, 1980, 35.

Kermode, Mark. Review of *Thor*, Paramount and Marvel, May 3, 2011. http://www.bbc.co.uk/programmes/poogpwxk.

Kerr, Paul. "*Babel*'s Network Narrative: Packaging a Globalised Art Cinema." *Transnational Cinemas* 1, no. 1 (2010): 37–51. doi 10.1386/trac.1.1.37/1.

Kesting, Piney. "The Next Generation of Superheroes." *Saudi Aramco World*, January 2007. http://www.saudiaramcoworld.com/issue/200701/the.next.generation.of.superheroes.htm.

Ketchell, Melissa. "Warner to Link with Roadshow." *The Courier-Mail* (Brisbane), November 18, 1988.

Khan, Sher. "Nation Awakes, Pakistan's First Superhero Film." *The Express Tribune*, February 19, 2013.

Khouri, Andy. "99 Problems but a Cape Ain't One: Conservatives Attack Islamic Superheroes." *Comics Alliance*, October 19, 2010. http://www.comicsalliance.com/2010/10/19/the-99-muslim-islamic-superhero-comic/.

Kim, Joon-Yang. "Critique of the New Historical Landscape of South Korean Animation." *Animation: An Interdisciplinary Journal* 1, no. 1 (2006): 61–81. doi: 10.1177/1746847706070256.

Kim, Tae-Jong. "Animations Heat Up Local Screens." *The Korea Times*, November 24. 2004. http://www.hancinema.net/animations-heat-up-local-screens-1776.html.

King, Geoff. *New Hollywood Cinema: An Introduction*. London: IB Tauris, 2002.

Klock, Geoff. *How to Read Superhero Comics and Why*. NY and London: Continuum, 2002.

Koven, Mikel J. *La Dolce Morte: Vernacular Cinema and the Italian* Giallo *Film*. Lanham: Scarecrow Press, 2006.

Kuipers, Richard. Review of *Thor*, Paramount/ Marvel. *Variety*, April 17, 2013. http://variety.com/2011/film/reviews/thor-1117945029/.

Langer, Jessica. Review of *Endhiran* (Robot), Sun Pictures. *Science Fiction Film and Television* 5, no. 1 (2012): 147–51.

Langford, Barry. *Film Genre: Hollywood and Beyond*. Edinburgh: Edinburgh University Press, 2005.

Leach, Jim. *Doctor Who*. Detroit: Wayne State University Press, 2009.

Lee, Hyangjin. *Contemporary Korean Cinema: Identity, Culture and Politics*. Manchester and New York: Manchester University Press, 2000.

———. "Chunhyang: Marketing an Old Tradition in New Korean Cinema." In *New Korean Cinema*. Edited by Chi-Yun Shin and Julian Stringer, 63–78. Edinburgh: Edinburgh University Press, 2005.

Lee, J. Y., and Julian Stringer. "Korean Blockbusters: Yesterday, Today and Tomorrow." In *Discovering Korean Cinema*. Edited by Daniel Martin and Mark Morris, 57–69. London: The Korean Cultural Centre UK, 2010.

Lee, Stan, and George Mair. *Excelsior! The Amazing Life of Stan Lee*. New York: Simon and Schuster, 2002.

Lent, John A., ed. "Comic Strips: An International Symposium." Special Issue, *International Journal of Comic Arts* 14, no. 1 (2012).

Lent, John A., and Kie-Un Yu. "Korean Animation: A Short But Robust Life." In *Animation in Asia and the Pacific*. Edited by John A. Lent, 89–101. Bloomington and Indianapolis: Indiana University Press, 2001.

Little, Ben. "2000 AD: Understanding the 'British Invasion' of American Comics." In *Comics as a Nexus of Cultures: Essays on the Interplay of Media, Disciplines and International Perspectives*. Edited by Mark Berninger, Jochen Ecke, and Gideon Haberkorn, 140–53. Jefferson, North Carolina: McFarland, 2010.

Loock, Kathleen, and Constantine Verevis, eds. *Film Remakes, Adaptations and Fan Productions: Remake/Remodel*. Basingstoke: Palgrave-MacMillan, 2012.

Lotman, Yuri. *Universe of the Mind: A Semiotic Theory of Culture*. Bloomington: Indiana University Press, 1990.

Lu, Amy Shirong. "The Many Faces of Internationalization in Japanese Anime." *Animation: An Interdisciplinary Journal* 3, no. 2 (2008): 169–87. doi: 10.1177/1746847708091893.

———. "What Race Do They Represent and Does Mine Have Anything to Do With It? Perceived Racial Categories of Anime Characters." *Animation: An Interdisciplinary Journal* 4, no. 2 (2009): 169–90. doi: 10.1177/1746847709104647.

MacDonald, Myra. "Muslim Women and the Veil." *Feminist Media Studies* 6, no. 1 (2006): 7–23. doi: 10.1080/14680770500471004.

Magnan-Park, Aaron H. J. "Technologized Tae Kwon Do Millennialism: Robot Taekwon V and the Assertion of a Triumphant South Korean National Identity." *Journal of Japanese and Korean Cinema* 2, no. 2 (2010): 109–130. doi: 10.1386/jjkc.2.2.109_1.

"Malala Yousafzai Opens New Birmingham Library." *The Guardian* (Manchester). September 3, 2013. http://www.theguardian.com/world/2013/sep/03/malala-yousafzai-opens-birmingham-library.

Mallat, Chibli. "Shari'a." *The Oxford Companion to the Politics of the World.* Oxford: Oxford University Press, 2012. http://www.oxfordreference.com/10.1093/acref/9780195117394.001.0001/acref-9780195117394-e-0688.

Marrison, James. "Arabs Not The First To Be Blown Away By The Movies." *Afterimage* 31, no. 5, (2004): 14.

Marshall, Rick. "Zoe Saldana Explains Why Her Character Was 'Softened' For 'The Losers' Movie." Splash Page, *MTV*. April 6, 2010. http://splashpage.mtv.com/2010/04/06/zoe-saldana-aisha-the-losers/.

Martin, Daniel. "How *Wonderful Days* Became *Sky Blue*: The Transnational Circulation of South Korean Animation." *Acta Koreana* 14, no. 1 (2011): 137–52. http://www.actakoreana.org./issue_file/233_Daniel_Martin_137_152.pdf.

Mathur, Suchitra. "From Capes to Snakes: The Indianization of the American Superhero." In *Comics as a Nexus of Cultures*. Edited by Mark Berninger, Jochen Ecke and Gideon Haberkorn, 175–86. Jefferson: McFarland, 2010.

McAllister, Matthew P., Edward H. Sewell, Jr., and Ian Gordon, eds. *Comics and Ideology*. New York: Peter Lang Publishing, 2001.

McCoy, Dan. "The Death of Baldur." *Norse Mythology: The Ultimate Online Resource for Norse Mythology and Religion.* http://norse-mythology.org/tales/the-death-of-baldur/.

———. "Loki Bound." *Norse Mythology: The Ultimate Online Resource for Norse Mythology and Religion.* http://norse-mythology.org/tales/loki-bound/.

———. "Ragnarok." *Norse Mythology: The Ultimate Online Resource for Norse Mythology and Religion.* http://norse-mythology.org/tales/ragnarok/.

———. "Thor the Transvestite." *Norse Mythology: The Ultimate Online Resource for Norse Mythology and Religion.* http://norse-mythology.org/tales/thor-the-transvestite/.

Meehan, Eileen. "'Holy Commodity Fetish, Batman!': The Political Economy of a Commercial Intertext." In *The Many Lives of the Batman: Critical Approaches to a Superhero and his Media.* Edited by Roberta E. Pearson and William Uricchio, 47–65. New York: Routledge, 1991.

Merica, Dan. "Muslim Superheroes Series Meets Resistance in U.S." *CNN*, October 6, 2011. http://www.cnn.com/2011/10/05/showbiz/tv-muslim-superheroes/index.html.

Miller, Laura. "Extreme Makeover for a Heian-Era Wizard." In *Mechademia 3: Limits of the Human*. Edited by Frenchy Lunning, 30–45. Minneapolis: University of Minnesota Press, 2008.

Miller, Toby, Nitin Govil, John McMurria, and Richard Maxwell. *Global Hollywood 2*. Berkeley: University of California Press, 2005.

Mittell, Jason. "A Cultural Approach to Television Genre Theory." *Cinema Journal* 40, no. 3 (2001): 3–24. doi: 10.1353/cj.2001.0009

Morrison, Grant. *Supergods: What Masked Vigilantes, Miraculous Mutants, and a Sun God from Smallville Can Teach Us about Being Human*. New York: Spiegel and Grau, 2011.

Müller-Wood, Anja and Karin Kukkonen. "Whatever Happened to All The Heroes? British Perspectives on American Superhero Comics." In *Comics as a Nexus of Cultures: Essays on the Interplay of Media, Disciplines and International Perspectives*. Edited by Mark Berninger, Jochen Ecke, and Gideon Haberkorn, 153–63. Jefferson, North Carolina: McFarland, 2010.

Murdoch, Blake. "Selling the Outback." *Hollywood Reporter* 336, no. 5, February (1995): S3–S4. Australia Special Issue supplement.

Murray, Chris. "Signals from Airstrip One: The British Invasion of American Mainstream Comics." In *The Rise of the American Comics Artist: Creators and Contexts*. Edited by Paul Williams and James Lyons, 31–45. Jackson: University of Mississippi Press, 2010.

Murray, Will. "The Phantom Walks on the Silver Screen." *Comics Scene* 4, October 1988, 68.

———. "Lee Falk: Father of Superheroes." *Comic Book Marketplace* 3, no. 121, (2005): 34–49.

"My Hero." *My Hero*. BBC One. Written by Paul Mayhew-Archer and Paul Mendelson, directed by John Stroud, aired February 4, 2000. Television.

Nagib, Lucia, Chris Perriam, and Rajinder Durdah, eds. *Theorizing World Cinema*. London: IB Tauris, 2011.

Napier, Susan J. *Anime from Akira to Howl's Moving Castle: Experiencing Contemporary Japanese Animation*. Updated Edition. New York: Palgrave Macmillan, 2005

Nayar, Sheila. "The Values of Fantasy: Indian Popular Cinema through Western Scripts." *Journal of Popular Culture* 31, no. 1 (1997): 73–90.

Ndalianis, Angela, ed. *The Contemporary Comic Book Superhero*. New York: Routledge, 2009.

———. "Do We Need Another Hero?" In *Super/Heroes: From Hercules to Superman*. Edited by Wendy Haslem, Angela Ndalianis, and C. J. Mackie, 1–10. Washington: New Academic Publishing, 2007.

Neale, Steve. *Genre and Hollywood*. London: Routledge, 2000.

Newman, Kim. *Doctor Who*. London: BFI, 2005.

Nolan, Hamilton. "Muslim Cartoon Will Make Your Kids Sharia Terrorists!" *Gawker*, October 11, 2010. http://gawker.com/5660849/muslim-cartoon-will-make-your-kids-sharia-terrorists.

Nowell Smith, Geoffrey, ed. *The Oxford History of World Cinema*. Oxford: Oxford University Press, 1996.

O'Brien, Denis. *The Weekly: A Lively and Nostalgic Celebration of Australia through 50 Years of its Most Popular Magazine*. Ringwood, Victoria: Penguin Books Australia, 1982.

The Observer. "The Comics Business." *The Observer* (Australia) 3, no. 25, December 10, 1960, 5–6.

Ong, Aihwa. *Flexible Citizenship: The Cultural Logics of Transnationality*. Durham: Duke University Press, 1999. Quoted in Leon Hunt and Leung Wing-Fai, "Introduction." In *East Asian Cinemas: Exploring Transnational Connections on Film*. Edited by Leon Hunt and Leung Wing-Fai, Leung, 1–13. London: IB Tauris, 2008.

Onoue, Ittō, Kenta Makuta, and Naoe Kimura. "Subete wa Urutoraman kara Hajimatta." [It All Started with Ultraman]. *Nikkei Entertainment!* 181, April 2012, 28–30.

O'Regan, Tom. *Australian National Cinema*. London: Routledge, 1996.

O'Rouke, Dan, and Pravin A. Rodrigues. "The 'Transcreation' of a Mediated Myth: Spider-Man in India." In *The Amazing Transforming Superhero! Essays on the Revision of Characters in Comic Books, Film and Television*. Edited by Terrence R. Wandtke, 112–28. Jefferson, North Carolina: McFarland & Company, 2007.

Orwell, George. "Riding Down From Bangor." *Essays*. London: Penguin, [1946] 2000.

Overman, Howard. "Misfits Interview." *The Last Broadcast*. http://www.lastbroadcast.co.uk/tv/interviews/v/9430-howard-overman-misfits-interview.html.

Pacific Film and Television Commission, Queensland, Australia. Promotional brochure. Ca. 1990s.

Paramount Pictures. *The Phantom: Handbook of Production Information*, 1996.

Partridge, Des. "Coast Movie Shuts Down." *The Courier-Mail* (Brisbane), September 20, 1994.

Passel, Jeffrey S., and D'Vera Cohn. "U.S. Population Projections: 2005–2050." *Pew Research Center for the People and the Press*, 2008. http://pewsocialtrends.org/files/2010/10/85.pdf.

Patrick, Kevin. "Jim Shepherd: The Man behind The Phantom." *Chronicle Chamber*, December 21, 2007. http://www.chroniclechamber.com/2007/12/jim-shepherd-the-man-behind-the-phantom/.

———. "The Cultural Economy of the Australian Comic Book Industry, 1950–1986." In *Sold by the Millions: Australia's Bestsellers*. Edited by Toni Johnson-Woods and Amit Sarwal, 162–81. Newcastle upon Tyne: Cambridge Scholars Publishing, 2012a.

———. "'Phans, Not Fans': The Phantom and Australian Comic-Book Fandom." *Participations: Journal of Audience and Reception Studies* 9, no. 2 (November 2012b): 133–58. http://www.participations.org/Volume%209/Issue%202/contents.htm.

Pearce, Drew. "Drew Pearce Interview." *Comedy.co.uk*. http://www.comedy.co.uk/guide/tv/no_heroics/interview/drew_pearce/.

Pearson, Roberta E., and William Uricchio, eds. *The Many Lives of the Batman: Critical Approaches to a Superhero and his Media*. New York: Routledge, 1991.

Peaslee, Robert M. "Superheroes, 'Moral Economy' and the 'Iron Cage': Morality, Alienation and the Super-Individual." In *Super/Heroes: From Hercules to Superman*. Edited by Wendy Haslem, Angela Ndalianis, and C. J. Mackie, 37–50. Washington: New Academic Publishing, 2007.

Persaud, Walter H. "Gender, Race and Global Modernity: A Perspective from Thailand." *Globalizations* 2, no. 2 (2005): 210–27. doi: 10.1080/14747730500202214

Pew Research Center. "Growing Number of Americans Say Obama Is a Muslim." *Pew Research Center for the People and the Press*, August 19, 2010. http://www.people-press.org/2010/08/19/growing-number-of-americans-say-obama-is-a-muslim/.

Peyser, Andrea. "Trading Cape for the Burqa." *New York Post*, October 11, 2010. http://www.nypost.com/p/news/local/trading_cape_for_the_burqa_SVLKS5gF1HlJugmRPFJepL.

Pilcher, Tim, and Brad Brooks. *The Essential Guide to World Comics*. London: Collins and Brown, 2005.

Porter, Charlene. "Superheroes Arise From a Life in Two Nations." *IIP Digital*, August 7, 2009. *http://www.america.gov/articles/webcontent/2009/080/20090807175620cMretroPo.8330761.xml.*

Porter, Jennifer E. "To Boldly Go: Star Trek Convention Attendance as Pilgrimage." In *Star Trek and Sacred Ground: Explorations of Star Trek, Religion, and American Culture*. Edited by Jennifer E. Porter and Darcee L. McLaren, 245–70. Albany: SUNY Press, 1999.

Porter, Liz. "TV Takes Over from Comics." *Sunday Telegraph* (Sydney), January 4, 1981, 30.

Porter, Lynnette. *Tarnished Heroes, Charming Villains and Modern Monsters: Science Fiction in Shades of Gray on 21st Century Television*. Jefferson, North Carolina: McFarland, 2010.

Powers, Tom. "'The Phantom': An Empty Suit." *Cinefantastique*, June 21, 2010. http://cinefantastiqueonline.com/2010/06/the-phantom-an-empty-suit/.

"President Obama Gives Naif Al-Mutawa and THE 99 A Shout Out." 2010. http://www.youtube.com/watch?v=xULeq3JrAEk&feature=youtube_gdata_player.

Puig, Claudia. Review of *Thor*, Paramount and Marvel, *USA Today*, May 6, 2011. http://usatoday30.usatoday.com/life/movies/reviews/2011-05-06-Thor06_ST_N.htm.

Rafer, David. "Mythic Identity in Doctor Who." In *Time and Relative Dissertations in Space: Critical Perspectives on Doctor Who*. Edited by David Butler, 123–37. Manchester: Manchester University Press, 2007.

Reynolds, Richard. *Super Heroes: A Modern Mythology*. Jackson: University Press of Mississippi, 1992.

Richards, Justin. *Doctor Who The Legend: 40 Years of Time Travel*, London: BBC Books, 2003.

Richards, Rashna Wadia. "(Not) Kramer vs. Kumar: The Contemporary Bollywood Remake as Glocal Masala Film." *Quarterly Review of Film and Video* 28, no. 4 (2011): 342–52.

Robson, Frank. "Phantom Freaks." *Australian Penthouse*, February 1985, 78–83.

Rogers, Mark. "Political Economy: Manipulating Demand and 'The Death of Superman.'" In *Critical Approaches to Comics: Theories and Methods*. Edited by Matthew J. Smith and Randy Duncan, 145–56. New York: Routledge, 2012.

Rolfe, Patricia. *The Journalistic Javelin: An Illustrated History of The Bulletin*. Sydney: Wildcat Press, 1979.

Ruh, Brian. "*Last Life in the Universe*: Nationality, Technology, Authorship." In *East Asian Cinemas: Exploring Transnational Connections on Film*. Edited by Leon Hunt and Leung Wing-Fai, 138–52. London: IB Tauris, 2008.

Ruth, Richard A. *In Buddha's Company: Thai Soldiers in the Vietnam War*. Honolulu: University of Hawaii Press, 2011.

Saeed, Henna. "Pakistani Cartoon Superhero." *Channel News Asia*. August 13, 2013. http://www.channelnewsasia.com/news/asiapacific/pakistani-cartoon/774878.html.

Saffel, Steve. *Spider-Man the Icon: The Life and Times of a Pop Culture Phenomenon*. London: Titan Books, 2007.

Sandhu, Sukhdev. Review of *Avatar*, 20th Century Fox. *Daily Telegraph* (London), December 17, 2009. http://www.telegraph.co.uk/culture/film/filmreviews/6832593/Avatar-full-review.html.

Sassaman, Gary, and Jackie Estrada. *Comic-Con: 40 Years of Artists, Writers, Fans and Friends*. San Francisco: Chronicle Books, 2009.

Scapperotti, Dan. "The Phantom." *Cinefantastique*, 27, no. 10, June 1995, 8–9 and 60.

Schatz, Thomas. *Hollywood Genres: Formulas, Filmmaking, and the Studio System*. Boston: McGraw-Hill, 1981

Schindler, Rick. "Islamic Superheroes: Role Models or Propaganda?" *TODAY.com*, October 13, 2011. http://today.msnbc.msn.com/id/44861088/ns/today-books/t/islamic-superheroes-role-models-or-propaganda/.

Schroeder, Christopher M. "Naif Al-Mutawa Fights to Bring 'THE 99' and Its Message to Wide U.S. Audience." *The Washington Post*, October 11, 2011. http://www.washingtonpost.com/lifestyle/style/naif-al-mutawa-fights-to-bring-the-99-and-its-message-to-wide-us-audience/2011/10/07/gIQAmZdqdL_story.html.

Schumaker, Justin S. "Super-Intertextuality and 21st Century Individualized Social Advocacy in Spider-Man and Kick Ass." In *The 21st Century Superhero: Essays on Gender, Genre and Globalization in Film*. Edited by Richard J. Gray II and Betty Kaklamanidou, 129–43. Jefferson, North Carolina: McFarland and Company, 2011.

Screen Australia. "Australian Content Box Office: Australia Top 100 All Time." *Screen Australia*, January 2012a. http://www.screenaustralia.gov.au/research/statistics/mrboxaust.asp.

———. "Audio Visual Markets—Cinema: Top-Grossing Films/Top All Time." *Screen Australia*, January 2012b. http://www.screenaustralia.gov.au/research/statistics/wctopalltime.asp.

———. "Audio Visual Markets—Cinema: Top 50 Films in Australia Each Year since 1992." *Screen Australia*, January 2012c. http://www.screenaustralia.gov.au/research/statistics/wctopfilms.asp#Rab28853

Seidl, Jonathon M. "Debuts 01/2011 on The Hub: 'The 99' TV Cartoon With Sharia-Compliant Muslim Superheroes." *Mayrant&rave*, October 11, 2010. http://mayrantandrave.com/2010/10/11/debuts-012011-on-the-hub-the-99-tv-cartoon-with-sharia-compliant-muslim-superheroes/.

Shaheen, Jack G. "Reel Bad Arabs: How Hollywood Vilifies a People." *The Annals of the American Academy of Political and Social Science* 588, (2003): 171–193. doi: 10.1177/0002716203255400.

Shaw, Deborah, and Armida De La Garza. "Introducing *Transnational Cinemas*." *Transnational Cinemas* 1, no. 1 2010: 3–6. doi 10.1386/trac.1.1.37/1.

Shedden, Bryan. "The Phantom: A Publishing History in Australia—Australian Newspapers (1957–Present)." *The Deep Woods*, ca, 2006. http://www.deepwoods.org/newspapers_australia.html.

———. "Phantom Fan Clubs and Fanzines—Australia." *The Deep Woods*, ca.2007. http://www.deepwoods.org/fanclubs_australia.html.

Sheehan, Paul. "Ghost Who Walks Hits the Screen—with Eyes Open." *Sydney Morning Herald*, September 28, 1996, 5.

Sheehy, Danny. "Paramount Spooked by 'The Ghost Who Walks.'" *Encore* (Australia) 12, no. 5, October 3–16, 1994, 5.

Shepherd, Jim. "The Phantom Goes to War: Introduction." *The Phantom* 910A, 1988, 5–9. Sydney: Frew Publications.

Shin, Jae-Hyo. *The Tale of Chun Hyang*. Translated by C. R. Chul. Rockville, Maryland: Silk Pagoda, 2010.

Shin, Jun-Sup. "The Seoul Ani Cinema Releases 'New Royal Secret Commissioner' Again." From *Korea Creative Content Agency*, February 14, 2005. http://www.hancinema.net/the-seoul-ani-cinema-releases-new-royal-secret-commissioner-again-2230.html.

Shoebridge, Neil. "Village, the Blue-Chip Blockbuster." *Business Review Weekly* (Australia), July 1, 1996, 7–12.

Short, Sue. *Cult Telefantasy Series: A Critical Analysis of The Prisoner, Twin Peaks, The X-Files, Buffy the Vampire Slayer, Lost, Heroes, Doctor Who and Star Trek*. Jefferson, North Carolina: McFarland, 2011.

Skender, A. L. Letter to the editor. *The Phantom* 1126, 1996, 34. Sydney: Frew Publications.

Smith, Iain Robert. *The Hollywood Meme: Global Adaptations of American Film and Television*. Edinburgh: Edinburgh University Press, 2004.

———. "'Beam Me up, Ömer': Transnational Media Flow and the Cultural Politics of the Turkish *Star Trek* Remake." *Velvet Light Trap* 61 (2008): 3–13.

Smith, Matthew J., and Randy Duncan, eds. *Critical Approaches to Comics: Theories and Methods*. New York: Routledge, 2011.

Smith, Virginia. "Council of Conservative Citizens boycotts 'Thor' for casting a black actor." *Nerve*, December 21, 2010. http://www.nerve.com/news/movies/council-of-conservative-citizens-boycotts-thor-for-casting-a-black-actor.

Snowden, John. "Frew Publications Checklist: Part One." *Cooee* 7, September 1973.

Spanakos, Anthony Peter. "Exceptional Recognition: The U.S. Global Dilemma in *The Incredible Hulk, Iron Man* and *Avatar*." In *The 21st Century Superhero: Essays on Gender, Genre and Globalization in Film*. Edited by Richard J. Gray and Betty Kaklamanidou, 15–28. Jefferson, North Carolina: McFarland and Company, 2011.

Spider-Man. ABC. 1967–70.

Spider-Man. CBS, 1977–70.

Spurlock, Morgan. *Comic-Con: Episode IV: A Fan's Hope*. New York: Dorling Kindersley, 2011.

Staiger, Janet. "Hybrid or Inbred: The Purity Hypothesis and Hollywood Genre History." In *Perverse Spectators: The Practices of Film Reception* by Janet Staiger, 61–76. New York: New York University Press, 2000.

Stanley, Di. "Billy's Phantastic Role." *TV Week* (Australia), September 17, 1994, 9.

Steinberg, Marc. *Anime's Media Mix: Franchising Toys and Characters in Japan*. Minneapolis: University of Minnesota Press, 2012.

Steinbrunner, Chris. "The Four-Panelled, Sock-Bang-Powie Saturday Afternoon Screen." In *All in Color for a Dime*. Edited by Dick Lupoff and Don Thompson, 2nd edition [1970], 193–207. Iola, Wisconsin: Krause Publications, 1997.

Stevens, J. Richard. "'Let's Rap With Cap': Redefining American Patriotism through Popular Discourse and Letters." *The Journal of Popular Culture* 44, no. 3 (2011): 606–32. doi: 10.1111/j.1540-5931.2011.00851.x

Stratton, David. "Justifiably Violent Descent into Hell." *Weekend Australian*, September 28–29, 1996, 11.

Stretton, Rowena. "Comic Book Phantom Is No Superman as an Investment." Collector's Corner, *Weekend Australian*, December 28–29, 1985, 16.

Strom, Marc. "Essential Thor: Thor's Exile." *Marvel.com*, October 21, 2010. http://marvel.com/news/story/14467/essential_thor_thors_exile.

Suh, Jung-Bo. "The Phantom Master Opens the PISAF 2004." *The Dong-A Ilbo*, November 2, 2004. http://english.donga.com/srv/service.php3?bicode=130000&biid=2004110350748.

The Sun. "Local Keen for Phantom Role." *The Sun* (Brisbane), September 21, 1988.

"Supergroupie." *No Heroics*. ITV2. Written by Drew Pearce, directed by Ben Gregor, aired September 18, 2008.

Supaidāman (Spider-Man), Tokyo Channel 12 [TV Tokyo], 1978–79.

"The Phantom May Appear in Australia." *Sydney Morning Herald*, March 18, 1988, 3.

Tasker, Yvonne. *Spectacular Bodies: Gender, Genre and the Action Cinema*. London: Routledge, 1993.

Tetsuwan Atomu [Astro *Boy*]. Directed by Osamu Tezuka. NTV. 1963–66.

"The 99 Muslim Animation Series to be in around 100 Million American Homes from October"." *Middle East Inside*, May 20, 2012. http://middleeastinside.wordpress.com/2010/05/20/the-99-muslim-animation-series-to-be-in-around-100-million-american-homes-from-october/.

Thomas, Rosie. "Indian Cinema: Pleasures and Popularity." *Screen* 26, no. 3 (1985): 116–31.

Thompson, Luke Y. "Comic-Con Move From San Diego to Anaheim Or LA? (Hell No! We Won't Go!)" *Deadline Hollywood*, May 2010. http://www.deadline.com/2010/05/comic-con-move-from-san-diego-to-anaheim-or-la-hell-no-we-wont-go/

Topsfield, Jewel. "Wham! Bam! Drawing on Islam." *The Sydney Morning Herald*, December 31, 2011. http://www.smh.com.au/national/wham-bam-drawing-on-islam-20111230-1pffk.html.

Tryon, Charles. "TV Time Lords: Fan Cultures, Narrative Complexity, and the Future of Science Fiction Television." In *The Essential Science Fiction Television Reader*. Edited by J. P. Telotte, 301–314. Lexington, Kentucky: The University Press of Kentucky, 2008.

Tsutsui, William M., and Michiko Ito, eds. *In Godzilla's Footsteps: Japanese Pop Cultural Icons on the Global Stage*. New York: Palgrave Macmillan, 2006.

Tulloch, John, and Manuel Alvarado. *Doctor Who: The Unfolding Text*. London: Macmillan Press, 1983.

Turner, Victor. *The Ritual Process: Structure and Anti-Structure*. London: Routledge and K. Paul, 1969.

UltraQ. Tokyo Broadcasting System and Tsuburaya Productions, 1966.

Ungpakorn, Giles Ji. "Class Struggle between the Coloured T-Shirts in Thailand." *Journal of Asia Pacific Studies* 1, No 1 (2009): 76–100. http://www.japss.org/upload/5ungpakorn.pdf.

"Unicorn Joins Teshkeel to Fund Comic Publisher." *Gulf News*, September 28, 2006. http://gulfnews.com/business/banking/unicorn-joins-teshkeel-to-fund-comic-publisher-1.256877.

Urban, Andrew. "Coote Does Hollywood." *The Bulletin* (Australia), 29 August 29, 1989, 13–14.

Urry, John. *Consuming Places*. London: Routledge, 1995.

Urutoraman [*Ultraman*]. Tokyo Broadcasting System and Tsuburaya Productions, 1967.

Van Gelder, Lawrence. "The Ghost Who Walks and His War with Evil." *The New York Times*, June 7, 1996.

Varia, Kush. *Bollywood: Gods, Glamour, and Gossip*. New York: Columbia University Press, 2013.

Variety. "Aussies Get Aggressive." *Variety* 354, no. 2, February 14–20, 1994, 45 and 53.

———. "Variety Box Office." *Variety* 363, no. 7, June 17–23, 1996, 10.

Variety Deal Memo. "Village Roadshow: Oz Film Giant Takes its Exhibition Show on the Road." *Variety Deal Memo* 2, no. 10, May 15, 1995, 10–11.

Vasudevan, Ravi. "The Politics of Cultural Address in a 'Transitional' Cinema." In *Reinventing Film Studies*. Edited by Christine Gledhill and Linda Williams,130–64. London: Bloomsbury, 2000.

Vitali, Valentina. *Hindi Action Cinema: Industries, Narratives, Bodies*. Bloomington: Indiana University Press, 2010.

Waddell, Callum. "Not Quite Superman." *SFX Bookazine: The Ultimate Guide to Superheroes* 5, 2013, 108–111.

Wandtke, Terrence R., ed. *The Amazing Transforming Superhero! Essays on Revision of Characters in Comic Books, Film and Television*. Jefferson, North Carolina: McFarland and Co, 2007.

Ward, Jens. "Phantastic." *People* (Australia), March 17, 1989, 10–12.

Watson, Bronwyn. "Holy Cow, It's a Race for Gotham City." *Sydney Morning Herald*, February 11, 1989, 83.

Weinstein, Simcha. *Up, Up, and Oy Vey! How Jewish History, Culture, and Values Shaped the Comic Book Superhero*. Baltimore, Maryland: Leviathan Press, 2006.

Wilding, Josh. "Interview With Iron Man 2 and THOR Set Decorator, Lauri Gaffin!" *ComicBookMovie.com*, April 22, 2011. http://www.comicbookmovie.com/fansites/joshw24/news/?a=35748#Ac8FAqQKqkykzG4B.99.

Winichakul, Thongchai. *Siam Mapped: A History of the Geo-Body of a Nation*. Honolulu: University of Hawai'i Press, 1994.

Wise Kwai. Review of *The Red Eagle* [Insee Daeng], Five Star Production. *Thai Film Journal*, 2010. http://thaifilmjournal.blogspot.com/2010/10/review-red-eagle-insee-dang.html.

Wonder Woman. ABC and CBS, 1975–1979.

Wright, Bradford W. *Comic Book Nation: The Transformation of American Youth Culture*. Baltimore: The Johns Hopkins University Press, 2001.

Wright, Peter. "Expatriate! Expatriate! Doctor Who: The Movie and Commercial Negotiation of a Multiple Text." In *British Science Fiction Film and Television: Critical Essays*. Edited by Tobias Hochscherf and James Leggott, 128–42. Jefferson, North Carolina: McFarland, 2011.

Xu, Gary. "Remaking East Asia, Outsourcing Hollywood." In *East Asian Cinemas: Exploring Transnational Connections on Film*. Edited by Leon Hunt and Leung Wing-Fai, 191–202. London: IB Tauris, 2008.

Yamanaka, Akira. *Spider-Man J*. 2004-2005.

Yoon, Ae-Ri. "In between the Values of the Global and the National: The Korean Animation Industry." In *Cultural Studies and Cultural Industries in Northeast Asia: What a Difference a Region Makes*. Edited by Chris Berry, Nicola Liscutin, and Jonathan D. Mackintosh, 103–115. Hong Kong: Hong Kong University Press, 2009.

Yoon, Hyun-Ok. "Simultaneous Screening of New Secret Royal Commissioner in Korea and Japan." *Korean Film Council*, November 2, 2004. http://www.hancinema.net/simultaneous-screening-of-new-secret-royal-commissioner-in-korea-and-japan-1729.html.

CONTRIBUTORS

Based in Kuala Lumpur, **Mary J. Ainslie** is Head of Film and Television Programs at the University of Nottingham Malaysia campus and specializes in Thai cinema. She is co-editor of the forthcoming volume *The Korean Wave in Southeast Asia: Consumption and Cultural Production* and a contributor to *Asian Cinema Journal*. She is currently the Malaysia and Thailand regional president for the World Association of Hallyu Studies (WAHS) and a fellow of the Dynamics of Religion in Southeast Asia (DORISEA) network. Her current research is focused on using the Thai film archives to display and write about significant yet unexplored Thai fims. This also includes investigating Hollywood interests in Southeast Asia during this period and the impact this had on the development of indigenous film industries.

Rayna Denison is a lecturer and researcher specializing in Asian media cultures at the University of East Anglia (UK). Her main focus of research is on Japanese media, particularly contemporary popular media forms like anime and live action television and film. Rayna has received funding from the UK Arts and Humanities Research Council for a project examining transmedia connectivity in Japan, titled *Manga Movies: Contemporary Japanese Cinema, Media Franchising and Adaptation* (more information available at: www.mangamoviesproject.com). She is widely published in these areas, including articles in the *International Journal of Cultural Studies*, *Mechademia*, *Japan Forum*, and *Animation: An Interdisciplinary Journal*.

Jochen Ecke teaches British literature and culture at Mainz University, Germany, where he has recently completed his PhD thesis, entitled *The British Invasion of American Comics: A Poetics*. He is particularly interested in historical and analytical stylistics of comic books, and has published widely on topics such as the representation of time and space in comics, authorship in US mainstream comics, and superhero fiction as autobiography. Alongside Mark Berninger and Gideon Haberkorn, he has also edited the essay collection *Comics as a Nexus of Cultures* (McFarland, 2010).

Vincent M. Gaine is an independent researcher with expertise in film philosophy, contemporary Hollywood authorship, and genre. His monograph, *Existentialism and Social Engagement in the Films of Michael Mann*, is published by Palgrave-MacMillan (2011). Vincent has published extensively in journals and edited collections on Hollywood auteurs, gender, and genre, as well as production cycles. He is a regular contributor to the Journal of World Cinema (Intellect), a founding member of the Thinking Film Collective, and also publishes a blog, vincentgaine.wordpress.com. He is currently researching science fiction television and critical reception.

Lincoln Geraghty is Reader in Popular Media Cultures in the School of Creative Arts, Film and Media at the University of Portsmouth. He is author of *Living with Star Trek: American Culture and the Star Trek Universe* (IB Tauris, 2007) and *American Science Fiction Film and Television* (Berg, 2009). He has edited *The Influence of Star Trek on Television, Film and Culture* (McFarland, 2008), *Channeling the Future: Essays on Science Fiction and Fantasy Television* (Scarecrow 2009), *The Smallville Chronicles: Critical Essays on the Television Series* (Scarecrow, 2011), and, with Mark Jancovich, *The Shifting Definitions of Genre: Essays on Labeling Film, Television Shows and Media* (MacFarland, 2008). He is currently serving as Editor of the *Directory of World Cinema: American Hollywood*, an online and print publication from Intellect Books (2011 and 2015), and his most recent book, entitled *Cult Collectors: Nostalgia, Fandom and Collecting Popular Culture*, was published by Routledge in 2014.

Patrick Gill is a lecturer in English Literature and Culture at Mainz University (Germany), where he also received his PhD. His monograph, *Origins and Effects of Poetic Ambiguity in Dylan Thomas's Collected Poems* was published in 2014. Apart from English poetry of all periods, the subjects of his publications have included contemporary drama and fiction, as well as Shakespeare and Shakespearan adaptations. Canonical literature aside, he maintains a strong interest in popular culture, particularly British and American TV culture. He has enjoyed periods as a visiting lecturer at the University of Edinburgh, Jagiellonian University, Krakow, and York University, Toronto.

Derek Johnston is Lecturer in Broadcast Literacy at Queen's University, Belfast (UK). His research focuses on television history, particularly that of British genre television, with a range of articles and book chapters covering points across the history of British television science fiction from its origins in 1938 up to *Life on Mars* and *Ashes to Ashes*. He has also published on British and American science fiction film and television in the 1950s as well as the music biopic, and is currently researching seasonal television, in particular relation to horror.

Daniel Martin is Assistant Professor of Film Studies in the School of Humanities and Social Sciences at the Korean Advanced Institute of Science and Technology (KAIST), and also holds a post as Honorary Researcher in the Institute for the Contemporary Arts at Lancaster University (UK). His recent research concerns the international circulation of films from South Korea, Japan, and Hong Kong. He is the co-editor of Korean Horror Cinema (Edinburgh University Press, 2013), and has published articles in *Cinema Journal, Film International, Acta Koreana, Asian Cinema* and *The Journal of Korean Studies*.

Rachel Mizsei-Ward graduated with her PhD from the University of East Anglia in 2014. Her research looks at popular media, including reception, transmedia, and licensing between film, television, and games. Rachel has contributed an essay on the film *Underworld* and the role-playing setting The World of Darkness to the edited collection *21st Century Gothic*, and has an article on Barack Obama as the Joker in *Comparative American Studies*. She is currently working on a monograph on quality American television.

Kevin Patrick completed his PhD thesis, titled *The Ghost Who Walks: A Cultural History of The Phantom Comic Book in Australia, India and Sweden*, at Monash University (Australia) in 2014. A former journalist, magazine editor and communications policy researcher, Kevin was appointed Guest Curator to the State Library of Victoria (Melbourne, Australia), where he staged the exhibition Heroes and Villains: Australian Comics and their Creators (2006–2007). His research on the history of Austrialian comic books has appeared in numerous peer-reviewed journals and he has taught courses on Australian media, culture and society at Monash University and the University of Melbourne.

Iain Robert Smith is Lecturer in Film Studies at the University of Roehampton, London. He is author of the monograph *The Hollywood Meme: Transnational Adaptations of American Film and Television* (Edinburgh University Press, 2014) and editor of a book-length special issue of the open-access journal *Scope*, entitled "Cultural Borrowings: Appropriation, Reworking, Transformation" (2009). He has published peer-reviewed articles in a range of international journals, including *Velvet Light Trap* and *Portal*, and he is currently a co-investigator on the AHRC funded research network Media Across Borders. Since 2012 he has been co-chair of the SCMS Transnational Cinemas Scholarly Interest Group.

INDEX

Lightning Source UK Ltd.
Milton Keynes UK
UKHW04f1100120918
328751UK00001B/73/P